D1549635

A Pictorial Record of
# Great Western Engines

# A Pictorial Record of GREAT WESTERN ENGINES

## by

## J. H. Russell

## (Volume One)

## Oxford Publishing Company

ISBN 0 86093 398 9

A FOULIS-OPC Railway Book

© Oxford Publishing Co. & J.H. Russell 1975
Reprinted 1988

Published by:
Haynes Publishing Group
Sparkford, Near Yeovil, Somerset. BA22 7JJ

Haynes Publications Inc.
861 Lawrence Drive, Newbury Park, California
91320, USA

All rights reserved. No part of this book may be reproduced or transmitted in any form or by any means, electronic or mechanical, including photocopying, recording or by any information storage or retrieval system, without written permission from the copyright owner.

The author and publishers wish to point out that these volumes do not claim to be a complete history of Great Western engines but are a pictorial record only. (The historic documentation of this fascinating subject can be found in the R.C.T.S. publications concerning Great Western locomotives.)

Many of the line drawings and sketches are taken directly from offical Swindon originals and due to the age of these the reproduction is not as clear as they would wish. The drawings have been reduced to 4mm scale as near as possible, but again, due to the condition of some of the drawings, variation in scale may exist.

## PREFACE

This series of Great Western Railway books was started with a collection of wagon pictures and drawings, which proved successful and so two similar volumes were produced, dealing with the carriage stock of the Great Western Railway. As the readers reception of these three works have been so favourable, I have been emboldened to attempt a third series, this time dealing with the steam locomotives of the 'Great' Company.

As before, this is not a technical book in any sense, only touching on the historical in that many of the photographs and drawings are now extremely rare, but the main objective has been to portray the evolution of the engines of the Great Western Railway through the medium of an enthusiast's private collection of pictures and drawings. The format is as before, namely with diagrams where possible, to accompany the photographs, and although it is just one more in the ever-growing library of railway engine books, the author hopes that readers might find it of immense interest. Please forgive any omissions and lapses, taking into consideration that it constitutes a 'labour of love', the compilation of which has given great pleasure.

JIM RUSSELL, 1975

# INTRODUCTION

I feel greatly privileged to have been born in the Great Western Railway era, and to have grown up with, worked amongst, and known intimately, those fascinating steam engines in the polished brass and green livery.

Without giving away my age too directly, let it suffice to say that I can just remember *La France*, and the saddle tanks shunting here at Banbury. I can recall the khaki-painted engines of the First World War, returning to Swindon works, coupled together, to have their rightful Brunswick green restored. I remember an excursion to the 'Works' as a small boy to see *The Great Bear,* and being more intrigued by the quaint little crane engines standing outside 'A' shop. Also those never-to-be-forgotten Sunday morning visits to Banbury loco shed, with my hot little hand clutched in my father's, whilst he and the shed foreman talked "shop".

Time passed, and eventually I too joined the Company in a very humble capacity at 16/- per week, but at least I was on the strength and working with steam engines. Those days saw the 'Stars', 'Saints' and '4300s' at their best, and even when, as a soldier in the Second World War, I joined the colours as a reservist, fortune still smiled, and in the (G.W.) Royal Engineers Operating Corps, I worked in France with, of course, the ubiquitous 'Dean Goods'!

Small wonder then, that, after giving up a railway career in 1945, the enthusiasm for steam engines has remained with me, and shows no signs of waning, thank goodness, even now in 1975. I am still thrilled to find a loco-motive or vehicle photograph which I have not seen before and did not know even existed.

The astonishing thing is that I am not alone in this railway mania, and many of my friends have often suggested that my collection of pictures and drawings would be of use and interest to other devotees and in particular to those of us who model steam engines of the railways.

This then is the *raison d'être* for this work, and I stress again that I am no historian or qualified engineer, just an enthusiast who has collected data and detail about railways for a very long time.

The Great Western Railway was most unusual, in that its existence of over one hundred  years contained an unbroken line of locomotive development, and this feature has always fascinated me, not in the actual mechanics of the engines so much, as in the general outline and design, and it is this that my collection sets out to show. If you are looking for technical detail I cannot help you; my approach is of one who was closely associated with the engines, admired their quality as well-built machines and appreciated the ease with which they did their work.

Many eminent gentlemen before me have fallen to the spell of the Great Western steam engines, and we enthusiasts have a great deal to owe to a small band of modellers who, in the 'between wars' years not only photographed and kept meticulous records, but also realized that models could be made to fine scale, and to this purpose produced excellent drawings from the original official blueprints.

I had the honour of knowing several of these charming people, to whom the mention of Great Western was the 'open sesame' to their valued friendship. It is, therefore, a great delight to be able to dedicate this work to those pioneers of railway modelling, as not only did they set me off on a never-ending trail of miniature railways, but they left behind such a store of information, which surely must be invaluable to all who model locomotives.

I have had difficulty in tracing many of the drawings, but through the kindness of Mrs. Maskelyne and Miss Anne Templer, many have been found, and are reproduced here by courtesy of the Bristol Museum and Roye Dock, who are the custodians of the originals. Also I would like to thank Messrs. Ian Allan Ltd., Real Photographs, Photomatic and British Rail (Western Region), in particular Keith Montague, for the help and photographs they have supplied.

Wherever it has been possible, both the prototype diagram from Swindon and the reduced model drawing have been produced to 4mm scale, but with millimetre dimensions for 7mm scale added, in the case of the Templer drawings. A few drawings that are not to 4mm scale will be annotated to that effect.

Before leaving the reader to amble through these pages, and in the hope that several are tempted to start a particular model, I would repeat the words of that meticulous searcher for authenticity, J. N. Maskelyne, who said in 1935: 'If a model or drawing is to be made, be careful to have at hand a photograph showing the particular engine concerned, and of the period in time desired, as every engine seemed to differ in some way. Take, for instance, the bogie singles. There were eighty constructed and I doubt if any two were exactly alike!'

This still applies in these drawings. Take all the general dimensions for the making of a model, but watch out for the small details. Boiler fittings are always suspect, chimneys in particular, so always try to make the fittings please the eye and look like the photograph. So many models are ruined by trying to show the copper band on the chimney, which in real life was only 1/16" thick!

Wherever possible I will mention likely pitfalls, at least those I know about, but as engines were rebuilt, converted and rebuilt again, almost any variation is possible. So the final advice is to go by the photograph. At least it is an authentic record of a loco of its class, even though some had their names changed for pictures! Also use the drawings with caution, for as I said somewhere before, a drawn line does not prove authenticity.

As the subject is so vast I have been forced to divide the work into two parts, otherwise one single volume would be too unwieldly. Therefore, Part 1 deals with the Gooch and Dean engines and their subsequent development, and the second part covers the Churchward and Collett locomotives and even a few Hawksworth designs.

## ... Gauge Index

| | Page |
|---|---|
| *Actaeon* | 5 |
| *Amazon* | 20 |
| *Antiquary* | 7 |
| *Argus* | 4 |
| Atmospheric | 7 |
| Bill of Sale | 5 |
| Boiler explosions | 2, 5, 8 |
| Bristol & Exeter | 16, 17 |
| *Bulkeley* | 19 |
| *Centaur* | 5 |
| Dean Goods | 12 |
| Dean Singles | 17 |
| *Dewrance* | 11 |
| *Dragon* | 178 |
| *Europa* | 12 |
| *Fenton* | 11 |
| *Firefly* | 4 |
| *Heron* | 9 |
| *Hirondelle* | 8 |
| *Hurricane* | 3 |
| *Leopard* | 2, 13 |
| *Lord of the Isles* | 10 |
| *North Star* | 6 |
| *Perseus* | 8 |
| *Rover* | 19 |
| *Sebastapol* | 18 |
| *Sir Watkin* | 14 |
| 'Star' class | 3 |
| *Stewart* | 13 |
| *Sultan* | 8 |
| Swindon sidings | 21, 22, 23 |
| *Sylph* | 178 |
| *Tartar* | 20 |
| *Taurus* | 15 |
| *Telford* | 11 |
| *Vulcan* | 2 |

| Wheel arrangement | Page |
|---|---|
| 2-2-2 | 1, 2, 4, 5, 6, 9, 17, 22, 178 |
| 4-2-2 | 3,8,10,16,17,18,19,20,23,178 |
| 0-2-4 | 9 |
| 2-4-0 | 11, 21 |
| 2-4-0T | 13, 21 |
| 4-4-0 | 7 |
| 4-4-0T | 9, 13 |
| 4-2-4T | 16 |
| 0-6-0 | 16, 23 |
| 0-6-0T | 14, 15, 21 |

## Standard Gauge Index

| | Page |
|---|---|
| *Achilles* | 49 |
| Alarm gong | 78 |
| *Alexander Hubbard* | 176 |
| *Amyas* | 167 |
| *Armstrong* | 52 |
| 'Armstrong' class | 50, 51, 52 |
| Armstrong Goods | 72-78, 80 |
| *Avon* | 63 |
| *Badminton* | 175 |
| 'Barnum' class | 64-68 |
| *Beaufort* | 43 |
| *Beaconsfield* | 28, 29 |
| Beyer-Peacock | 69, 71, 107, 145 |
| Beyer tanks | 107 |
| *Bessborough* | 170 |
| 'Bicycle' class | 54, 55 |
| *Blenheim* | 172 |
| *Brunel* | 50 |
| 'Buffalo' class | 88-94 |
| *Bulldog* | 177 |
| Cab details | 42, 81, 86 |
| Cambrian Rly. | 85 |
| Cardiff Rly. | 139 |
| Cattle train | 80 |
| 'Chancellor' class | 53 |
| *Charles Saunders* | 51 |
| Coaling crane | 87 |
| 'Cobham' class | 30, 33, 40 |
| Convertible | 39, 40 |
| 'Cornishman' train | 41 |
| *Corsair* | 46 |
| *Cotswold* | 166 |
| *Courier* | 41 |
| Dean Goods | 79, 80, 83, 84-87 |
| Dean Singles | 40, 41, 43, 45-49 |
| *Dee* | 62 |
| *Dragon* | 44 |
| 'Duke' class | 162, 163, 166 |
| *Duke of Connaught* | 44 |
| *Duke of Cornwall* | 161, 163 |
| *Earl Cawdor* | 171, 173, 174 |
| *Emperor* | 42 |
| *Empress of India* | 45 |
| Exeter shed | 82, 110 |
| Experimentals | 36, 37, 38 |
| *Flying Dutchman* | 41 |
| *Fowey* | 162 |
| *Frederick Saunders* | 49 |
| *Glenside* | 47 |

| | Page |
|---|---|
| *Gooch* | 51 |
| *Goonbarrow* | 141 |
| *Grasshopper* | 145 |
| *Guinevere* | 166 |
| *Hercules* | 47 |
| *Hotspur* | 170 |
| *Insignia* | 168 |
| *Isis* | 62 |
| *Isle of Tresco* | 166 |
| *John Owen* | 141 |
| *King Arthur* | 163 |
| *Lambert* | 45 |
| Large 'Metro' class | 136-140, 142 |
| List of names | 42, 48, 62 |
| *Lorna Doone* | 43 |
| Lot index | 186-188 |
| *Marlborough* | 170, 175 |
| *Maristowe* | 166 |
| *Merlin* | 164 |
| *Mersey* | 164 |
| 'Metro' class | 126-135 |
| *Mortimer* | 169 |
| *Mount Edgcumbe* | 165 |
| *Nelson* | 48 |
| No. 1 | 143 |
| No. 13 | 146, 147 |
| No. 34, 35 | 148, 149 |
| No. 36 | 150, 151 |
| No. 101 | 145 |
| No. 1490 | 144 |
| Painting and lining | 185 |
| *Pembroke* | 178 |
| *Prince of Wales* | 27 |
| Princes Risborough Rly. | 142 |
| *Princess Beatrice* | 46 |
| *Princess of Wales* | 27 |
| 'Queen' class | 25-29 |
| *Royal Albert* | 38 |
| *Royal Sovereign* | 46 |
| 'River' class | 62, 63 |
| *Samson* | 176 |
| *Shakespeare* | 174 |
| Sharp Bros. | 24 |
| 'Sharpies' | 30, 32, 33 |
| 'Sir Daniel' class | 24, **32**, 33 |
| Small engines (diagrams)141, (photos)145 | |
| Snowplough | 76, 84, 106 |
| South Devon Rly. | 142 |
| Spark arresting chimney | 94 |

|  | Page |
|---|---|
| Standard Goods (Armstrong) | 72-78, 80 |
| *St. Ives* | 167 |
| 'Stella' class | 151-153 |
| Tenders | 179-184 |
| *Thames* | 41 |
| *Trevithick* | 164 |
| *Victoria* | 37 |
| *Worcester* | 47, 48 |
| Worcester shed | 81 |
| War Dept. engines | 83 |
| *Waterford* | 171 |
| '57' class | 70 |
| '111' class | 56 |
| '119' class | 95, 98 |
| '131'class | 70 |
| '157' class | 25, 30, 31 |
| '322' class | 71 |
| '388' class | 69, 74 |
| '517' class | 120-123, 125 |
| '633' class | 103-105 |

|  | Page |
|---|---|
| '645' class | 98, 100 |
| '727' class | 95 |
| '806' class | 54, 55, 57 |
| '850' class | 108-112, 114, 119 |
| '1016' class | 102 |
| '1076' class | 88-94 |
| '1501' class | 106 |
| '1661' class | 97 |
| '1701' class | 99, 100 |
| '1813' class | 96 |
| '1850' class | 95, 100 |
| '1901' class | 113, 115, 116, 118 |
| '2021' class | 117-119 |
| '2201' class | 57, 58 |
| '2721' class | 93, 101 |
| '3226' class | 56 |
| '3232' class | 59, 60, 61 |
| '3501' class | 154-156 |
| '3521' class | 146, 157-161 |
| '3571' class | 124, 125 |

**Wheel arrangement**

|  | Page |
|---|---|
| 2-2-2 | 24-33, 35-38, 40, 41 |
| 4-2-2 | 43-49 |
| 2-4-0 | 36, 53-68 |
| 2-4-0T | 39, 126-137, 141, 142, 143 |
| 2-4-2T | 138-140, 146, 147 |
| 0-4-0T | 141, 145 |
| 0-4-4T | 146-149 |
| 4-4-0 | 50, 51, 157-174, 176-178 |
| 4-4-0T | 144, 146, 147 |
| 0-4-2T | 120-124, 146, 147 |
| 0-6-0 | 34, 69-79, 83-87 |
| 0-6-0T | 39, 88-119, 141 |
| 4-6-0 | 150 |

The very first engine delivered to the Great Western Railway was a primitive 2-2-2 class built by the Vulcan Foundry Company and called appropriately enough *Vulcan*. She was in steam officially on January 9th, 1838, and was employed on the 7′ (broad) gauge track which was being laid between Paddington and Maidenhead. Isambard Kingdom Brunel, the architect and engineer of the Great Western Railway, having planned, surveyed and started construction of a line of rails from London to Bristol, searched, found and finally accepted for the post of Locomotive Engineer, Daniel Gooch, who was at that time working on the Manchester-Leeds Railway.

Gooch entered the service of the Company on August 18th, 1837, and as there were no engines at that time to superintend, started to plan engine houses at Paddington and Maidenhead.

In these early days, engines were made to order by various firms specialising in locomotive construction, and these included Mather Dixon Co., Tayleur Co., Vulcan Foundry, Sharp Roberts Co., and the Haigh Foundry. The Great Western gave orders for six engines from Mather Dixon, namely *Premier, Ajax, Ariel, Planet, Mercury* and *Mars;* six also from Vulcan Foundry named *Vulcan, Aeolus, Bacchus, Apollo, Neptune* and *Venus;* three from Sharp Roberts, *Lion, Eagle* and *Atlas;* and two from the Haigh Foundry, *Viper* and *Snake.* All 17 were built to the broad gauge adopted by the Company, namely 7′ between the running rails, and were peculiar in that they were all of the small boiler and large driving wheel style to comply with Brunel's specification. This stated that 'a velocity of 30 m.p.h. was to be considered as standard and this to be attained without requiring the piston to travel at a greater rate than 280 per minute. The engine to be able to exert a tractive force of 800 lb. on level track, independent of the power required to move itself and at a pressure of 50 lb. per square inch. Total weight not to exceed 10½ tons and if above 8 tons to be carried on six wheels.'

This then was the beginning of the long line of engines which served the Great Western Railway, and these brief sentences have only been penned in order to set the scene, and to endeavour to show how the very earliest locomotives had many characteristic features and details of design which were perpetuated throughout the subsequent building of engines at the Company's own workshop at Swindon.

Returning to the first engines of the Great Western, Daniel Gooch next received *Premier* from Mather Dixon Co., and as the only track then laid was a couple of miles at West Drayton, this is where the official trial runs took place on January 9th, 1838.

It may be of interest to record that these first two engines had travelled by sea to London Docks, and thence by canal to West Drayton, where they were unloaded and moved overland to the engine-house a mile away. The famous engine *North Star*, which was built by Robert Stephenson Co., was also delivered to the Company by canal, but to Maidenhead, where she had to remain from November, 1837 to May, 1838 owing to the lack of rails at that station. Readers who are interested in more details and drawings of these three engines should refer to three sources for information, (a) *pp 52-3* of MacDermot's *History of the Great Western Railway, Vol I, Part I* (b) *Great Western Magazine, April, 1910, pp 82-3* and (c) *Great Western Magazine, June, 1913, pp 165-79.*

*Figure 1* is of great interest in that this drawing, located in the Railway archives, is inscribed on the reverse as being the first design submitted to the company for locomotives, by Messrs. Tayleur of Newton-Le-Willows.

It actually depicts *Aeolus,* makers No. 52, which was eventually delivered in November, 1837 and ran the first train carrying the public in June, 1838. She was finally condemned 30 years later in 1867.

Figure 1

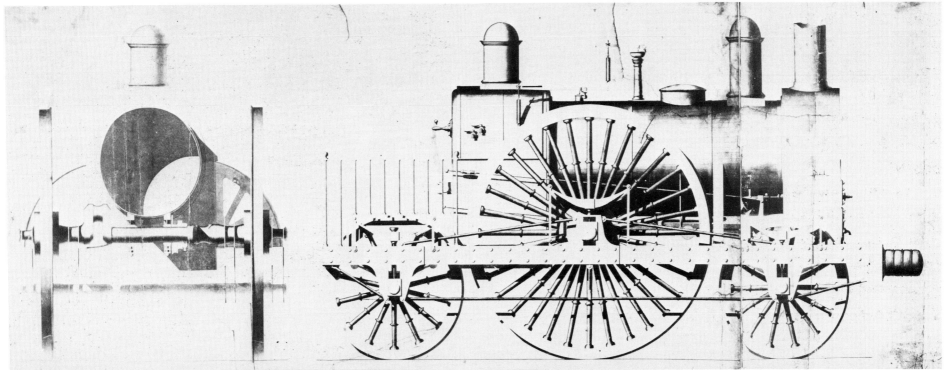

Figure 2

PAGE 2

Figure 3

Although *Aeolus* took the first fare paying passenger train on the Great Western, *Vulcan* was the first to be actually tried in steam, at Iver on December 28th, 1837. *Figure 3* shows a very early photograph of this engine after several years service, when the wheels had been altered from 8′ to 6′ and 4′ 6″ to 3′ respectively, and she had also been converted into a tank engine.

*Figure 2* illustrates graphically the hazards of the early steam railways. This engine *Leopard* was one of the 'Firefly' class of sixty-two which were built by various firms between 1840 and 1842. *Leopard* was a Sharp Roberts and Co. locomotive, delivered in May of 1840 and it exploded at Bristol in 1857. It was re-fitted with a steel firebox and carried on working until sold in 1878.

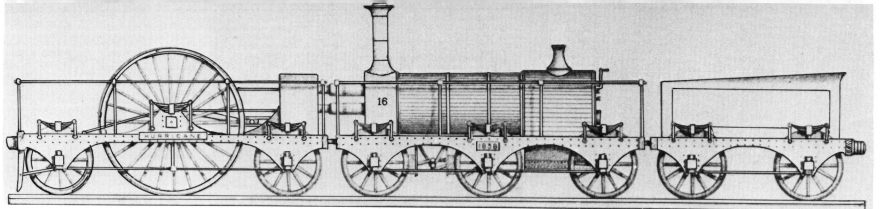

Figure 4

G.W.R. "Hurricane" built by Messrs. Hawthorne, Newcastle-on-Tyne, 1838.

Designed by T. E. Harrison, patented December 1836, ordered for G.W.R.
by Mr. I. K. Brunel. Ran to Taplow 22½ miles in 16 minutes.
Driving Wheel 10 feet diameter.     Cylinders 16 inches × 20 inches.

### DESCRIPTION

N3 This Class of Engine had originally but 3 pair of Wheels, and now the Boiler has been lengthened 2 feet with an additional pair of Leading Wheels. Cylinders of the Morning and North Star 16 in? in diam? with a 16 in? stroke, all the others have a 15 inch Cylinder with an 18 inch stroke. Boiler 18 feet long and now they are 10 feet long, by 4 feet in diam? Nor of Tubes vary from 114 to 170 from 2¼ in? to 1¾ in? in diam? Wheels Driving 7 feet in diam? Trailing, 4 feet in diam? Leading 2 pair of 3 feet 6 in? to replace a pair of 4 feet Wheels. Royal Star with 4 cwt of Coke and 6½ in? of Water in the Glass Weighs 23 Tons 7 cwt 2 qr? Leading 7 Tons. 6 cwt. Driving 11 Tons 13 cwt. Trailing 4 Tons 8 cwt 2 qr?

The drawing in *Figure 4* is of one of the two unusual engines made for the Company by Messrs. Hawthorne of Newcastle-on-Tyne, and shows the ingenuity of this firm in creating a large engine, but still keeping within Brunel's specification. This machine, named *Hurricane*, was one of two, the other being *Thunderer* which had a geared drive on to driving wheels of 6' diameter. *Hurricane* used the big-wheel principle, the two large drivers being 10' in diameter, whilst the smaller-carrying wheels were 4' 6" diameter. As can be seen in the drawing by Henry Greenly of 1895, the engine proper was on a separate carriage to that of the firebox and boiler, whilst the tender was of a four-wheel design which resembled future tenders built in the Company's workshops for many years. One unusual feature of this engine was that the firebox was divided into two compartments, with a door to each. Steam was conveyed to the cylinders by means of flexible joints, and one advantage claimed for the divided boiler and engine plan was that repairs could be carried out to one part whilst the other was still in service, replacements being available, of course! Strange machine she might have been, but it is on report that this engine completed a mileage of 10,527 before being scrapped in 1839, and even then the boiler gave further service, being utilized on a goods engine! Note also that for those days *Hurricane* was fast; she was recorded as running 22½ miles in 16 minutes to Taplow, which means in excess of 80 m.p.h.

Interesting features in these early engines are the smaller details such as the shape of the framing, spring buckles and anchorages, chimney and safety valve bonnet, all of which were carried through to future engines for 50 years or more.

In *Figure 5* we see what was probably the first tank engine on the Great Western, namely the 'Star' series, many of which were converted from 2-2-2 classification in the 1850's.

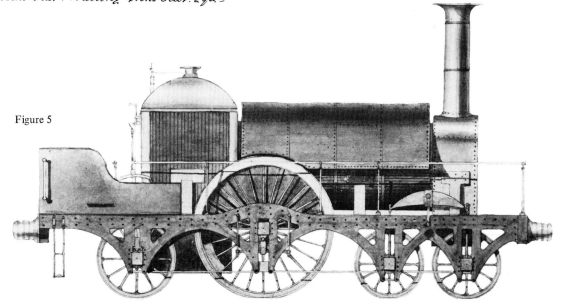

Figure 5

Figure 6

*PAGE 4*

Having illustrated the 'Firefly' class in an 'exploded' condition, *Figure 6* shows an early picture of the prototype engine, which was built by Jones Turner and Evans also of Newton-Le-Willows and delivered to the company in March of 1840. *Figure 7* shows *Argus* another of the same series, but built by Fenton Murray and Jackson of Leeds. She commenced work in August, 1852 and was sold out of the company in 1873. The picture is of great interest, as it includes one of the early short wheelbase tenders.

Sixty-two engines were built in the years of 1840 to 1842 by seven different firms, namely Jones Turner & Evans of Newton-Le-Willows, Sharp, Roberts & Co. of Manchester, Fenton, Murray & Jackson of Leeds, G.J. Rennie of Blackfriars, R.B. Longridge of Bedlington, Stothert & Slaughter of Bristol and Nasmyth Gaskell & Co. of Manchester. These little engines were all of the slotted sandwich-frame type, with the driving wheels of 7′ diameter and carrying wheels of 4′ diameter. The boilers were fitted to tall dome-shaped fireboxes and although Gooch did all he could to ensure standardisation of parts, and a reasonable measure of quality (by placing liability for material and workmanship on the shoulders of the builders) accidents could and did take place, as seen in *Figures 2* and *9*.

Figure 7

*North Star*, the first engine on the books of the company, was probably the most famous of all Great Western engines. Built by R. Stephenson of Newcastle, she was the first of 12 similar machines, all called after stars and differing slightly from one another in small details. She was delivered on November 28th, 1837, and worked the first passenger train six months later. The engine proved such a success that eleven more were ordered and delivered between 1839 and 1841.

Searching amongst the historical files at Paddington I came across the illustrated document, which I thought worthy of inclusion here, as it surprised me as to the cost of these early steam engines *(Figure 8)*. It is a bill of sale from Robert Stephenson Co. of Newcastle-on-Tyne, and dated February 24th, 1841, all in copperplate handwriting, with the following text: "One locomotive engine 15½″ cylinders 18″ stroke, copper firebox, 1 pair 7′ and 2 pair 4′ wheels. (No. 270) 'Rising Star' – £2150. With 1 set screw, large and small monkey wrench, 1 set fire irons, 3 oil cans, 1 hammer, 3 chisels, 2 ball valves, 4 large

packing cases hooped with iron – £13. One locomotive engine 15½" cylinders as above, 1 set tools (No. 271) – £2150. 4 large packing cases as above – £13. Total £4326 the 'John Capt Colledge' etc.

So in 1839 a small steam railway engine cost in excess of £2,000 and this when one pound would buy a tradesman's service for a week! According to Swindon records, 12 of the broad gauge 'Stars' were altered to saddle-tank engines in the years 1848-50 and *Figure 5* shows how these engines appeared when so rebuilt. Note that the leading wheels have been reduced to 3' 6" to replace the 4' diameter wheels *(see page 3). Figure 9* shows the other 'Firefly' class to go the same way as *Leopard* on *page 2.* This is an artist's impression of what was left of *Actaeon* after a 'big fire, no water' mishap at Gloucester in February of 1855. *Figure 10* depicts *Centaur* and shows the first four-wheeled tender.

The Great Western Railway Company

Newcastle upon Tyne 24th Feby 1841

Bo.t of Robert Stephenson & Co.

Engineers, Millwrights, Brass & Iron Founders.

Makers of locomotive, high pressure & portable steam engines and boilers of every description.

Hydraulic presses, paper machines and drying cylinders &c. on the most approved plan.

Weighing machines.

Dividing, planing & drilling machines, lathes, boring mills & copper work in general.

| | £ |
|---|---|
| One Locomotive Engine 15½ In Cylinder 18 Inch Stroke Copper Fire Box 1 pair 7 feet & 2 pair 4 feet Wheels (No 270) "Rising Star" With 1 Set Screw Keys Large & Small Monkey wrench 1 Set Fire Irons 3 oil Can, 1 Hammer 3 Chisel & 2 Ball valve, | 2150 " " |
| 4 Large Packing Cases Hooped with Iron Flannel | 13 " |
| One Locomotive Engine 15½ In Cylinder as above with 1 Set Tool, (No 271) | 2150 " |
| 4 Large Packing Case, as above, | 13 " |
| | 4326 " |

p the "John Capt. Colledge"

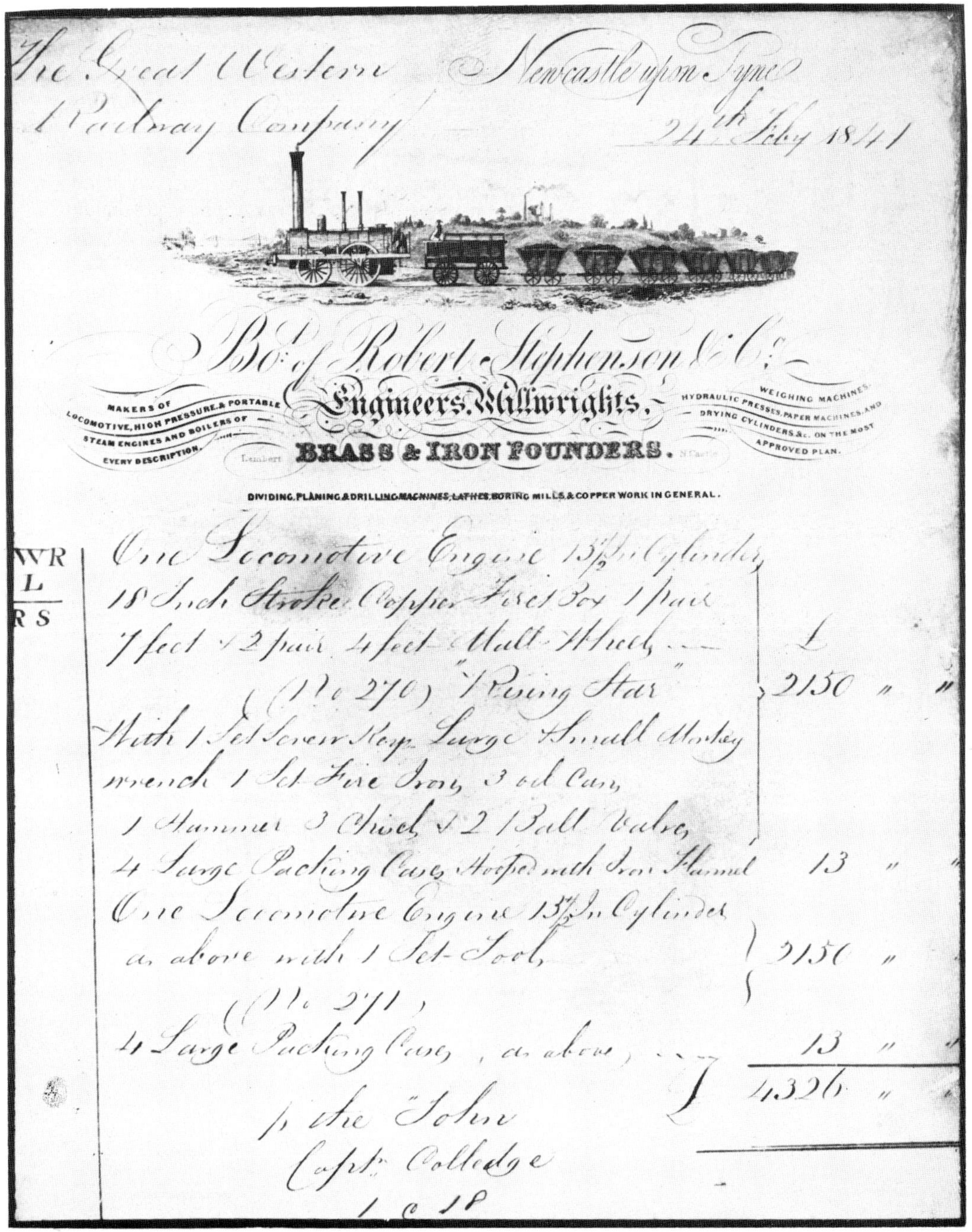

Figure 8

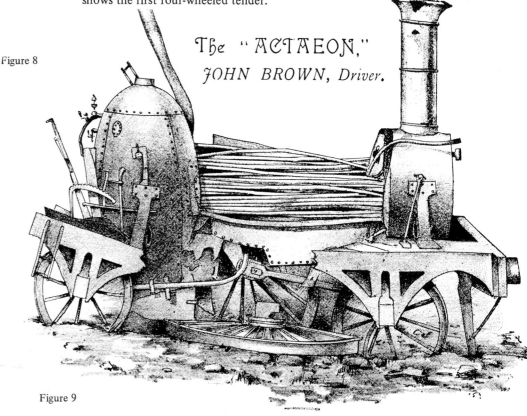

The "ACTAEON,"
JOHN BROWN, Driver.

Figure 9

**The boiler of this engine exploded, in Glo'ster Station yard, close to the water tank, on February 7th, 1855.**

Figure 10

CENTAUR

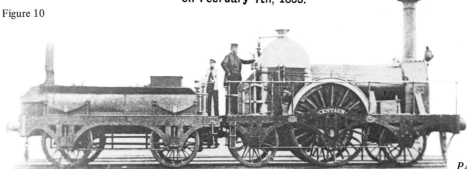

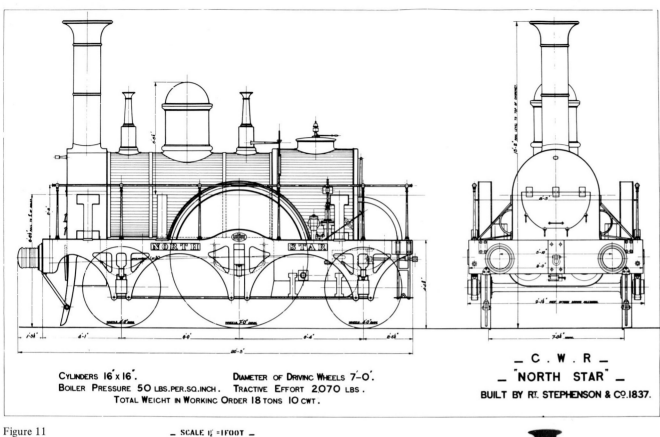

CYLINDERS 16ʺ x 16ʺ.  DIAMETER OF DRIVING WHEELS 7ʹ-0ʺ.
BOILER PRESSURE 50 LBS.PER.SQ.INCH.  TRACTIVE EFFORT 2.070 LBS.
TOTAL WEIGHT IN WORKING ORDER 18 TONS 10 CWT.

_ C . W . R _
_ "NORTH STAR" _
BUILT BY Rᵗ. STEPHENSON & Cº.1837.

_ SCALE 1½ʺ =1FOOT _

Figure 11

Figure 12

Figure 13

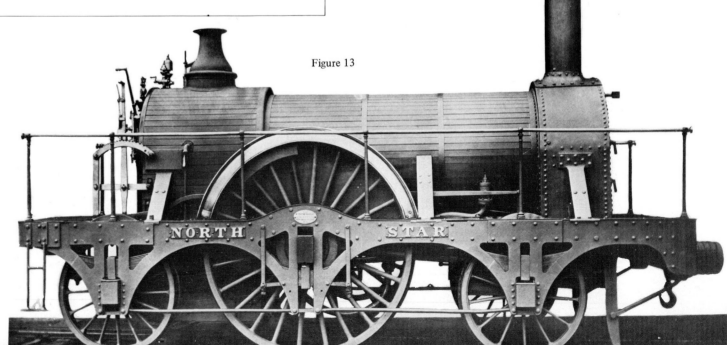

This page features both a drawing and photograph of the famous *North Star.* In the drawing the engine is shown exactly as delivered from Messrs. Robert Stephenson's, and it was in this condition that she worked the first passenger train (a Director's Special) in May 1938.

She ceased work in 1871, and was preserved at Swindon in the condition seen in *Figure 13,* until 1906, when she was cut up on Churchward's orders only to be resurrected as a full size replica in 1925 for the Darlington centenary exhibition *(Figure 12).* This model can still be seen at Swindon museum today.

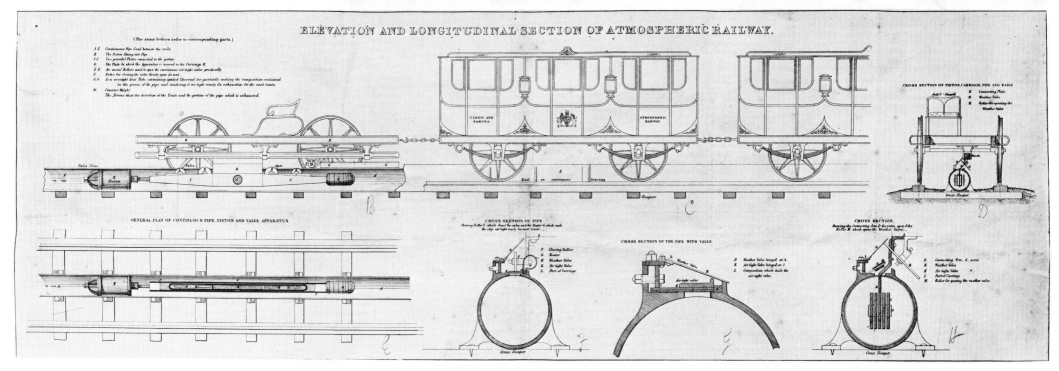

ELEVATION AND LONGITUDINAL SECTION OF ATMOSPHERIC RAILWAY.

GENERAL PLAN OF CONTINUOUS PIPE, PISTON AND VALVE APPARATUS

CROSS SECTION OF PIPE

CROSS SECTION OF THE PIPE WITH VALVE

CROSS SECTION

CROSS SECTION OF PISTON, CARRIAGE, PIPE AND RAILS

Between the years of 1846 and 1848, I. K. Brunel tried desperately to succeed with a new form of traction between Exeter and Teignmouth, on the South Devon Railway. This was the 'Atmospheric Railway' and although a complete failure, it has its place in Great Western history. So, as this is a book dealing with all types of Great Western engines, it was thought fit to include this diagrammatical sketch of the atmospheric system which shows in good detail how the engine carriage moved in the tubes.

In 1855, 10 broad gauge engines were built by R. Stephenson & Co. of Newcastle for the Great Western which were of the 4-4-0 type with tenders, the only series of this classification to run on the broad gauge. *Figure 14* shows *Antiquary* at Swindon. The class was known later as the 'Abbot' class, although recorded as the 'Waverley' class. None were rebuilt and were all withdrawn by 1876.

*Figure 15* is of *Rob Roy* in the same class. This engine was derailed in the Bullo Pill accident of 1868.

Figure 15

Figure 14

Figure 16

*Figure 16* is an early official photograph of one of the well-known 8′ 'Singles', named *Sultan*. First built in 1847, she was one of 24 engines of the 'Rover' class renewed at Swindon between 1871 and 1888. Several points of interest are worthy of note in this picture. For instance, the sandwich frames and inverted springs on the leading wheels (not a bogie incidentally!), and the sand boxes just in front of the leading wheels mounted on the running plate, a position they occupied for 80 years afterwards. Note also the braking, now transferred to the tender and applied by means of a crank handle, a feature also perpetuated. In those days, too, the engine crew wore *white* cord overalls so the engines just had to be clean or the driver's and fireman's uniform would soon suffer. Finally, note the 'Coffin' box on the tender rear for the use of a travelling porter to 'watch over' the following

Figure 17

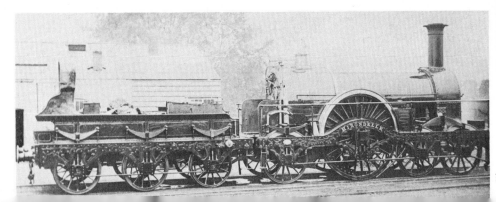

Figure 18

Figure 19

train. *Figure 17* is a picture of the same engine recorded at Paddington, where she was being used at the time as an artist's model for Frith's famous painting of the terminus. The right-hand side of the class can be seen in the picture of *Hirondelle (Figure 18)*, whilst *Figure 19* indicates that operating these early engines was still fraught with danger, another boiler explosion this time belonging to *Perseus* and shown in Westbourne Park shed in November 1862.

Figure 20

Figure 21

Figure 22

Absorbed and associated railways figure largely in any history of the Great Western, and here are shown three engines of widely different design and use.

No. 29 shown in *Figure 21,* was the first example of a steam rail-car to work over what later became the Great Western Railway, designed and built by W. B. Adams at Fairfield Works, Bow, to the order of the Bristol & Exeter Railway in 1848. Constructed to the broad gauge, it consisted of a carriage with four wheels of 3′ 6″ diameter and a type of articulated engine platform which supported an upright boiler, and cylinders set horizontally, driving onto the single drivers of 4′ 6″ diameter.

It was tried out by the Great Western on the West London Railway and spent most of its Bristol & Exeter life on the Tiverton, Clevedon and Weston branches.

The little well tank, No. 30, *(Figure 20)* was built by Longridge to 7′ gauge, for the Bristol & Exeter Railway also, this time in 1851, and was one of five similar tanks. Like No. 29, several were employed on the Tiverton and Clevedon branches, and two acted as Bristol pilots. Nos. 31 and 32 lasted into Great Western days, being renumbered 2054 and 2055, and were finally withdrawn in 1877 and 1878 respectively.

However, for a real chequered history, *Heron (Figure 22)* must win hands down. Built in 1861 by Sharp Stewart as a 4-4-0 side-tank engine, she was hired along with her sister *Magpie* to the Carmarthen & Cardigan Railway. When the line was changed to standard gauge in 1872, the two engines were sold to the South Devon Railway who altered them to saddle tanks. The picture shows No. 2134 at Newton Abbot, as altered by the Great Western, finally being withdrawn in May 1892. The toolbox on the front buffer is reminiscent of the 'Metro' class of 2-4-0Ts.

*Lord of the Isles,* probably the most famous broad gauge locomotive of all, was originally named *Charles Russell,* a name which was only used when it was exhibited at the Hyde Park exhibition of 1851. She did not in fact begin working until 1852 under the new name of *Lord of the Isles,* she headed a director's special and came to grief at Aynho Station of September 30th, 1852. However, little damage was sustained to the engine, and she ran on until being withdrawn in 1884. She was preserved at Swindon with *North Star* and was finally broken up in 1906. *Figures 23 and 24* show the left and right hand sides respectively. The tender brake blocks were on one side only, and this was the only brake on the engine!

Figure 23

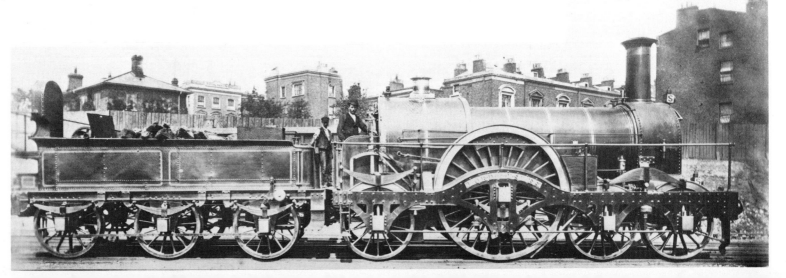

Figure 24

After the 4-4-0 'Waverley' class of 1855 *(seen on page 7),* a lighter form of engine was designed and built in the following year at Swindon. This was the 'Victoria' class, the series taking its name from the first engine turned out in August of 1856. They were built to two 'lots', the first batch on the fifth passenger lot of eight engines, and the second ten on the sixth passenger lot during 1863-64. This second batch took the names of the famous contemporary engineers. *Telford* is seen in *Figure 25* and it can be seen that the wheel configuration was that of a 2-4-0 tender engine. Coupled wheels were 6′ 6″ diameter and leading wheels 4′ diameter.

Nine years after the introduction of the 'Victoria' class came the 2-4-0 'Hawthorn' class. Very similar in outline to the 'Victoria' series, this latter class of twenty engines were made by what became the Avonside Engine Co., and a further six engines were made at Swindon approximately twelve months later. All this class had 6′ coupled wheels and 4′ leading wheels and *Figure 26* shows *Dewrance* (left hand side) and *Figure 27 Fenton* (right hand side); note that both engines have been fitted with a buffer plank to handle narrow gauge as well as broad stock.

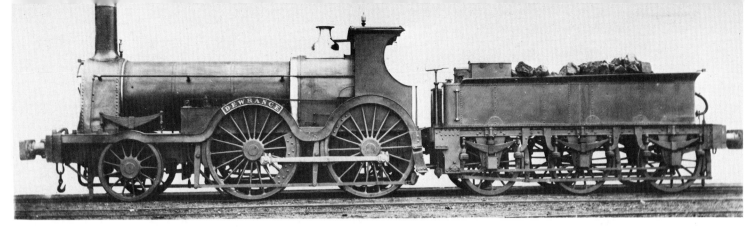

Figure 26

Figure 27

Figure 25

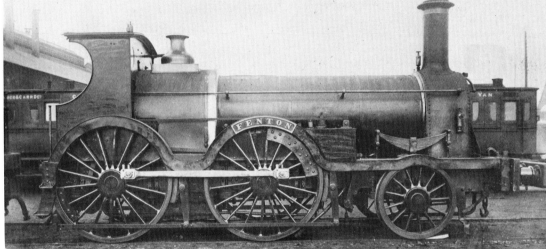

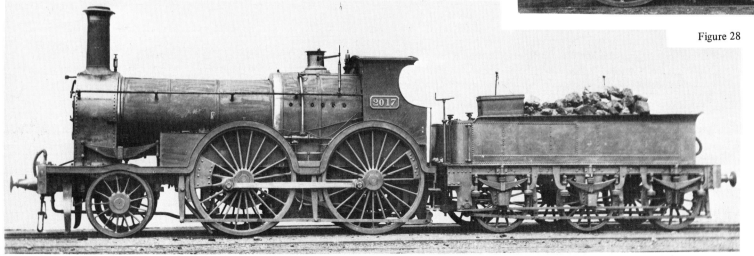

Figure 28

The 2-4-0 in the lower illustration *(Figure 28)* was one of the first passenger engines to be built by Pearson in 1870-72 for the Bristol & Exeter Railway. They were all replacements of earlier engines, constructed at Bristol, and came into the ownership of the Great Western in 1876, working mostly to Newton Abbot and back, but could have been seen occasionally on excursion and fast goods traffic to London. The driving wheels were 6′ 7½″ diameter, one inch less than Churchward 'Stars', and the leading wheels were 4′ diameter. Note that both these engines carried the same boiler fittings, namely, the Gooch safety valve bonnet and the early Dean chimney. Also, like the majority of the 'absorptions and convertibles', the characteristic Great Western number-plate was now fitted. This engine lasted until the gauge conversion in 1892.

Figure 29

PAGE 12

*Europa,* featured in the top photograph, *(Figure 29)* was built at Swindon in 1853 and was one of the 'Ariadne' class of 7′ gauge Gooch standard goods engines and even at this early date one can see signs of the eventual Dean goods. Note the cab shape and sand boxes on the running plate; also note that the only brake is a hand brake on the tender, making a brake whistle a necessity. There were 102 engines in the class under seven different lots, and *Europa* was the only one to be rebuilt at Swindon in 1869 with a new boiler and survived until the end of the broad gauge. In fact this was the last broad gauge locomotive to leave Plymouth for Swindon when pulling the early morning goods on May 21st, 1892.

During the years 1884-88 twenty of the 0-6-0 tender goods engines which had been built to standard gauge in 1876 at Swindon, were fitted with broad gauge axles and were used on the freight trains between London and Plymouth to relieve the shortage of the broad gauge engines, the stock at that time being run down prior to the abolition of the wide 7′ trackage. These engines had an unusual look about them as they were paired with the wide tenders of the broad gauge with outside frames. *Figure 30* illustrates No. 1205, which was built in 1876, fitted for broad gauge in 1888, and reconverted to standard gauge in 1892. (Another in the same series is shown on *page 16.*)

Figure 30

Figure 31

There were many odd looking engines on the Great Western during broad gauge days, and amongst them were these two saddle tanks. In *Figure 31* the 4-4-0 tank *Leopard* is shown. She was originally built by the Avonside Engine Co. for the South Devon Railway in 1872 and was especially designed to be easily converted to the standard gauge. However she was always a broad gauge engine and finished her days at the Swindon dump shunting all the condemned 7′ gauge stock until she was cut up in 1893. Coupled wheels were 5′ 9″ and bogie wheels 3′ 6″. Her only sisters were *Stag, Lance* and *Osiris*.

*Stewart* shown in *Figure 32* was one of the 'Hawthorn' class mentioned on *page 11*. She started life as a 2-4-0 tender engine, and then in 1877, with nine others of the class, was altered to the saddle tank design shown here. Driving wheels were reduced to 5′ diameter, and tanks to hold 860 gallons were fitted. She was finally withdrawn in 1892.

Figure 32

Figure 33

PAGE 14

*Figures 33 and 34* are shown together on this page to illustrate the Armstrong saddle-tanks. *Sir Watkin* shown in *Figure 34* was one of six engines built in 1866 with side-tanks and condensing gear for working over the Metropolitan Railway, but as the wide gauge on the 'Met' was converted to standard in 1869, the tanks lost this job, and three were sold to the South Devon Railway. When later rebuilt, all six were fitted with the long saddle-tank shown in the photograph, and *Sir Watkin* and a sister engine *Saunders* were the only two of the class to survive to the end of the broad gauge.

It is interesting to compare *Sir Watkin* with No. 1561 in *Figure 33* as they are both 'Armstrong' engines, but 10 years separate their building dates. As the end of the broad gauge was obviously in sight, it would have been imprudent to continue building broad gauge engines, so the compromise was reached in 1876 to construct engines as narrow gauge machines, but fitted with 7′ long axles enabling them to work over the wider gauge and then eventually be refitted with the standard gauge running gear when the change of gauge became a reality. All the engines so fitted were known as 'Convertibles' and could be recognised as such by carrying number-plates, but no names. Points of interest are the obvious relationship of the coal bunkers, size and shape of the wheels (4′ 6″ diameter), spring gear and boiler mountings. The large wooden blocks bolted to the buffers on *Sir Watkin* would be to enable this engine to work 'mixed' stock, to take up the difference in buffer widths.

Figure 34

Three more saddle tanks on this page. In *Figure 36* is No. 2048, one of the twenty six passenger 4-4-0 tanks built between 1855-73 by various firms, for the Bristol & Exeter Railway. It was one of this class (No. 2051) which, whilst running at full speed with a boat express, collided at Norton Fitzwarren with a goods train killing ten passengers.

*Figure 35* shows a small shunting engine built in 1869 for the South Devon Railway, by the Avonside Engine Co. She had 3' wheels and lived long enough to be converted to standard gauge, being scrapped in 1905. No. 2093 shown in *Figure 37* was one of a pair of 0-6-0 tank engines built at Bristol in 1866-7 and was exceptional in having that long extended tank. Her sister No. 2092 only had a short saddle tank of 950 gallons.

Figure 35

Figure 36

Figure 37

Figure 40

The drawing, *Figure 39,* and photograph, *Figure 40,* of No. 2002 shown at the bottom of this page illustrates a further development of engine design at Swindon. These engines started life as a 4-2-4 tank class for the Bristol & Exeter Railway and were built by Rothwell & Co. for the Exeter expresses *(Figure 38).* They had four-wheel bogies leading and trailing, with wheels of 4′ diameter, and the drivers were large, of 9′ in fact. Only four were taken into Great Western stock, Nos. 39-42, and were re-numbered 2001-2004. On July 27th, 1876, the up 'Flying Dutchman' was descending the Bourton incline when the engine, No. 2001, left the rails and rolled over and over, finishing up finally on the down line. Although condition of the track was blamed, the 4-2-4 class was under suspicion, and from then on the other three were rebuilt as 4-2-2 tender engines, becoming the first inside-framed bogie singles in the country. No. 2001 was not converted but scrapped, and 2004 was renumbered 2001. No. 2002 is the engine pictured at Swindon shops. There is a superb colour illustration of this class on the frontispiece of *Part 2 R.C.T.S. Great Western locomotives.*

Figure 38

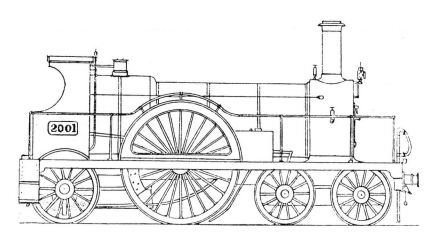

Figure 39

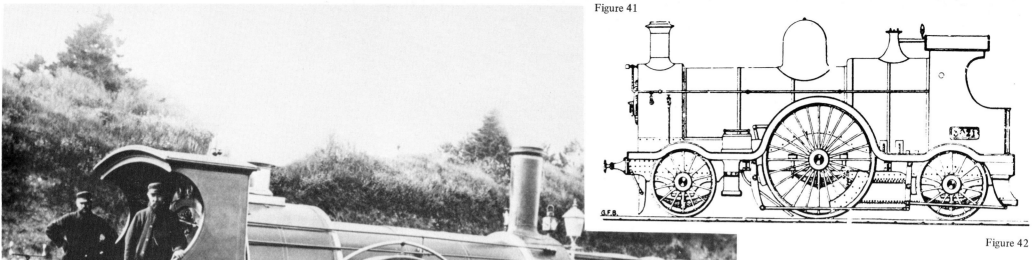

Figure 41

Figure 42

*Figure 41* shows what massive engines these rebuilds were. No. 2001 is seen here at the head of an up express, standing in Dawlish station in 1883. Before rebuilding she was numbered 2004 and finally took over No. 2001 when that engine was cut up after the Long Ashton accident.

Also on this page is the final example of the convertibles, the 2-2-2 express singles Nos. 3021-3028, which were built for the broad gauge, with 7′ axles and wide cabs, but with allowance for a quick conversion to the standard gauge when the change came about. These eight engines only worked on the 7′ track for approximately twelve months, before being taken into the '3001' class, from which they had originated. They were then given names in this class as under:

| | |
|---|---|
| 3021 *Wigmore Castle* | 3022 *Rougemont* |
| 3023 *Swallow* | 3024 *Storm King* |
| 3025 *St. George* | 3026 *Tornado* |
| 3027 *Thames* | 3028 *Wellington* |

Figure 43

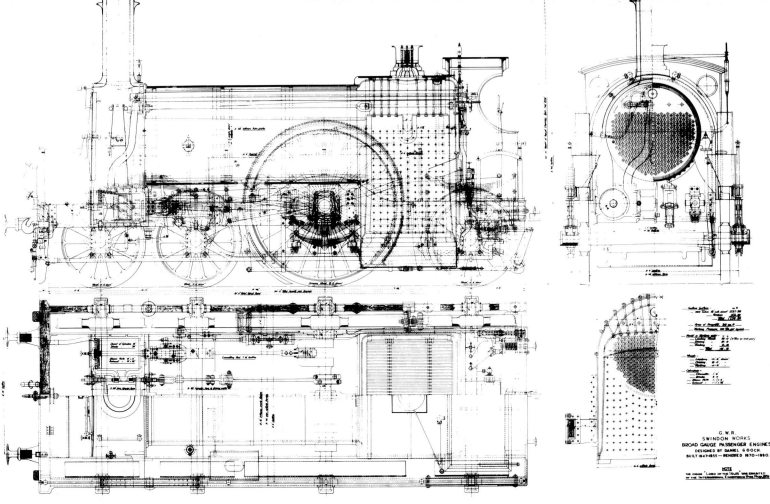

G.W.R.
SWINDON WORKS
BROAD GAUGE PASSENGER ENGINES.
DESIGNED BY DANIEL GOOCH.
BUILT 1847-1855 — RENEWED 1870-1880.

NOTE
THE ENGINE "LORD OF THE ISLES" WAS EXHIBITED
AT THE INTERNATIONAL EXHIBITION IN HYDE PARK 1851.

Figure 44

Without doubt, the most magnificent and fascinating engines of the whole broad gauge era were the Gooch 4-2-2 singles with driving wheels of 8′ diameter, known as the 'Rover' class.

There were 24 engines in all and, although classed as renewals, twenty of them were completely new in 1873. *Page 8* shows these engines as they were first built, and on this page is the general arrangement drawing from Swindon of the series as "Renewed" in 1870/80 *(Figure 44)*. Seen from the rear end in *Figure 45* is *Sebastapol* which complements the drawing.

Figure 45

Figure 46

Two superb studies from the photographic records of Swindon. *Figure 46* shows *Bulkeley* as seen in the works grey paint, posed expressly for the purpose of photography. Even the axleboxes are painted white.

*Figure 47* shows the initial engine of the 'Rover' class standing at Swindon on the mixed track, just notice the pride in the faces of the driver and fireman.

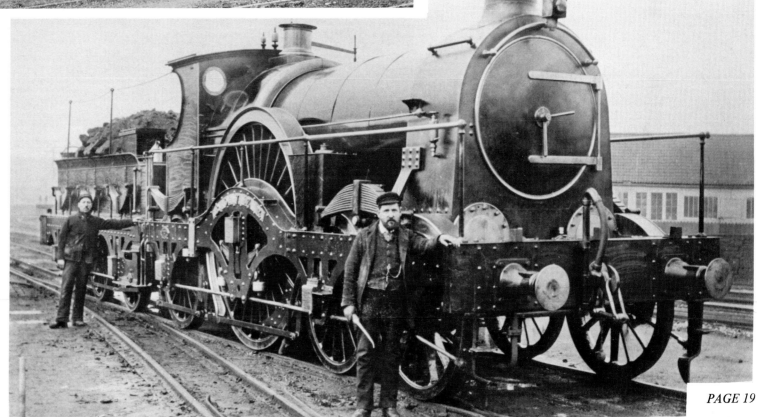

Figure 47

Figure 48

Two final pictures of these fine locomotives. *Figure 48* shows *Amazon* standing at Chippenham Station, and below, in *Figure 49 Tartar* is posed outside the drawing office at Swindon Works. Notice the stone carving on the wall of the building in the top left of the photograph.

Figure 49

Figure 50

Figure 51

The end of the broad gauge came in 1892, and all the non-convertible engines of the wide gauge were marshalled into temporary sidings, laid especially for that purpose at Swindon.

Pictures of this scene have been published many times before, but always in small format. In order to see more detail in these interesting photographs, the next three pages are occupied wholly by contact prints from Swindon archives. I trust the reader will find them as interesting as I do. The engine in the foreground, *Argo,* is one of a class of eight goods tanks taken over from the South Devon Railway in 1876. Built in Bristol by Slaughter & Gruning Co. in October of 1863, although carrying many Great Western fittings, the strange cab and bunker shape prove her 'private company' ancestry. *Roberts* is next in line and from the same lineage, originally built as a 2-4-0 tender engine. She was altered to a saddle-tank arrangement in 1877 and the driving wheels were changed from 6′ diameter to 5′ diameter. Notice that both engines are domeless, but carry the Dean chimney and Armstrong safety valve bonnet. Behind *Roberts* can just be seen No. 2133, *Heila.* She came from the Carmarthen & Cardigan Railway and was built in 1864 by Rothwell & Co. The classification was 4-4-0 saddle tank with 5′ 3″ coupled wheels, and after having many owners, she was sold to the South Devon Railway in 1872. A new boiler and saddle tank were fitted to her by Avonside Engine Co. in 1875.

*Buffalo* can be seen middle left, one of ten built in 1872 by the Avonside Engine Co., again for the South Devon, and she was eventually converted to standard gauge in 1893. Two other small points caught my eye in this enlargement – note the tiny star on the smoke box door of the saddle tank on the extreme right. Also the discrepancy in buffer widths between *Argo* and the tender in front of her, the tank engine having a buffer plank to cover both broad and standard gauges.

The odd-looking engine in *Figure 51* was a 'one-off' experimental engine of William Dean's design, to the 2-4-0 classification. She had six plate frames, a double sandwich carrying the driving axleboxes and the outer single frame forming the hornblocks for the leading wheels. The engine was fitted with four cylinders, two high pressure cylinders and two low pressure, the L.P.'s being set in front of the H.P.'s in tandem, the piston rods from the L.P. cylinders passing outside the high pressure cylinders and linked to common crossheads to the connecting rods. However, No. 8 gave a lot of trouble, and was never converted to the standard gauge, being withdrawn in 1892 and the number was used for a new standard gauge engine built in 1894.

Figure 52

Figure 53

An interesting picture for the historian. In the immediate foreground are discarded 'Mansell' coach wheels of 7′ gauge, and behind them two tenders of the same width, one showing the front, and one the rear end. Note the odd position of the lamp brackets. On the front end of these tenders is a 12-wheel boiler truck (the first picture I have seen of one of these wagons) and note that the flanges have been removed from the two centre pairs of wheels. Three more tenders on the second road, and I have found out that the tall round pillar was the outlet for the return flow of water from the pump.

Two saddle tanks, one numbered 2053 which would mean they were ex Bristol & Exeter 4-4-0 passenger saddle tanks built in 1873 by the Avonside Engine Co. Note the cab shape, reminiscent of G.N.R. practice. Next in line come Nos. 2016 and 2020 again from Bristol & Exeter, and the same class as on page 4. They were built be Pearson in 1871 and 1870 respectively. Right on the edge is No. 2159, *Saunders,* the sister engine to *Sir Watkin* on *Page 5.*

Other engines which can be identified are several of the passenger tank engines designed by Dean for working in South Devon. Originally 0-4-2 saddle tanks, they were changed later to 0-4-4 with side tanks, and a photograph of No. 3548 seen here, can also be seen on *page 130.*

*Figure 53* illustrates the one-off engine No. 9. Whilst the broad gauge was still at its height, William Dean was trying out many varied ideas i.e. tandem cylinders, compounding and others.

No. 9 on the other hand was totally different. She was first built in 1881 as a strange-looking 4-2-4 side tank, with single drivers of 7′ 8″ diameter, and was the only 'single' tank engine to be built by the Great Western for the standard gauge. On emerging from the shed for her first trials in May of 1881, she ran off the turntable in front of William Dean, and the little service she did perform was studded with de-railments. So much so, that in 1884 she reappeared as shown in *Figure 53* with the original large driving wheels and the 18″ diameter cylinders, with a very long stroke of 26″. Also retained was the outside valve motion, driven as can be seen from an eccentric mounted on the outside end of the main driving axle. This unusual engine ran like this until 1890, when together with No. 10, she was fitted with 7′ driving wheels, and was rebuilt to an approximation of the 'Queen' design.

More details of the engines already mentioned can be seen in this last large photo of the Swindon dump. On the right can be seen the 0-4-4 tanks referred to on the previous page. The number plate of No. 3542 can be identified with No. 3548 ahead of her. Right in the foreground is the cab of one of the big singles, the 'Rover' class, and many details are recognisable. Note the clack-boxes entering the boiler backplate, the sanding gear lever right across so that driver or fireman could operate same, and the connecting rods in the tender. On the left can just be seen No. 1199, one of the convertible 0-6-0 goods engines and note the difference in width of engine and tender. In front of her is a row of saddle tanks of 0-6-0 classification, the first one being No. 1250 and so on.

Figure 54

Although originally constructed solely as a broad gauge system, lines of standard gauge were taken over in the Midlands and North with the absorption of the Shrewsbury-Chester and the Shrewsbury and Birmingham Railways. In the early 1850s the Great Western Railway became a Company of two systems, the majority of the southern section being broad gauge, whilst the northern division was to the standard gauge of 4' 8½". All the 7' gauge engines made by the Company were constructed at Swindon Works, whereas the standard gauge engines, other than those absorbed, were made firstly at Wolverhampton. Thus the situation arose of a railway company having two distinct locomotive engineers pursuing their individual designs, one to each of the two systems. As related briefly in the last section, Daniel Gooch was in charge of the Southern Broad Gauge division, whilst at the Wolverhampton Works,

Figure 55

Joseph Armstrong reigned supreme. (However, it must be stated that overall control was with Gooch at Swindon.) The Wolverhampton engines were always distinctive and different in many ways from the Swindon machines, having boiler fittings of a different pattern to those of the southern division. Even the frames were unlike the Swindon product, having no cut-outs. This no doubt derived from the style of the absorbed engines which were taken into stock at Stafford Road, and maintained there. It was only in 1864 when Daniel Gooch resigned at Swindon and Joseph Armstrong succeeded him in the post of Locomotive Engineer, that the two styles started to amalgamate. William Dean who was Works Manager at Wolverhampton in 1868, was summoned to Swindon by Armstrong to act as his assistant, and so it was that the traditions of Brunel and Gooch were gradually added to, and replaced by the designs and ideas from Stafford Road.

The first illustration of the standard gauge engines is of No. 14 *(Figures 55 and 56)*. Built by Sharp Brothers in July 1848 for the Shrewsbury & Chester Railway, she came into Great Western hands in 1854. Although only a tiny engine by comparison, one can nevertheless

Figure 56

see the well-tried designs of 'framing' as used in 1838 by Hawthorne in *Hurricane* on *page 3*. Both sides of the engine are shown, and one picture shows the tender used with this engine. Although withdrawn in 1885, she was preserved at Wolverhampton until 1920. Perhaps it should also be stated here that the livery of the Northern division engines was different to that of Swindon, Armstrong locomotives being painted in a blue/green shade, picked out with red instead of white lines, and underframes were of a darker red/brown shade, different to the more Indian red colour of the Southern division.

At this point in time, and in fact right up to 1882 period, the majority of the standard gauge engines were singles, by which I mean there were few locomotives at work on the system with coupled driving wheels. The opinion amongst loco men at that time was that an engine

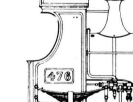

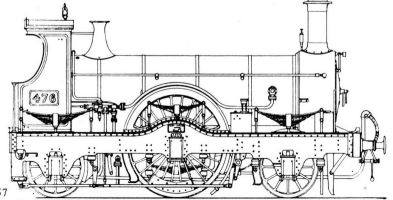

Figure 57

with single drivers would run more freely than a similar machine encumbered with coupling rods and several pairs of driving wheels. Thus it was that the large majority of the express working was handled by engines of the 2-2-2 class which were taken into stock from the absorbed companies. The first Great Western proper narrow gauge passenger engines were the '69–76' class which were constructed for the Great Western by Beyer-Peacock, to Gooch's specifications. The first engine was built in 1855 and looked very much like a narrower version of the broad gauge singles *(see Figure D2 in Part 4 of R.C.T.S. locos of Great Western Railway)*. Eventually in the 1890s these engines were rebuilt finally as 2-4-0s and became the 'River' class, and are referred to on *page 52* of this volume. In 1862 the Great Western purchased a further ten 2-2-2s by Gooch, this time from Sharp Stewart & Co. which were very similar to the '69–76' class except that driving wheels were 7' diameter instead of 6' 6". As they were eventually considerably rebuilt and had a long history on the Great Western, they are dealt with in more detail on *page 30*. The first passenger lot built by the company for the standard gauge was the 'Sir Daniel' class, and the drawing in *Figure 57* shows No. 476 of this class as rebuilt in 1881. It is shown on *page 24* along with No. 14, as they compare very well in details such as shape of framing, overhung springing system, wheel guards, sandboxes and even number plates. Although there were thirty engines made, only four were named.

No. 378 *Sir Daniel*              No. 380 *North Star*
No. 381 *Morning Star*            No. 471 *Sir Watkin*

They were later converted to 0-6-0s. *See page 35.*

Figure 58

Figure 59

The 'Queen' class of 2-2-2 wheel configuration began with the single engine so named, built in 1873 at Swindon. A further twenty were constructed in 1875, but only ten of the class received names.

No. 55 *Queen*                    No. 999 *Sir Alexander*
No. 1118 *Prince Christian*       No. 1119 *Princess of Wales*
No. 1122 *Beaconsfield*           No. 1123 *Salisbury*
No. 1128 *Duke of York*           No. 1129 *Princess May*
No. 1130 *Gooch*                  No. 1132 *Prince of Wales*

Figure 60

As suggested by the name, 'Queen' was the engine used on most of the Royal train work and apart from the pictures in this book, a good official photograph showing her at the head of an early Royal special can be seen in the companion book to this, *Great Western Coaches, vol. 1, page 32.*

This class of express engine was larger in dimensions than the earlier 'Sir Daniel' class, and was different in having underhung springs to the drivers instead of on top of the framing. Also the motion was arranged for two slide bars instead of four.

The photograph *(Figure 58)* shows the engine as built with no cab, open splashers and coupled to the early tender with no rails, whereas *Figure 59* illustrates No. 55 in 1897 rebuilt with cab, new chimney and with Royal decorations. Note that the tender has now received coal rails. *Figure 60* shows the engine later still at Oxford, and is included as the right hand side of *Queen* can be seen. Note that she now has a more modern tender with the springs directly over the axleboxes.

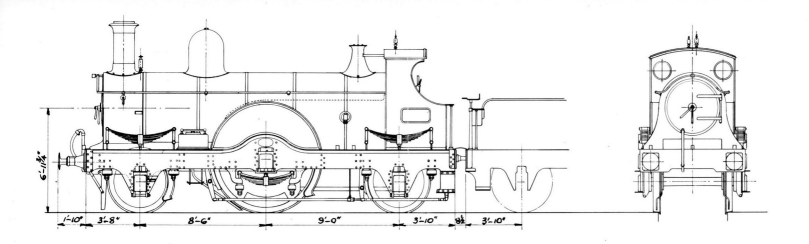

These drawings are of interest in that they show the 'Queen' class in two stages of rebuild. In the top diagram, *Figure 61* — shows the engine having the dome on the front ring of the boiler, whereas in the lower illustration this fitting is on the back ring. Also the two drawings show the two different types of tender, overhung and underhung springs, and the longer capacity and length of the later variety, shown in the Swindon diagram 'A', in *Figure 63*.

Figure 61

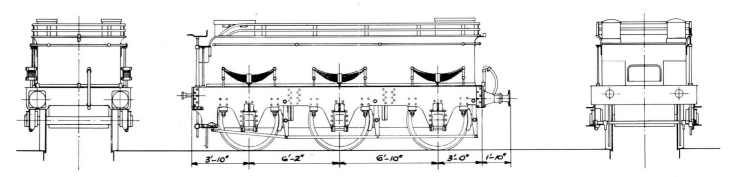

Figure 62

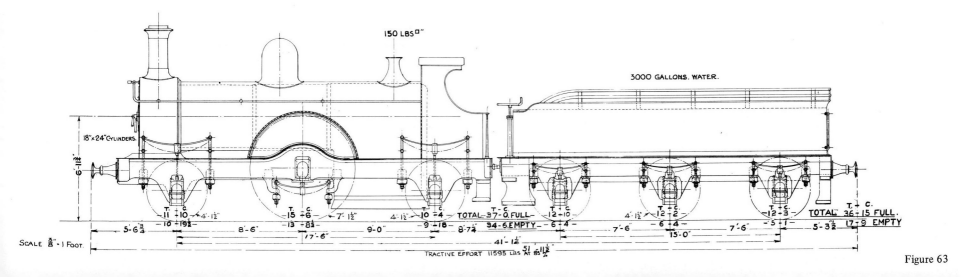

150 LBS ◻"

3000 GALLONS. WATER.

18"x24"CYLINDERS.

SCALE ⅜" = 1 FOOT.

TRACTIVE EFFORT 11595 LBS AT 85 ½

Figure 63

These two photographs show both sides of the 'Queen' class, and illustrate two more of the named engines, No. 1132, *Prince of Wales* seen in works undercoat and No. 1119, *Princess of Wales* shown actually in service. The two views also show the steam dome mounted in the two different positions. The 'Prince' has this fitting on the front boiler ring, whereas 'Princess' shows the dome on the second ring. The dates of the pictures would be 1896 for the upper illustration, and approximately 1899-1900 for the lower photograph *(Figure 66)*. The utter simplicity of these early engines can be seen in the creased and tattered drawing reproduced in *Figure 64*. We apologise for the condition but the drawing is 100 years old!

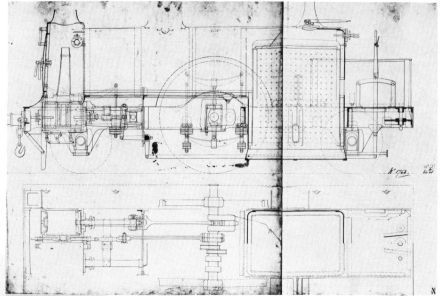

Figure 65

Figure 64

Figure 66

Two more drawings of the 'Queen' class are seen on this page, both official Swindon diagrams. The bare outline in the upper drawing is of the engine No. 1122 which was named *Beaconsfield* and shows the class at its stage in 1880 with the small tender. The lower diagram, *Figure 68*, shows the class fitted with the Belpaire firebox which was flush with the boiler top, but still carrying the steam dome on the second ring. Also note that the tender is now of the modern variety as built under Churchward.

In *Figure 69* the rebuilt version of the '157' class is shown and illustrates well how close was this design to that of the 'Queens', the only main difference being in the sandwich-slotted frames of the former design. This official diagram is 'B' of *Lot 51*, the only one issued by Churchward showing the Belpaire boiler and firebox.

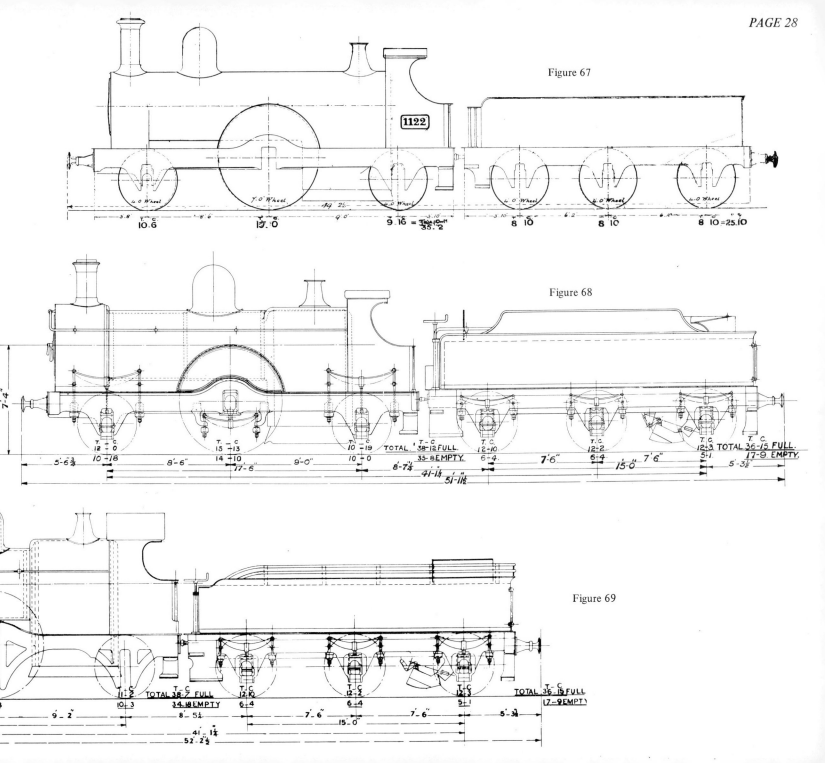

Figure 67

Figure 68

Figure 69

The final form of the famous 'Queen' class appears on this page and one can see that now the boiler has the raised Belpaire firebox, type BRO, which carried the safety valve on the second boiler ring in place of the dome. I would assess the date of these pictures to be around 1903 and modellers should note the shorter chimney now fitted, the higher cab, with larger windows, and the different arc to the cab's rear sides. Contrast No's. 1120 and 1122 with No. 1132 in *Figure 72*.

It should perhaps be said that these engines, together with the '157's, carried the whole burden of the express working from London to Wolverhampton and London to Swindon in the 1890's on the standard gauge with five and sometimes six eight-wheeled carriages. The 141 miles to Wolverhampton was reached from the terminus in three hours four minutes, and this was via Oxford of course. Mr. Ahrons, in his book on *Locomotive and Train Working in The Latter Part of the 19th Century* published by Heffer, deals at length with the sound work these engines performed, and gives some idea of their importance in the evolution of the Swindon locomotive.

Figure 70

Figure 71

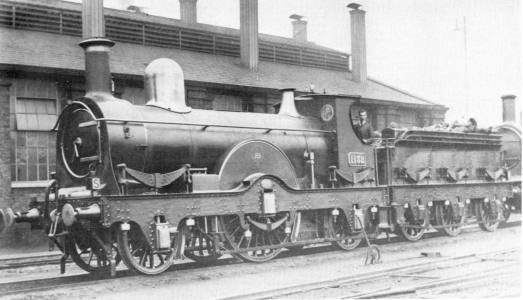

Figure 72

Figure 73

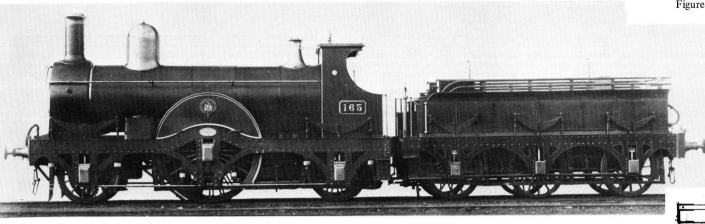

The year 1878 also saw the introduction of the '157' class of 2-2-2's which performed the same work as the 'Queens' previously referred to. These engines were also known as 'Cobhams' or 'Sharpies', the latter because they were probably replacements for the 2-2-2 constructed by Sharps in 1862. The main difference between these engines and the 'Queens' was in the sandwich frames, which, as can be seen from the illustrations, was of the open-slotted pattern, and originally had the open splashers with a broad brass band fixed on the side. The lower picture

Figure 74

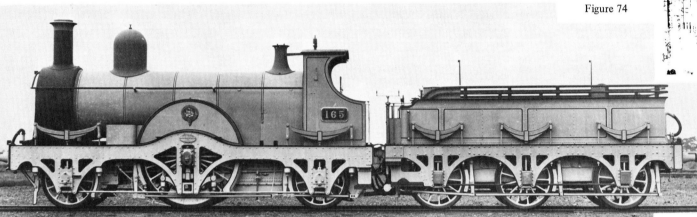

*(Figure 75)* shows No. 158 as originally built, without dome, whereas the two Swindon pictures *(Figures 73 and 74)* illustrate No. 165 in works undercoat, and finished livery. The upper picture is dated 1895, and the middle illustration 1896, and it is interesting to note that the old type of axles boxes have been changed for a more modern pattern. (The drawing on

Figure 76

*page 31* shows the class rebuilt.) The tiny works drawing in *Figure 76* is reduced from the original Swindon general arrangement of 1863 and shows the internal layout.

Figure 75

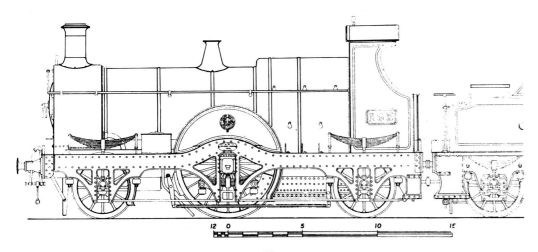

Figure 77

Figure 78

The three stages of rebuild to the '157' class can be clearly seen on this page. The large Swindon picture, *Figure 79,* shows a three-quarter view of No. 165 with the dome on the front ring of the boiler, and the smaller photograph of No. 166 gives the dome on the second ring, and with the clack boxes mounted on the firebox side *(Figure 78).* The drawing, *Figure 77,* illustrates the final stage of the class, now fitted with raised Belpaire boiler, domeless, and with the safety valve on the second ring. This engine, No. 165, outlived her sisters by several years, and ended up at Oxford before being scrapped in 1914. There were 10 built altogether, Nos. 157-166, and there were many changes in various engines, as some were rebuilt at Swindon and some at Wolverhampton, so modellers are advised to check carefully on the particular engine chosen to model.

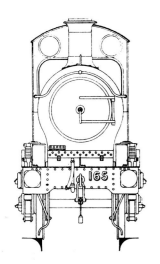

Figure 79

Three more pictures of the 'Sharpies' again to show how different engines in the class varied slightly from their sisters. All three have the final raised Belpaire firebox and the tall cab. In the upper picture, *Figure 80,* the detail of the framing is very good, and note the mudguards which these engines always carried on leading and driving wheels, also the square-shanked head-lamps and brackets. No. 160 shown in the lower left photo has the dome on the second boiler ring, and an unusually wide cab with side windows, whereas No. 165 again, bottom right, *Figure 82,* is seen at Oxford at the end of her days. Note that she has the Churchward tender, clackboxes in the front side of the boiler barrel, and is fitted with the flat iron lamp brackets in this picture.

Figure 80

Figure 81

Figure 82

Figure 83

Figure 84

Four pictures on this page illustrate the subtle differences between the 'Sir Daniel' class and the 'Sharpies'. In *Figure 83,* No. 162 *Cobham* is seen (upper left) at Oxford, still fitted with her early boiler and polished dome, and (top right) No. 159 is seen with the raised Belpaire firebox and outer gauge glass handle on the cab *(Figure 84).*

In contrast, (bottom right), *Figure 86* is No. 480 of the 'Sir Daniel' class,

built in 1869 at Swindon, but altered at Wolverhampton to the rolled top chimney and small cab. With this little cab came the characteristic brass number plate in place of the painted numerals. Note the smoke box wing plates with which the early Cobham was fitted and also the outside framed tender as shown in *Figure 85.*

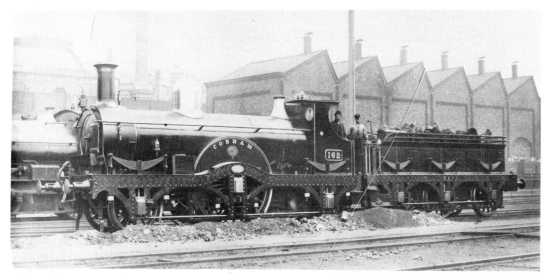

Figure 85

Figure 86

Figure 87

Figure 88

There were thirty engines built to the 'Sir Daniel' class, and when loads at the turn of the century became too much for these little machines, Dean had the idea of converting them to 0-6-0 goods engines. Seven were scrapped as singles between the years of 1898-1904, but the other twenty-three had their large 7′ drivers taken away, and were fitted with six coupled drivers of the standard 5′ 2″ diameter.

Two of these converted engines can be seen on this page. Top left, *Figure 87,* shows No. 381, which was the longest lived of the class, lasting in fact in this form until December 1919. Bottom right, *Figure 88,* shows No. 384 performing local goods duty judging by the position of the headlamp on the front buffer beam. It was always easy to identify these conversions, as the curved frame and higher centre spring showed from where these engines stemmed.

A small point of interest is the S & T plaques hanging outside the signal box windows which was an indication that the signalman required the attention of both signal and telegraph linesman at his box.

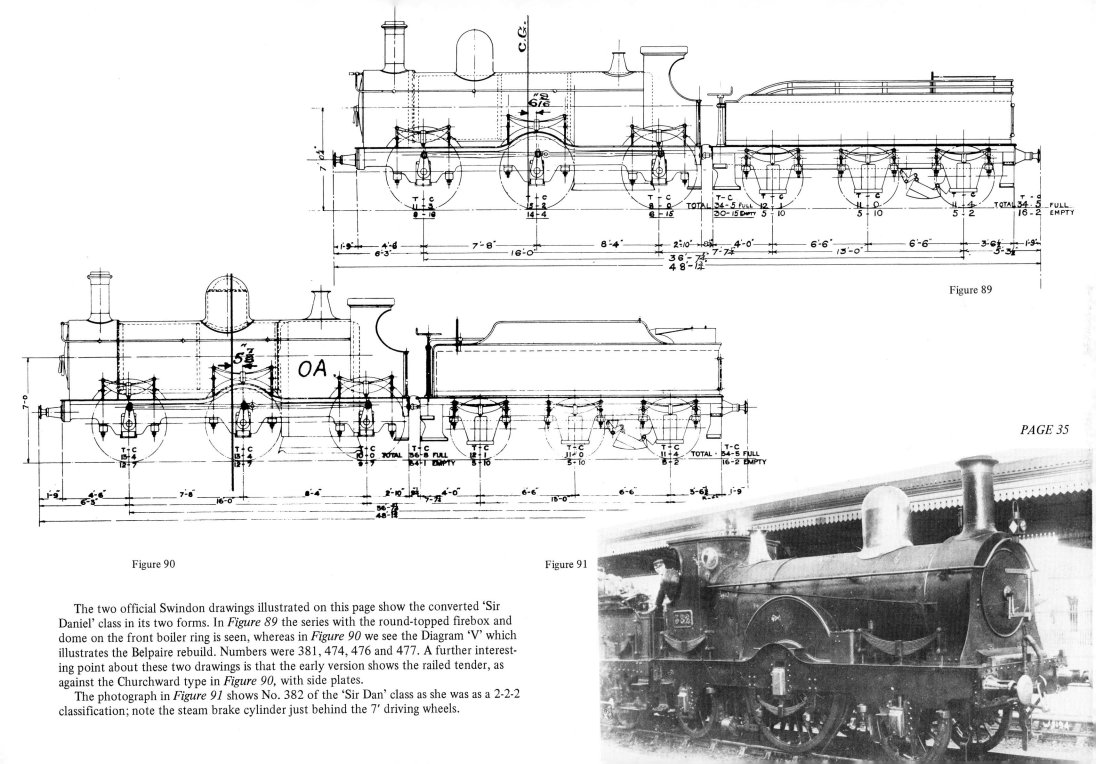

Figure 89

Figure 90

Figure 91

The two official Swindon drawings illustrated on this page show the converted 'Sir Daniel' class in its two forms. In *Figure 89* the series with the round-topped firebox and dome on the front boiler ring is seen, whereas in *Figure 90* we see the Diagram 'V' which illustrates the Belpaire rebuild. Numbers were 381, 474, 476 and 477. A further interesting point about these two drawings is that the early version shows the railed tender, as against the Churchward type in *Figure 90,* with side plates.

The photograph in *Figure 91* shows No. 382 of the 'Sir Dan' class as she was as a 2-2-2 classification; note the steam brake cylinder just behind the 7' driving wheels.

Four experimental engines were constructed by William Dean to try out the various innovations which were being tested by railway engineers at this time. Their numbers were 7, 8, 9 and 10, and they were all different in cylinder and motion design. *Figure 93* shows No. 7 which started life in 1886 at Swindon under *Lot 68* as a tandem compound with coupled wheels of 7' 0½" diameter, but with the usual two-ring boiler with Great Western standard boiler mountings. The tandem compounding drive was arranged by installing the 23" diameter low pressure cylinders in front of the high pressure, with the valves of the low pressure cylinders above, and those of the high pressure below the cylinders. Piston rods carried both L.P. and H.P. pistons, and the valve spindles were united for attachment to the normal valve gear.

However, this experiment was not successful, difficulty in maintenance due to inaccessible motion being the main cause and, after a couple of years service on minor routes, the engine was laid aside and finally dismantled in 1890.

No. 8 was another similar engine to No. 7, but ran on the broad gauge as a convertible, the only difference, apart from the gauge, being that there were two sets of piston rods, joined to a common crosshead, and boiler pressure was up to 180 lbs. This engine gave much trouble and never entered regular service, being completely rebuilt into a 4-4-0 of the 'Armstrong' class in 1894 together with No. 7 to standard gauge.

*Figure 92* is another picture of No. 9 as described on *page 22* and *Figure 53,* and is placed here to show the same boilers used, with totally different framing and springs.

Figure 92

Figure 93

Figure 94

This picture and drawing, *Figures 94, 95* illustrate the engine No. 9 in her later days, when rebuilt with new frames and standard axleboxes etc. She was named *Victoria* in the early 1890's together with No. 10 which bore the title *Royal Albert*. According to the R.C.T.S. book, these two engines then worked over the London-Swindon route, and later No. 9 was shedded at Stafford Road. Our picture shows her doing station pilot duties at Cardiff. Note that in the rebuilding, the leading and trailing axleboxes now have the springs on the side of the frames, rather than above as previously. The diagram is Swindon 'C' of the 2-2-2 class.

Figure 95

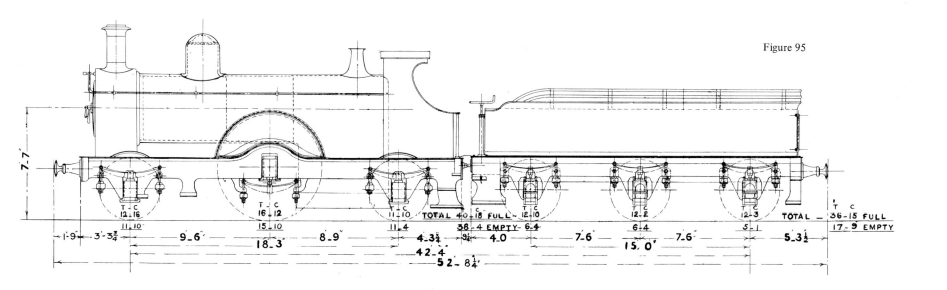

Finally the last of this batch of specials, No. 10. Originally this engine was to have been fitted with Joy's valve gear but, due to the troubles with No. 9, this order was cancelled and No. 10 appeared with normal motion, but was otherwise similar to No. 9, with large 7′ 8″ drivers and 4′ 6″ diameter carrying wheels. Slightly longer than No. 9 the two illustrations show both sides of the engine, and it can be seen clearly that the larger carrying wheels necessitated splashers on top of the running plate. Note also that this engine had the side hung springs, and the lower photograph, *Figure 97,* gives a good illustration of the early 1885 Dean tender, without rails or undergear. As mentioned before she was reconstructed in 1890 with 7′ wheels, and eventually named *Royal Albert,* and finally withdrawn in January 1906. *Figure 97A* is a reduced 4mm scale drawing of the original Swindon frame plan for engine No. 10 dated 1887. The Lot No. was 66.

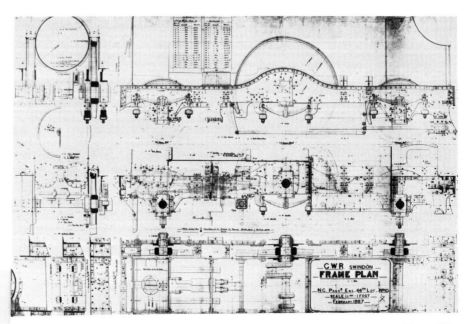

Figure 97A

Figure 96

Figure 97

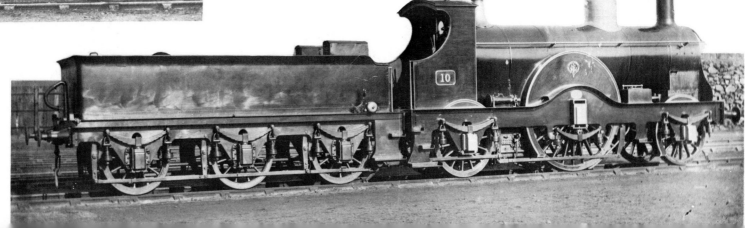

Two tank engines are shown here with a very chequered history. In *Figure 98,* the 0-6-0 saddle tank started life in 1867 built by the Worcester Engine Co. as an 0-6-0 tender goods engine for the Bristol & Exeter Railway. There were six made, and five of them were converted to the broad gauge in 1870 and back to standard gauge in 1875. On being taken into Great Western stock the engine shown (No. 77) was given No. 1360 and altered to an 0-6-0 saddle tank. In January 1890 she was fitted with an extension shaft on the centre drivers and put to work as a stationary engine at Messrs. Spillers of Cardiff. Being condemned in April of 1890 she was used as 'Stationary 076' at Swindon works brickfield in November. In the middle of 1902 she was fitted with a domed boiler and transferred to Kemble, returning to Swindon as spare the following year. She then went on to Old Oak Common carriage shed in 1909, back as spare to Swindon in 1913, hired out as power for a sawmill at Blandford in 1917, Swindon again in 1919, Newton Abbot 1922, Gloucester 1923, Newport 1924 and finally to Swindon again in 1925, and was finally cut up in 1944. I get the impression nobody wanted her!

Figure 99

Figure 98

On the other hand, *Figure 99* shows No. 3509, another of the 'convertibles', a standard gauge engine, built for service on the broad gauge as a tank and converted to narrow gauge as tender engine. There were ten in the class, numbering 3501-3510, and all built in 1885 as side tanks as shown. Five of them were altered to tender engines for the broad gauge in 1890-91, and all the class were converted back to standard gauge in 1892 in this form. Photographs of these engines thus treated can be found on *pages 154-156.*

The two photographs on this page show the difference between the famous 'Cobham' class No. 162, and the larger Dean singles as portrayed by No. 3026 in *Figure 101.* As mentioned previously, 'Cobham' was one of the 'Sharpies' of 1878, and was the only one in the class to have a name and keep it until scrapping. It was named incidentally after Lord Cobham, who was Deputy Chairman from 1889 to 1891, having been a director of the Company since 1878. Ahrons always spoke highly of 'Cobham', relating that in one Paddington-Birmingham run in the 90s, hauling a load of 160 tons, although stopped twice by signals, and badly checked six times, she nevertheless managed the 130 miles in 138 mins. 9 secs., which was nine minutes under time!

Figure 100

Figure 101

*Figure 101* shows No. 3026, a large Dean single with the underhung springs, having just been re-converted back to the standard gauge, after her year's spell on the broad gauge *(see page 17).* Notice that as a 'convertible' she did not carry a name, but after being changed eventually into a 4-2-2 in June of 1894, she was named *Tornado.*

She was finally withdrawn in February of 1909.

Figure 102

Figure 103

William Dean's last development of the 2-2-2 singles was the famous '3001' class, which finally culminated in the handsome bogie singles, known wherever enthusiasts gather. As can be seen from the photograph and drawing they had double frames, and all the springs on the engine were underhung. The boiler was still of the narrow 4' 3" diameter type, which could not be exceeded because of the large driving wheels, and to overcome this defect the boiler was made longer, and the firebox was raised to give a greater heating surface.

Figure 104

The first eight of the class, numbered 3021-3028, were fitted out for the broad gauge as convertibles in 1891, and have already been mentioned on *pages 17 and 40*. Nos. 3029 and 3030 were built to the standard gauge in November and December of 1891 and the others in 1892. In service, these large singles were unsteady owing to large cylinders and too much weight at the front end and, when No. 3021 was derailed in 1893 passing through Box tunnel, it was decided to fit them with a bogie leading instead of the fixed carrying wheels under the smoke box and so was born the bogie single class! Their names and numbers arc appended so that the reader can be acquainted with the original standard gauge engines, the convertibles, and the various rebuilds and name changes.

*Figure 104* shows No. 3006 *Courier* at the head of the 'Cornishman' corridor train of 1893.

Figure 105

| | | Built | Altered to 4-2-2 | | | | | |
|---|---|---|---|---|---|---|---|---|
| 3001 | Amazon | 1/1892 | 10/94 | Built as standard gauge engine | | | | |
| 3002 | Atalanta | 1/1892 | 6/94 | ” | ” | ” | ” | |
| 3003 | Avalanche | 2/1892 | 5/94 | ” | ” | ” | ” | |
| 3004 | Black Prince | 2/1892 | 11/94 | ” | ” | ” | ” | |
| 3005 | Britannia | 2/1892 | 11/94 | ” | ” | ” | ” | |
| 3006 | Courier | 3/1892 | 6/94 | ” | ” | ” | ” | |
| 3007 | Dragon | 3/1892 | 8/94 | ” | ” | ” | ” | |
| 3008 | Emperor | 3/1892 | 10/94 | ” | ” | ” | ” | |
| 3009 | Flying Dutchman | 3/1892 | 11/94 | ” | ” | ” | ” | |
| 3010 | Fire King | 3/1892 | 9/94 | ” | ” | ” | ” | |
| 3011 | Greyhound | 3/1892 | 10/94 | ” | ” | ” | ” | |
| 3012 | Great Western | ” ” | 6/94 | ” | ” | ” | ” | |
| 3013 | Great Britain | ” ” | 11/94 | ” | ” | ” | ” | |
| 3014 | Iron Duke | 4/1892 | 10/94 | ” | ” | ” | ” | |
| 3015 | Kennet | ” ” | 8/94 | ” | ” | ” | ” | |
| 3016 | Lightning | ” ” | 11/94 | ” | ” | ” | ” | |

| | Built | | | Altered to 4-2-2 |
|---|---|---|---|---|
| 3017 | 4/92 | | Nelson | 9/94 |
| 3018 | ” | | Racer | 8/94 |
| 3019 | ” | | Rover | 5/94 |
| 3020 | ” | | Sultan | 9/94 |
| 3021 | 4/91 | To broad gauge | To standard gauge 1892 | Wigmore Castle | 3/94 |
| 3022 | 5/91 | ” | ” | Rougemont | 7/94 |
| 3023 | 7/91 | ” | ” | Swallow | 9/94 |
| 3024 | 7/91 | ” | ” | Storm King | 12/94 |
| 3025 | 8/91 | ” | ” | St. George | 10/94 |
| 3026 | 8/91 | ” | ” | Tornado | 6/94 |
| 3027 | ” | ” | ” | Thames | 11/94 |
| 3028 | ” | ” | ” | Wellington | 7/94 |
| 3029 | 11/91 | Standard gauge | | White Horse | 7/94 |
| 3030 | 12/91 | ” ” | | Westward Ho | 10/94 |

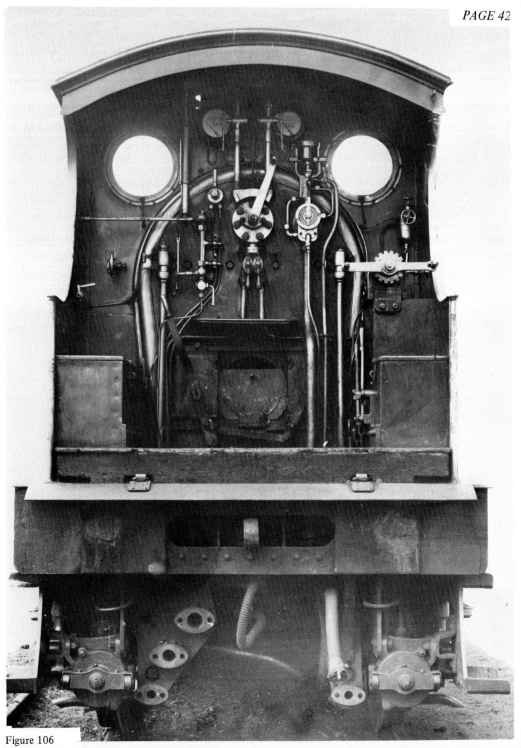

Figure 106

It is interesting to record that these 'singles' seemed to be the first series which had their names running in alphabetical order (with the exception of No. 3021) in spite of being built at different times, which must mean that names were allotted on the drawing board. This system was maintained in general to the end of the Company's existence.

*Figure 106* shows the cab details of No. 3009 *Flying Dutchman* as a 2-2-2 in 1893, (see *Figure 102*) and several features are perhaps of interest. For instance, the extension rod for shutting off the water gauge in case of a broken glass can be seen, although by this time the small lever outside the cab had been dispensed with. The safety valve spring balance lever is not inside the cab, and fixed to the back plate. The blower valve can be seen just above and to the right of the water gauge. Whistle valves show just by the steam gauges, and note that reversing is now accomplished by screw gear in place of lever. Look also at the steam brake cylinders just over the rail head; this type was used right up to the 1950s on the Dean goods. *Figure 105* shows *Emperor* outside Westbourne Park shed.

The next six pages are devoted to the classic bogie singles, which as mentioned before, derived from the Dean '3001' class of 2-2-2. What a successful rebuild this was, resulting in what to many devotees' minds was the most handsome of railway locomotives ever to run on British rails.

Much has been written about them, and as this book does not set out to be either technical or historical, I will content myself with one or two pointers about variations and rebuilds. The superb drawing on this page by J.N. Maskelyne shows *Lorna Doone* as built. She left the works in February of 1895, ran for seventeen years in this condition and was one of the few which were not rebuilt, being withdrawn in 1912. The official photograph of No. 3035, *Figure 108* shows the engine after receiving the name *Beaufort* in December of 1895. Originally when constructed in July of 1894, she was named *Bellerophon*. Note the clackbox on the side of the front boiler ring, not shown in the drawing of No. 3047.

Figure 107

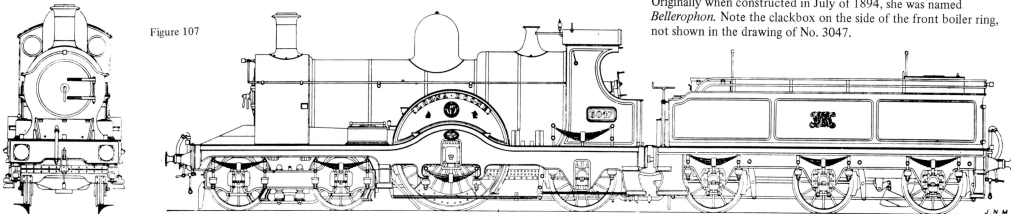

Figure 108

Figure 110

Figure 109

Two more of the class, *Duke of Connaught (Figure 109)* built in July of 1897 showing the boiler feed entering at the side of the firebox this time, and, below, No. 3007 *Dragon* as converted from the original 2-2-2 design to conform to the bogie single class. The photograph does manage to show what large engines these were, with that huge driving wheel and its splasher dwarfing the cleaner and shunter. Proof that these engines were earning their keep for the operating department in the '90s, is given by the fact that there were twenty in steam daily, seven at the London terminus, eight at Bristol, and five at Newton Abbot in 1894.

*Duke of Connaught,* shown at the top of the page, was the engine which took over where *City of Truro* left off, on the record run of May 9th, 1904, covering the journey from Bristol to Paddington at an average speed of 71.3 m.p.h. with a load of 120 tons. At one point on the journey she was travelling at 91.8 miles per hour.

Figure 111

Figure 112

Another pair of these beautiful engines on this page, both from Swindon photographic archives. *Figure 111* shows *Lambert* in full side view, and *Empress of India* is in three quarter view *(Figure 112)*. According to the register at the works, No. 3040 was photographed thus in May 1895, whereas the date of No. 3055 is given as January 1901, which means that the design was fairly static over these six years. Just for the record, the engine 3055 was renamed *Lambert* in honour of Henry Lambert, who had joined the Company in 1865 and was General Manager from 1887 until 1896. This happy knack of naming engines after chief officers was perpetuated long into the Great Western's history. No. 3055's original name was *Trafalgar* until 1901. The small fitting on the smoke box side was a displacement lubricator for the cylinders. I have an old portable farm engine of 1890 which I have restored, and this machine has a similar fitment.

Figure 115

No. 3076, *Princess Beatrice* in *Figure 113,* shows the right-hand side and a good frontal view for modellers, and being fitted with the flat iron lamp brackets, is pictured just before being withdrawn in July 1912. Note the different style of feed water clackbox entering the front boiler ring. *Figure 115,* No. 3037 *Corsair,* seen top right was a comparatively short-lived engine, built in September 1894. She only ran for fourteen years before being scrapped in 1908, and so was never rebuilt with Belpaire firebox.

Figure 113

In comparison, No. 3050, *Royal Sovereign,* in *Figure 114* seemed to be a guinea pig. Note (bottom left) the unusual front bogie springing, which was replaced later when rebuilt. The final stage is shown in *Figure 116,* when No. 3050 had a normal bogie, a domeless Belpaire firebox and boiler, and a very wide cab covering the trailing springs.

Figure 114

Figure 116

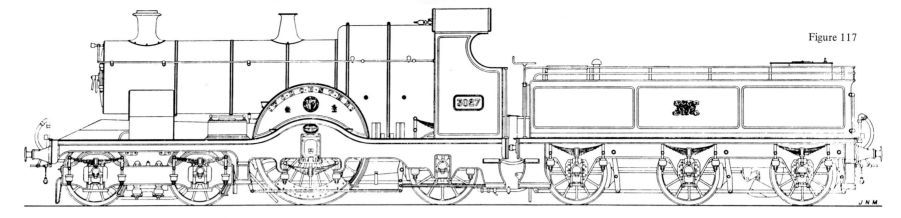

Figure 117

We now see the hand of Churchward showing in the rebuilding of the 'Singles'. From 1900 onwards in order to keep abreast with up-to-date modifications, and to give these engines a longer lease of life, two different types of boiler and firebox arrangements were fitted to thirty one of the class. The first change was to Diagram C, and consisted of replacing the old original boiler with a standard No. 2 type having the high Belpaire firebox, with no dome, and the safety valve mounted on the second ring. This meant also, of course, the fitting of a different chimney and some engines had the cast-iron style

Figure 118

shown in the drawing of No. 3027 *Worcester, Figure 117,* and others had the handsome built-up type with copper top as in *Figure 119* of *Glenside.* Notice that with the rebuilds a new wider and higher cab has also been fitted, with rectangular side windows as well as spectacles, and side-plates extending down over the trailing springs to the edge of the valance. The tender at first remained unaltered, but later the coal rails were replaced by side-plates, thus bringing it to the final tender shape. The second change was to a domed boiler and Belpaire firebox, and this started in 1910 and carried on to 1913. The diagram was F, and *Figure 76* shows this rebuild well. In *Figure 118,* No. 3043 *Hercules* is seen also in this final condition but with the addition of a top feed clack-box mounted on the boiler.

Figure 119

Diagram F was the last and final rebuild of the 'Singles', as, although, Churchward looked into the possibility of re-building again as a 4-4-0 with taper boiler, the cost of such a complicated refit was just too much, and so the class ended their lives in the Diagram F condition as seen on this page. Points to note are the different shape of cab sides to that of Diagram C, and also that a new pattern of bogie designed by Churchward has now replaced that of Dean. Incidentally there was an intermediary Diagram D which seemed to be a mixture of C and F. An example of the three engines so converted can be seen in *Figure 116, Royal Sovereign,* the other two being No. 3015 *Kennett* and No. 3049 *Nelson.*

Figure 120

Figure 121

There were only eight engines which had the three diagrams applied, namely:

| | No. | Built | Rebuilt | | Cut up |
|---|---|---|---|---|---|
| | | | C. Dia | F. Dia | |
| *Great Britain* | 3013 | 1892 | 1902 | 1910 | 1914 |
| *Worcester* | 3027 | 1891 | 1900 | 1911 | 1914 |
| *Dreadnought* | 3039 | 1894 | 1902 | 1913 | 1915 |
| *Majestic* | 3048 | 1895 | 1904 | 1910 | 1913 |
| *Prometheus (Nelson)* | 3049 | 1895 | 1903 | 1910 | 1913 |
| *Duchess of Teck* | 3067 | 1898 | 1902 | 1910 | 1914 |
| *Earl of Warwick* | 3070 | 1898 | 1900 | 1910 | 1914 |
| *Sir Walter Raleigh* | 3052 | 1895 | 1904 | 1913 | 1913 |
| *Royal Sovereign* | 3050 | 1895 | 1909 | 1914 | 1915 |
| | | | To D | To F | |

| | | | |
|---|---|---|---|
| Driving wheels until 1898 | 7′ 8½″ | after | 7′ 9″ |
| Bogie      ”      ”      ” | 4′ 1″ | ” | 4′ 1½″ |
| Trailing   ”      ”      ” | 4′ 7″ | ” | 4′ 7½″ |
| Wheelbase  7′ 0″ and 7′ 6″ and 9′ 0″ | | | |

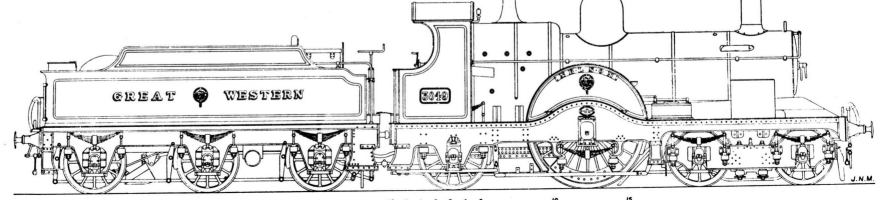

Figure 122

Here are two singles, one as built, and one at the final phase. In *Figure 123* is shown No. 3042 *Frederick Saunders* photographed at Swindon factory in 1895, and in contrast in *Figure 124* we see No. 3031 *Achilles,* which was built in March 1894, and kept the same boiler throughout her 18 years of existence. Note the copper-topped chimney with capuchon and the green-painted dome. In my opinion, the 'Singles' were still handsome, even in the green and black livery, and with a modern tender.

Figure 123

Figure 124

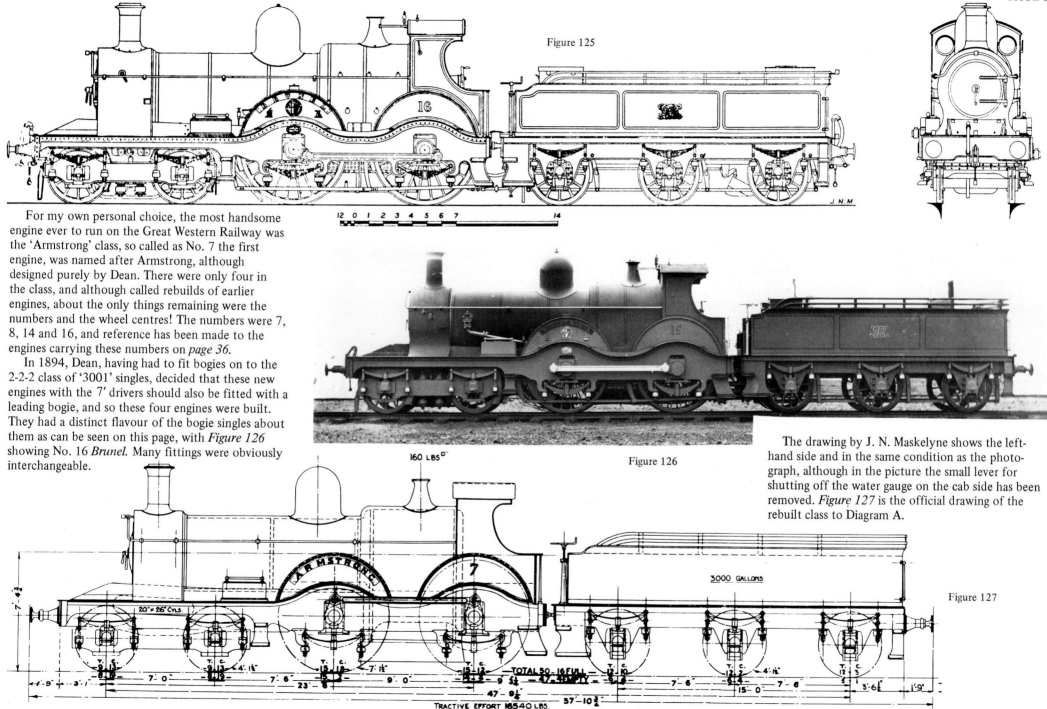

Figure 125

For my own personal choice, the most handsome engine ever to run on the Great Western Railway was the 'Armstrong' class, so called as No. 7 the first engine, was named after Armstrong, although designed purely by Dean. There were only four in the class, and although called rebuilds of earlier engines, about the only things remaining were the numbers and the wheel centres! The numbers were 7, 8, 14 and 16, and reference has been made to the engines carrying these numbers on *page 36*.

In 1894, Dean, having had to fit bogies on to the 2-2-2 class of '3001' singles, decided that these new engines with the 7' drivers should also be fitted with a leading bogie, and so these four engines were built. They had a distinct flavour of the bogie singles about them as can be seen on this page, with *Figure 126* showing No. 16 *Brunel*. Many fittings were obviously interchangeable.

Figure 126

The drawing by J. N. Maskelyne shows the left-hand side and in the same condition as the photograph, although in the picture the small lever for shutting off the water gauge on the cab side has been removed. *Figure 127* is the official drawing of the rebuilt class to Diagram A.

Figure 127

Figure 128

No. 14 *Charles Saunders* is illustrated on this page in *Figures 128 and 129* and the drawing is of the right-hand side of No. 8 *Gooch.* This diagram shows the feed water clack box entering the boiler side, whereas J.N.M.'s drawing does not reveal this feature, the water pump having been removed.

The four engines were rebuilt extensively between 1905 and 1911, carrying various styles of boilers and fireboxes and finally in 1915, 1917 and 1923 respectively, they received 6′ 8½″ wheels and were absorbed into the 'Flower' class renumbered thus:

No. 7 *Armstrong* becoming No. 4171
No. 8 *Gooch* becoming No. 4172
No. 14 *Charles Saunders* becoming No. 4170
No. 16 *Brunel* becoming No. 4169

Figure 129

Before being rebuilt these engines worked between London and Bristol, but after 1909 they were all sent to the Wolverhampton Division, and before being absorbed in to the 'Flower' class worked as station pilots and handled local traffic in the northern section.

For myself, I have 30 or more 4mm. scale locomotives, and if I had to sell all but one, 'Gooch' would be the one I would keep till the last. Coupled to a train of contemporary four-wheelers in the early chocolate and cream livery, the picture created is of elegance and grace.

Driving wheels 7′ 1″ later with thick tyres 7′ 1½″ diameter
Bogie wheels 4′ 1″ later with thick tyres 4′ 1½″ diameter
Wheelbase 7′ 0″ and 7′ 6″ and 9′ 0″

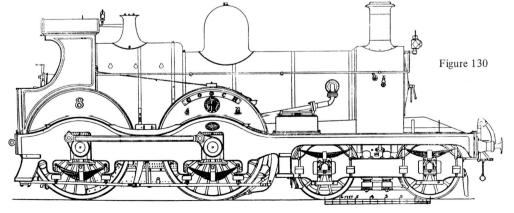

Figure 130

The 'Armstrong' class of four engines were eventually rebuilt with taper boilers and cast-iron chimneys, also their big 7' drivers were changed for the more standard 6' 8½". This change came about as they were renumbered in 1915-1923 and taken into the 41XX series, becoming No. 4171 *Armstrong*, No. 4172 *Gooch*, No. 4170 *Brunel* and No. 4169 *Charles Saunders*. In this final condition they ran until the late '20s, No. 4169 being withdrawn as the last survivor in 1930.

*Figure 131* shows *Armstrong* still carrying No. 7 outside Old Oak Common shed in 1911, and note one of the 'Frenchmen' under the coal stage, extreme right. The drawing in *Figure 132* is by Layland Barratt and is to 4mm. scale with millimetre measurements for 7mm modellers.

Figure 131

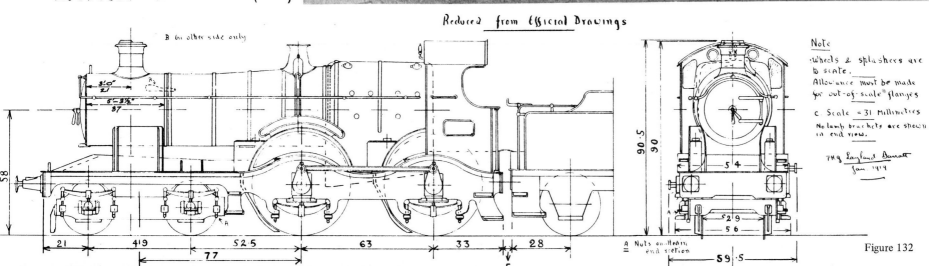

G.W.R. 'ARMSTRONG' (4171)

Reduced from Official Drawings

Note
Wheels & splashers are to scale.
Allowance must be made for out-of-scale flanges
c Scale = 31 Millimetres
No lamp brackets are shown in end view.

FHg Layland Barratt
Jan. 1919

Figure 132

Having dealt with some of the early 'top link' passenger engines of the 19th century, space must be found for some of the locomotives which operated the secondary services.

Amongst the first of these are the early 2-4-0 tender engines with the sandwich frames, made by George England in 1862 to designs by Gooch. Although originally meant for express work at Wolverhampton with trains for the north, their capacity was limited and between 1878 and 1883 all eight were 'renewed' at Wolverhampton as shown in *Figure 133*. The renewal was drastic. Very little of the original engines remained, cabs were fitted and the Wolverhampton 'W3' boiler was installed. Only one engine was named, and this was No. 154, called *Chancellor* in honour of the visit to Stafford Road works in 1878 of the Chancellor of the Exchequer (Sir William Harcourt) whilst this engine was being rebuilt. From here on the class was known as the 'Chancellor' class and numbers were 149 to 156. Two lasted until 1920 and six of them ran more than one million miles apiece. The Maskelyne drawing shows the rebuild of 1914, and the official diagram L in *Figure 135* illustrates the final form with water scoop on the tender. Most of their work was performed in the Wolverhampton area, but one or two made appearances in Oxford and London, usually working via Worcester.

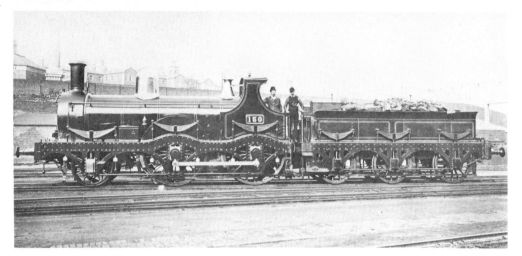

Figure 133

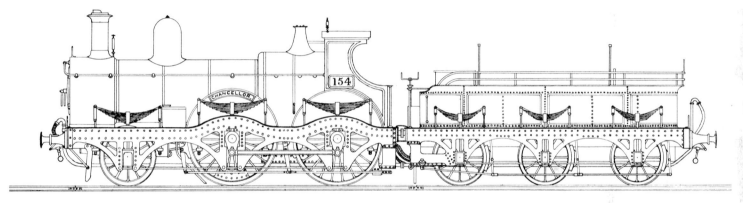

Figure 134

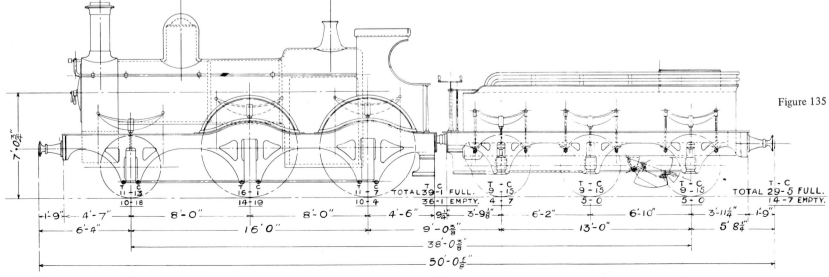

Figure 135

At first glance these two engines would seem to be of the same class, but in fact they are of very different years and types. The earliest one is shown in *Figure 137*, and is No. 444 of the 'Bicycle' class of 1868 built originally under *Lot 14*. They were the first 2-4-0s to be built at Swindon, having inside frames and bearings to all wheels. As originally built the whole driving of 6′ 1″ was exposed and this earned them the nickname of 'Bicycles'. However, when renewed at Wolverhampton in 1885, the whole design was transformed and the engine turned out in the style shown in *Figure 137* with wavy framing and deep valance to provide bearings for the leading wheels. There were only seven in the class and all were scrapped by 1918, some examples having had three or even four rebuilds.

Figure 136

Figure 137

The same Wolverhampton outline can be seen in *Figure 136* of No. 810, as running in 1920, with the S4 type of boiler. This engine had the longest life of the '806' class, being built at Swindon in 1873, *Lot 32*, and surviving many rebuilds at Wolverhampton until final withdrawal in 1926. As built at Swindon the framing and valance were as shown in *Figure 136*, but the splashers were open, and of course, there was no cab. Consequent renewals and rebuilds at Wolverhampton brought them to a great similarity with the 'Bicycles'. Built under *Lot 32*, there were twenty engines, and they were the last of the Armstrong 2-4-0 designs, the 22XXs being a Dean version of the class.

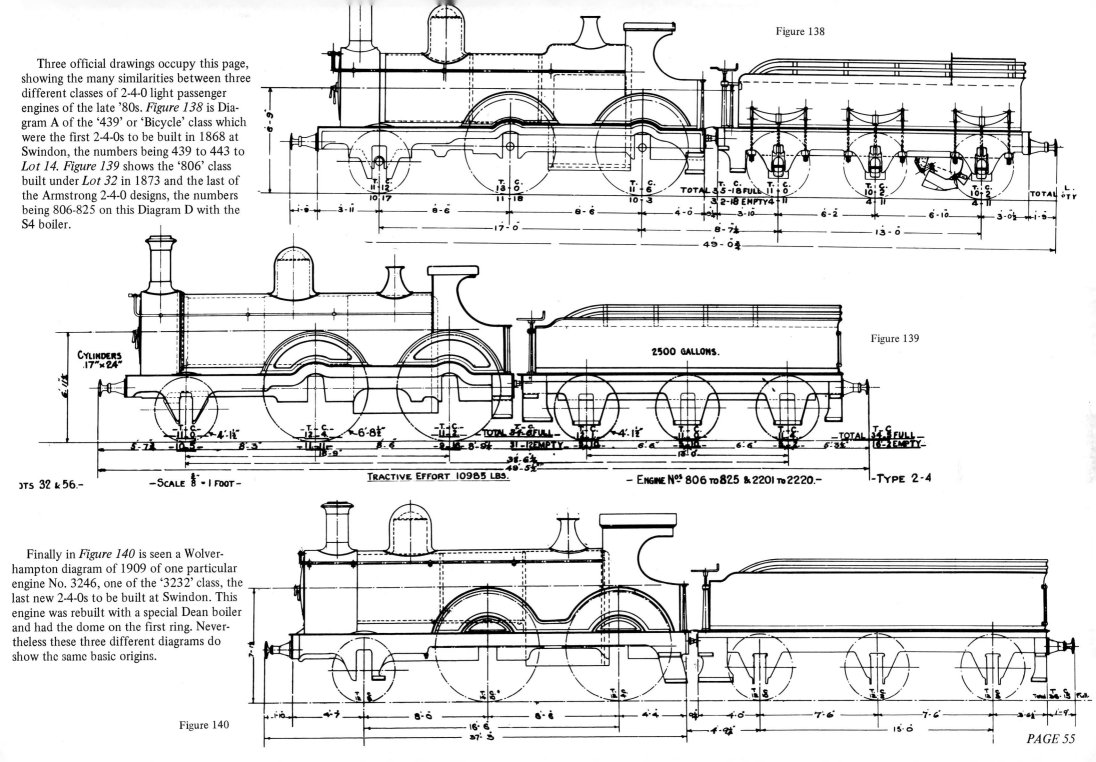

Three official drawings occupy this page, showing the many similarities between three different classes of 2-4-0 light passenger engines of the late '80s. *Figure 138* is Diagram A of the '439' or 'Bicycle' class which were the first 2-4-0s to be built in 1868 at Swindon, the numbers being 439 to 443 to *Lot 14*. *Figure 139* shows the '806' class built under *Lot 32* in 1873 and the last of the Armstrong 2-4-0 designs, the numbers being 806-825 on this Diagram D with the S4 boiler.

Figure 138

Figure 139

CYLINDERS .17" × 24"

2500 GALLONS.

TRACTIVE EFFORT 10985 LBS.

─ SCALE ⅛" = 1 FOOT ─

─ ENGINE Nᵒˢ 806 ᴛᴏ 825 & 2201 ᴛᴏ 2220. ─

─TYPE 2-4

Finally in *Figure 140* is seen a Wolverhampton diagram of 1909 of one particular engine No. 3246, one of the '3232' class, the last new 2-4-0s to be built at Swindon. This engine was rebuilt with a special Dean boiler and had the dome on the first ring. Nevertheless these three different diagrams do show the same basic origins.

Figure 140

Figure 141

Figure 142

Six engines built at Wolverhampton in 1889 were 2-4-0 tender engines, and the first to be built to this design since 1867. Nos. 3226-3231, built under *Lot 52,* were modifications of the earlier '111' class, and in fact they were so alike that at first it was intended they be numbered 104-109·but this was changed for the '3226' series.

*Figure 142* shows the class, as built in 1889, the design from which they all stemmed. In *Figure 143,* No. 110 of the '111' class, and in *Figure 141* shows the final form of No. 3230 with the very small wheelbase tender of 2,000 gallon capacity; the picture was taken in the 1920s, presumably. J. N. Maskelyne's drawing shows No. 3230 at the same period when she was used for working over the Berks and Hants line.

Most of the class worked in the West Midland area, and consequently had frequent boiler changes at Swindon instead of their home shops, Stafford Road. Nos. 3230 and 3231 lasted until 1922 before being withdrawn. Their other claim to fame is that they were the last tender engines to be constructed at Wolverhampton.

Figure 143

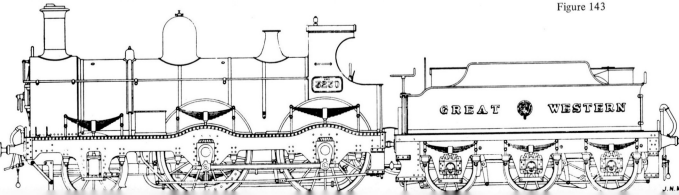

GREAT WESTERN

Figure 144

Figure 145

The next class illustrated is the '2201' series which were Dean's version of the '806' class, already mentioned on *page 54*. Twenty engines were built in 1881-82 at Swindon, the first ten being very similar to the '806' class as regards outward appearance and framing. However, the series 2211-20 had a different style of framing, in that the running platforms were in a straight line from front to back, whilst the splashers were closed in (unlike the earlier ten which had open splashers) and the number followed a small arc, which was affixed to the rear driving splasher. It is odd to report that the sixteen engines of the '806' series when rebuilt, also were modified to follow this same pattern of straight framing and closed splashers, etc. One small way of identifying the '806' rebuilds and the '2210' class, was in the brass beading around the driving splashers; the '806's had one continuous strip over the two wheels,

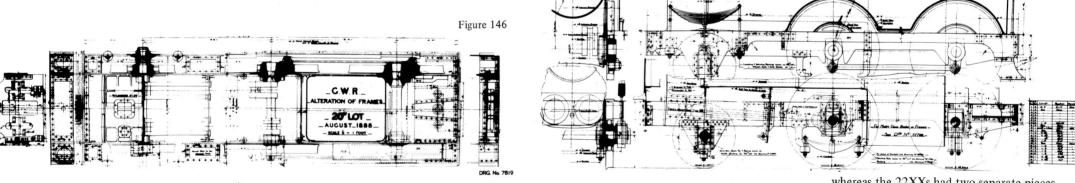

Figure 146

DRG. No. 7819

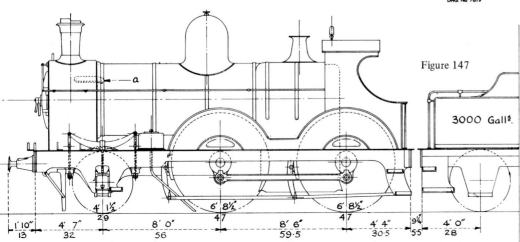

Figure 147

3000 Galls.

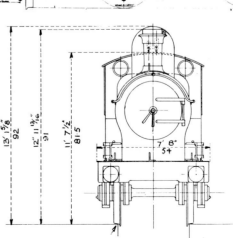

whereas the 22XXs had two separate pieces, one to each splasher. *Figure 145* illustrates this well in No. 824, which has been rebuilt to the 22XX outline. The drawing from Col. Templer shows the class at the later stage, with the small Belpaire firebox and boiler. This drawing is to 4mm scale, but full size measurements are in feet, and 7mm. scale dimensions are in millimetres *(Figure 147)*.

Further information covering the conversion of sixteen engines of the '806' class to the straight framing style *(Figure 146)* is in a reduced copy of the works drawings dealing expressly with this rebuild, and it can be seen that this plan is dated 1888.

Figure 149

*PAGE 58*

Figure 148

Four pictures of the '22XX' class are seen on this page, two showing the round-topped firebox, and two with the Belpaire design as per the drawing on the previous page.

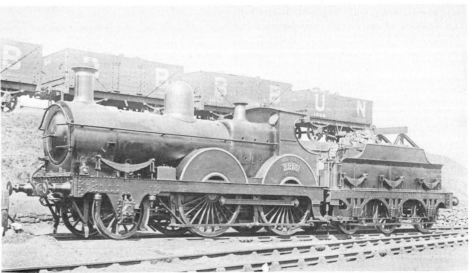

*Figure 148* is of No. 2208 at an early date, as this engine still retains the extending water gauge stop-cock lever on the cab side. Notice also the polished smokebox hinges and rim. *Figure 151* shows No. 2206 at Bristol shed, still with round-topped firebox but with the tender rails changed for side plates. *Figures 149 and 150* are of No. 2213 and No. 2220, at later date, just prior to with-drawal, and fitted with the Belpaire boiler and box. Note the unpolished dome and bright copper-banded chimney. Only No. 2208 has the Swindon works plate on the valance, the other three having lost theirs in the course of the several rebuilds.

Figure 150

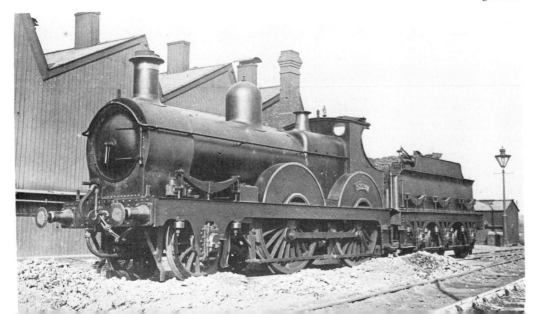

Figure 151

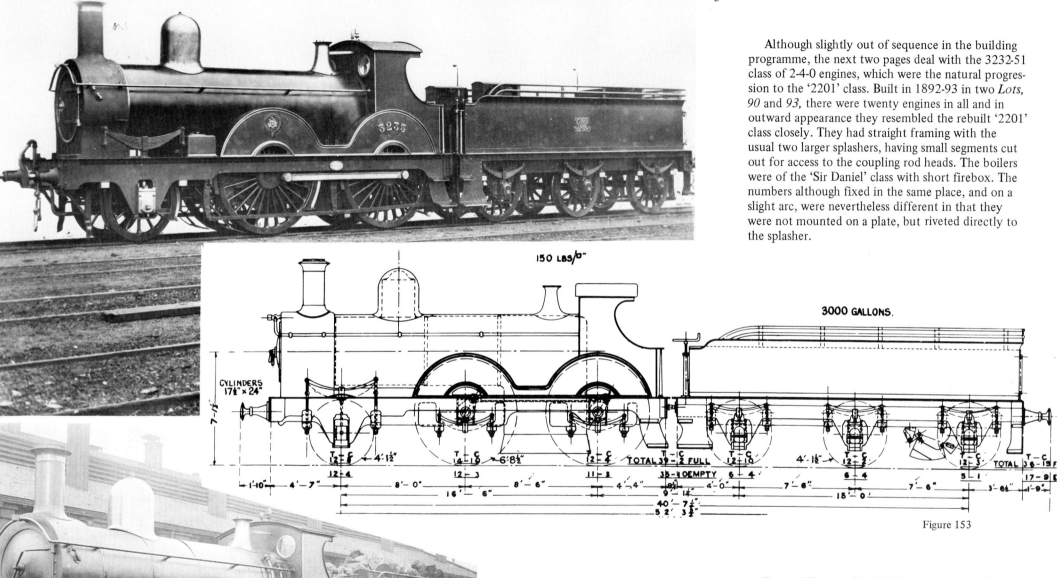

Figure 152

Although slightly out of sequence in the building programme, the next two pages deal with the 3232-51 class of 2-4-0 engines, which were the natural progression to the '2201' class. Built in 1892-93 in two *Lots*, *90* and *93*, there were twenty engines in all and in outward appearance they resembled the rebuilt '2201' class closely. They had straight framing with the usual two larger splashers, having small segments cut out for access to the coupling rod heads. The boilers were of the 'Sir Daniel' class with short firebox. The numbers although fixed in the same place, and on a slight arc, were nevertheless different in that they were not mounted on a plate, but riveted directly to the splasher.

150 LBS/▯″

3000 GALLONS.

CYLINDERS
17½″ × 24″

Figure 153

Figure 154

*Figure 152* shows No. 3235 as built with boiler feed to back plate, whilst *Figure 154* illustrates No. 3233 with live steam injector supply entering the left-hand firebox top. The Swindon diagram is 'G' with dome on the front ring. Note the early superheater damper lever on the smoke-box side, and the control passing through the handrail to the cab.

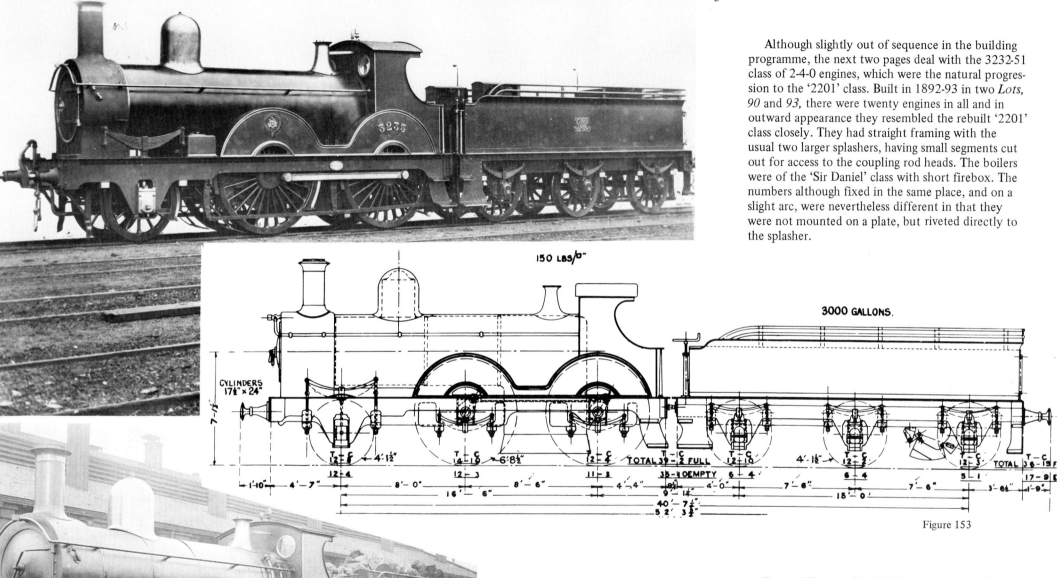

No. 3241 of the '3232' class is seen at the top of the page in *Figure 155,* as photographed at Swindon in works grey, which always showed the detail up well. Notice that this is one of the six which were fitted with Westinghouse brake for working trains from other companies using this type of gear. The Westinghouse pump was mounted on the right-hand side of the firebox. During the next fifteen years this equipment was removed, and handed on to the 4-4-0s (see second Volume, engine named *White).*

Swindon's drawing shows them with the more modern Churchward tender, but the outline of the engine is almost as built. These engines' working rosters included the Reading and Newbury line, and also that they used to power the South Wales expresses up to the 1907 period. The delightful picture in *Figure 157* is from the camera of my

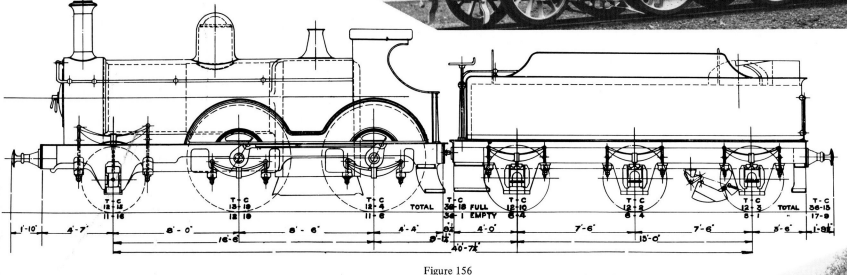

Figure 155

Figure 156

friend Maurice Earley and shows No. 3236 on an up stopping train at Tilehurst in 1923. Note that the engine has been rebuilt now with B4 Belpaire boiler and firebox, which has the dome on the second ring. As built this fitting was on the front ring. These engines were slightly more powerful than the 2201s as the cylinder diameter had been increased from 17″ to 17½″ and at least six of the class lasted until 1906.

The diagram letter was 'Q', which applied to engines rebuilt with Belpaire boilers of the 'Sir Daniel' class, *Figure 156.*

Figure 157

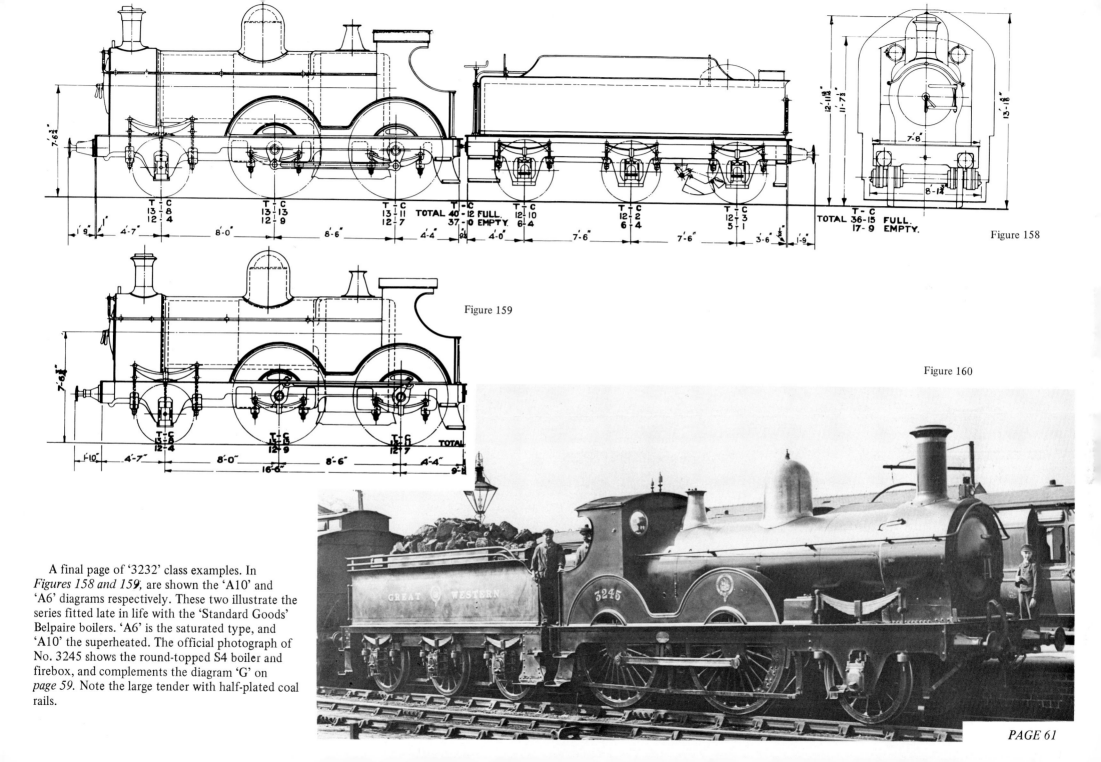

Figure 158

Figure 159

Figure 160

A final page of '3232' class examples. In *Figures 158 and 159,* are shown the 'A10' and 'A6' diagrams respectively. These two illustrate the series fitted late in life with the 'Standard Goods' Belpaire boilers. 'A6' is the saturated type, and 'A10' the superheated. The official photograph of No. 3245 shows the round-topped S4 boiler and firebox, and complements the diagram 'G' on *page 59.* Note the large tender with half-plated coal rails.

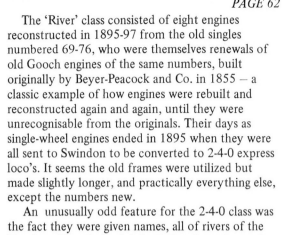

The 'River' class consisted of eight engines reconstructed in 1895-97 from the old singles numbered 69-76, who were themselves renewals of old Gooch engines of the same numbers, built originally by Beyer-Peacock and Co. in 1855 — a classic example of how engines were rebuilt and reconstructed again and again, until they were unrecognisable from the originals. Their days as single-wheel engines ended in 1895 when they were all sent to Swindon to be converted to 2-4-0 express loco's. It seems the old frames were utilized but made slightly longer, and practically everything else, except the numbers new.

An unusually odd feature for the 2-4-0 class was the fact they were given names, all of rivers of the kingdom. Namely in alphabetical and number order they were:-

|       |        | Reconstructed | Withdrawn |
|-------|--------|---------------|-----------|
| No. 69 | *Avon*  | 1/96  | 3/07  |
| No. 70 | *Dart*  | 10/95 | 1/07  |
| No. 71 | *Dee*   | 10/95 | 6/13  |
| No. 72 | *Exe*   | 8/95  | 6/13  |
| No. 73 | *Isis*  | 10/95 | 10/18 |
| No. 74 | *Stour* | 3/97  | 12/18 |
| No. 75 | *Teign* | 12/95 | 6/15  |
| No. 76 | *Wye*   | 11/95 | 5/14  |

It has been recorded that No. 74 was to have been given the name *Thames,* but as a six letter word did not fit nicely in the small space on the splasher, the name *Stour* was substituted.

*Figure 161* is an early picture of *Dee* seen at Hereford on a delightful train of clerestories. I would date the photograph at 1910, as a large Churchward carriage can be seen on the middle road. *Figure 163* is Mr. Maskelyne's drawing of No. 73 *Isis* as she appeared just before withdrawal.

*Figure 162* depicts the 'River' class with the 1893 S2 boiler, the driving wheels were 6′ 8″ and leading 4′ 1½″ diameter. Diagram is H.

Figure 161

Figure 162

Figure 163

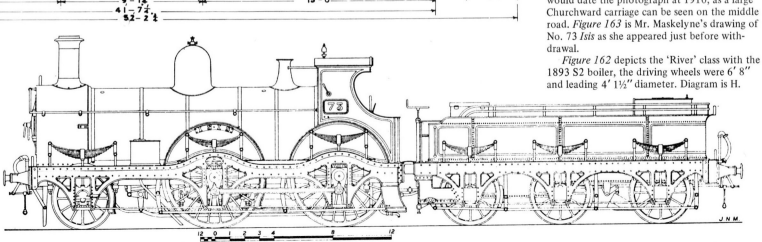

*Avon* shown in *Figure 164,* is straight out of Swindon factory and resplendent in her Works grey undercoat. Note that even the framing has been lined out for the photograph. The picture is dated 1902.

*Figure 165* shows the same engine in service with the highly polished dome and safety valve bonnet. What handsome engines these were.

J. N. Maskelyne's drawing in *Figure 163* shows *Isis* with a boiler renewal, which has put the dome back on to the second ring, similar to *Avon* in *Figure 164.* It is perhaps relevant to mention here that No. 70 was scrapped in 1907, owing to a severe collision which wrote her off, and that for some reason *Avon* was also withdrawn in the same year.

Two of the class, *Isis* and *Stour,* spent their last years here at Banbury, and although I cannot recall them personally, some of my older colleagues remember them with great affection. Perhaps it would also be of interest to record that *Teign* was fitted with a shorter chimney in 1913, which changed her appearance somewhat, and that three engines were given Belpaire boilers and fireboxes in 1910-11, being Nos. 72, 74 and 76. Wheelbases 9′ 0″ and 8′ 6″, total 17′ 6″.

Figure 164

Figure 165

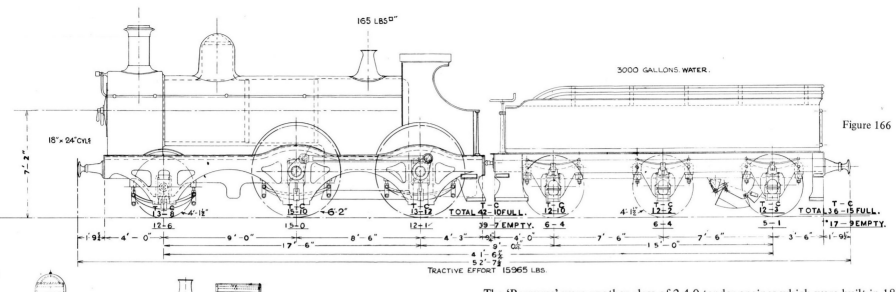

165 LBS⁰˝

3000 GALLONS. WATER.

Figure 166

18˝ × 24˝ CYLS

7′-2˝

TRACTIVE EFFORT 15965 LBS.

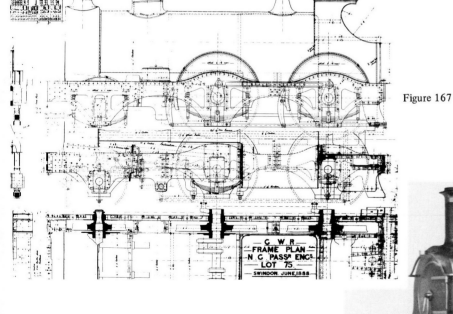

Figure 167

G W R
FRAME PLAN
N G PASSᴿ ENGˢ
LOT 75
SWINDON. JUNE,1888.

The 'Barnums' were another class of 2-4-0 tender engines which were built in 1889 under *Lot 75*. They were so called because, being quite powerful machines with comparatively light axle loading, they were used at one time for hauling the heavy train of rolling stock which was used for transporting Barnum & Bailey's Great Circus from town to town on their tour of Great Britain.

There were twenty engines in the class, and as built had underhung springs to the leading wheels which can be seen in both *Figures 166 and 168* on this page. As new, they were fitted with the Swindon S2 boiler with the dome mounted on the front ring and had Allen-Richardson balanced slide valves underneath the cylinders. The numbers were 3206 to 3225 and they were the last type in Britain to be made with the open sandwich frames. The drawing in *Figure 166* is the official Diagram E of Swindon, and shows the engines built with 1889 boiler, and in *Figure 167* we have a reduced works drawing of the original 'Frame plan' of 1888.

Figure 168

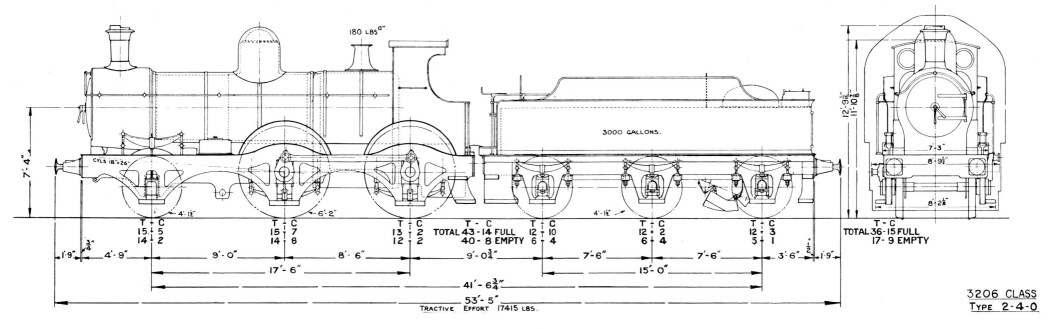

180 LBS □″

3000 GALLONS.

CYLS 18″x26″

7′-4″

12′-9½″
11′-10⅞″

7′-3″
8′-9½″
8′-2⅛″

| T | C | | T | C | | T | C | | T | C | | T | C | | T | C | | T | C |
|---|---|---|---|---|---|---|---|---|---|---|---|---|---|---|---|---|---|---|---|
| 15 | 5 | | 15 | 7 | | 13 | 2 | TOTAL 43-14 FULL | 12 | 10 | | 12 | 2 | | 12 | 3 | | TOTAL 36-15 FULL |
| 14 | 2 | | 14 | 8 | | 12 | 2 | 40- 8 EMPTY | 6 | 4 | | 6 | 4 | | 5 | 1 | | 17- 9 EMPTY |

1·9″  ¾″  4′-9″   9′-0″   8′-6″   9′-0¾″  4′-1½″  7′-6″   7′-6″   3′-6″ ½″ 1·9″

4′-1½″   6′-2″

17′-6″   15′-0″

41′-6¾″

53′-5″
TRACTIVE EFFORT 17415 LBS.

3206 CLASS
TYPE 2-4-0

Figure 169

3221

Figure 170

The diagram in *Figure 169* shows the class with superheated Belpaire boilers. No. 3221, shown in Works grey, was one of the majority that lasted into the 1930s. Notice that in *Figure 170* the springs for the leading axle have now been fitted above the running plate. The numerals of these engines were of brass, and were fixed without a background plate in an arc which followed the framing direct to the side of the rear splasher.

Driving wheels were 6′ 1½″, later 6′ 2″.

Leading wheels were 4′ 1″, later 4′ 1½″.

The wheelbase was 9′ and 8′ 6″, total 17′ 6″.

*PAGE 65*

As would be expected for locomotives which had a life of nearly 50 years, the 'Barnums' were rebuilt many times with different designs of boiler and firebox and *Figure 171* shows No. 3222 in immaculate condition, and equipped with the domeless BRO type of boiler in 1909. Note the high gloss finish on the paintwork, and it is possible in the original photograph to see the reflection of the motion in the underside of the boiler. There is an interesting detail in this picture, namely the two small pipes leaving the boiler cladding and entering the smokebox, just above the handrail. These are the pipes for the regulator-controlled sight feed lubricator, and from 1910 onwards they were covered with a small shaped hood, which have been a feature on Great Western locomotives ever since.

In the official drawing in *Figure 172* the 'Barnum' class is shown with domeless boiler, which was the 1909 rebuild of Nos. 3222 and 3214. As can be seen, the boiler is now the BRO type of Belpaire with no dome and flat-topped firebox. This engine is also shown with the cast-iron chimney which several of the class carried.

Figure 171

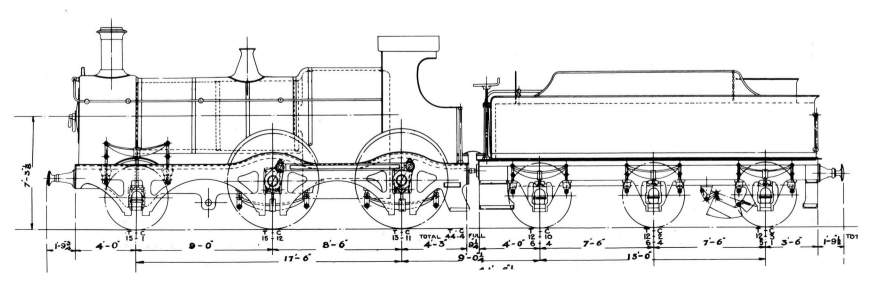

Figure 172

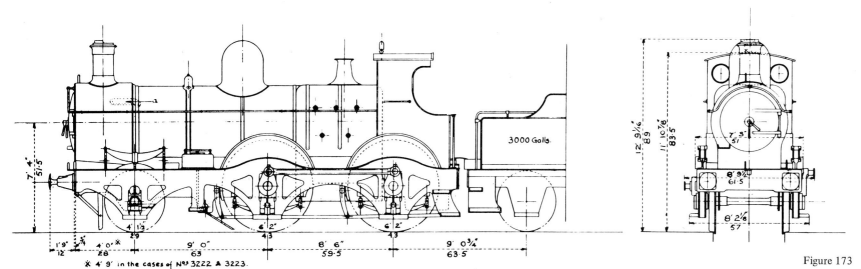

7' 4"
51·5

12' 9½"
89

11' 10⅞"
83·5

7' 3"
51

8' 9½"
61·5

8' 2⅛"
57

4' 1½"
29

6' 2"
43

6' 2"
43

1' 9"
12

¾
4

4' 0" X
28

9' 0"
63

8' 6"
59·5

9' 0¾"
63·5

3000 Galls.

X 4' 9' in the cases of Nos 3222 & 3223.

NOTE. 'a' on right side only. Dimensions in feet and millimetres for Gauge 'O'.

Figure 173

3214

The Templer drawing in *Figure 173* shows the 'Barnum' class at the end of their days, carrying the B4 boiler, and with top feed into the front ring. As usual with these superb drawings, which are reduced from the official general arrangement diagrams, dimensions are shown in feet whilst the millimetre sizes are for 7mm scale, the drawing as presented being to 4mm scale.

The photograph of No. 3214 in *Figure 174* was of the engine at Stourbridge shed taken in 1930 just after a major overhaul, which accounts for the shiny unlined paintwork. As can be seen from the group letter on the cab side, the power group of these engines was 'A' and the route colour was yellow. Note the dome and safety valve bonnet are painted green, but she still retains the old-style lettering.

Figure 174

The final page of 'Barnums' illustrates No. 3225 in *Figure 173A* at Aberdovey station in the 1930s. Note she is fitted with top feed to the boiler and has the vacuum brake pipe running along the left-hand side of the framing.

*Figure 174A* is a good frontal view of No. 3214 again at Stourbridge, and many constructional details can be seen. Note, for instance, the single step on the left-hand side of the smokebox, the cylinder drain cocks just below the buffer beam, the vacuum hose plug on the left and the hook for hanging the screw shackle on the right-hand side. These engines were known at most of the sheds on the Great Western. *Figure 173B* is the official Swindon diagram A.1. of the class.

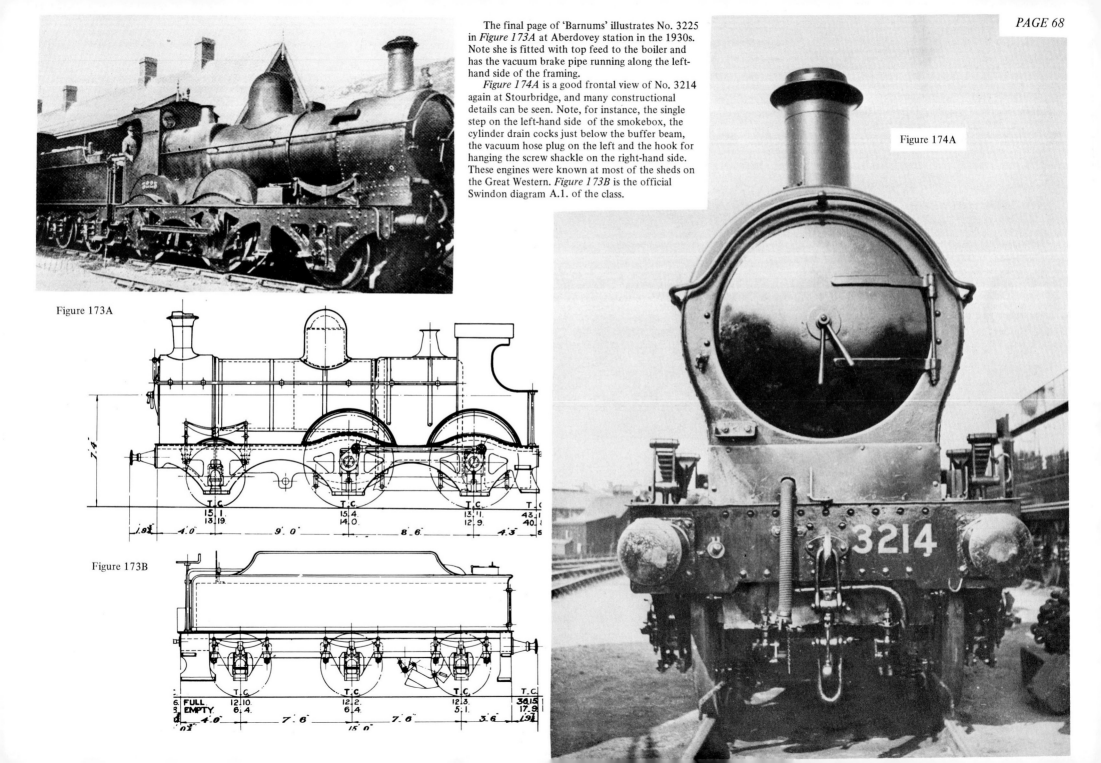

Figure 173A

Figure 173B

Figure 174A

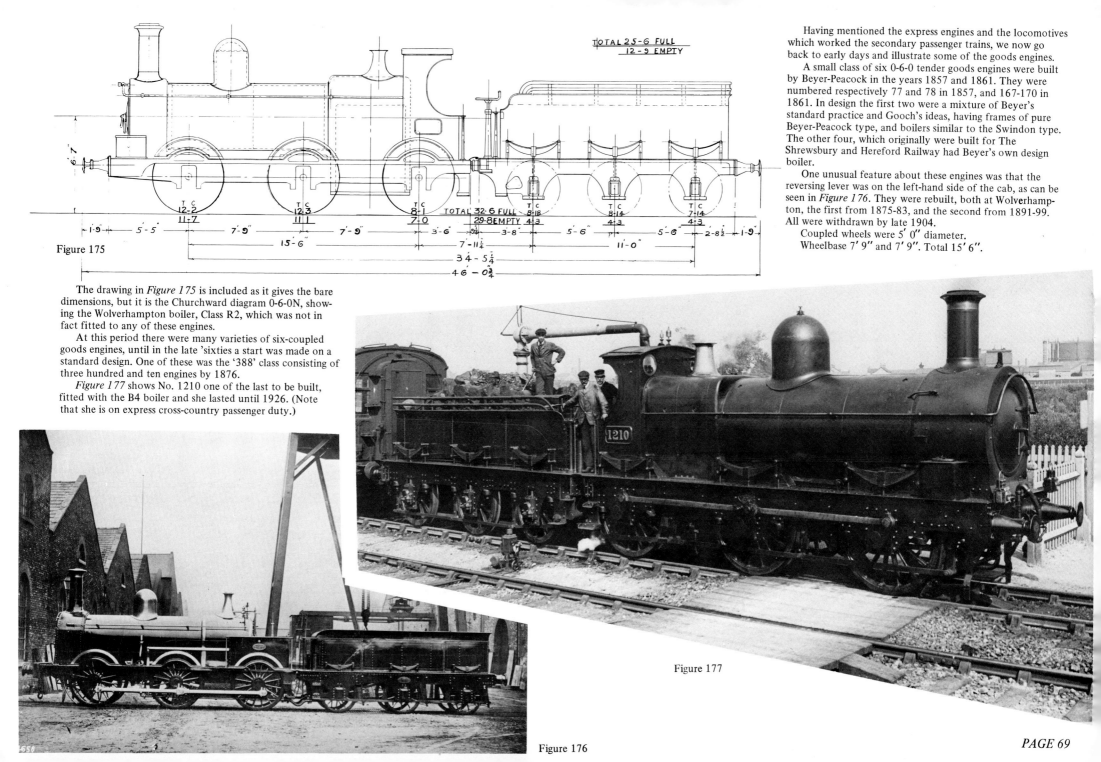

TOTAL 25-6 FULL
12-9 EMPTY

Figure 175

Having mentioned the express engines and the locomotives which worked the secondary passenger trains, we now go back to early days and illustrate some of the goods engines.

A small class of six 0-6-0 tender goods engines were built by Beyer-Peacock in the years 1857 and 1861. They were numbered respectively 77 and 78 in 1857, and 167-170 in 1861. In design the first two were a mixture of Beyer's standard practice and Gooch's ideas, having frames of pure Beyer-Peacock type, and boilers similar to the Swindon type. The other four, which originally were built for The Shrewsbury and Hereford Railway had Beyer's own design boiler.

One unusual feature about these engines was that the reversing lever was on the left-hand side of the cab, as can be seen in *Figure 176*. They were rebuilt, both at Wolverhampton, the first from 1875-83, and the second from 1891-99. All were withdrawn by late 1904.

Coupled wheels were 5′ 0″ diameter.

Wheelbase 7′ 9″ and 7′ 9″. Total 15′ 6″.

The drawing in *Figure 175* is included as it gives the bare dimensions, but it is the Churchward diagram 0-6-0N, showing the Wolverhampton boiler, Class R2, which was not in fact fitted to any of these engines.

At this period there were many varieties of six-coupled goods engines, until in the late 'sixties a start was made on a standard design. One of these was the '388' class consisting of three hundred and ten engines by 1876.

*Figure 177* shows No. 1210 one of the last to be built, fitted with the B4 boiler and she lasted until 1926. (Note that she is on express cross-country passenger duty.)

Figure 177

Figure 176

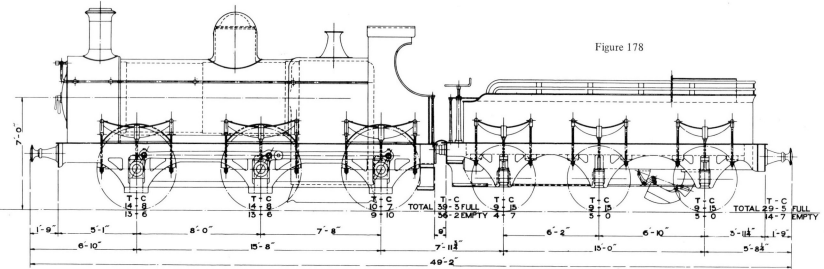

Figure 178

Having mentioned an outside frame 0-6-0 goods engine on the previous page, we come now to the earliest Swindon product.

No. 57 has the honour of being the first engine built by Gooch at the factory for the standard gauge lines of the Great Western Railway in 1855.

The original design showed the same elementary features as the broad gauge engines, namely the slotted sandwich frames and the domeless boiler with the characteristic fittings. Gooch's stationary link motion was used for the engines, and spring compensating beams were fitted between the axles, a feature which later found some favour on the Churchward engines.

After many rebuilds and renewals, with all sorts of boilers, the final form was as seen in *Figure 179*. Swindon's picture is dated 1910, and the engine was scrapped in November of 1912. Note that deep flat tie bars had been fitted between the hornplates in place of the original round rods, and the springs on the driving axle were so much lighter than those on the leading and trailing axles. The engines were numbered 57-68 rebuilt at Wolverhampton between 1873-1890 and three others, 316-18 were built at Stafford Road during 1890-91.

The '131' class illustrated in Maskelyne's drawing of *Figure 180*, was a modified version of the '57's, the main difference being that no compensating beams were fitted, and Stephenson's link motion took the place of the Gooch stationary link. Cylinders and stroke were increased slightly, but all other dimensions were identical.

The wheels were 5′ 2″ diameter, wheelbase 8′ 6″ and 7′ 9″. The official diagram is the Swindon *A3* which is as close as possible to the photograph *Figure 178*.

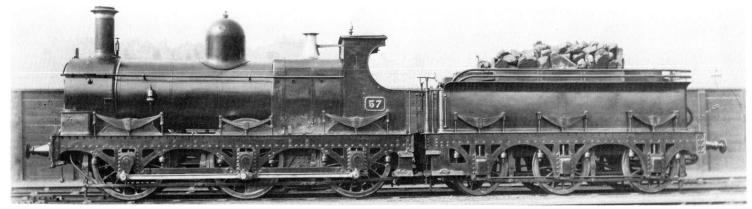

Figure 179

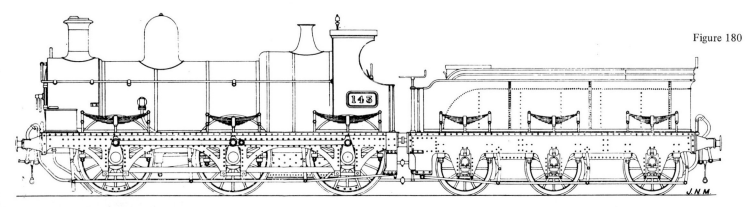

Figure 180

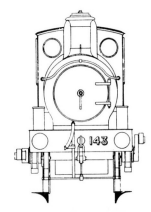

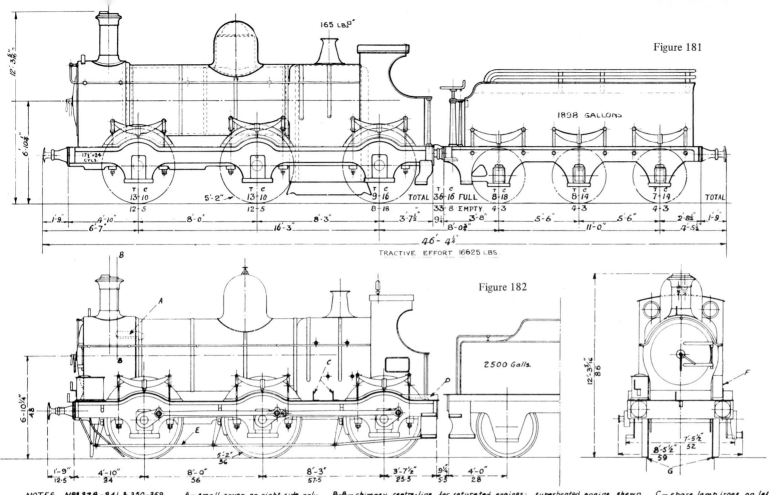

Figure 181

Figure 182

165 LBS

1898 GALLONS

TRACTIVE EFFORT 16625 LBS.

2500 Galls.

NOTES. Nos 328-341 & 350-359.   A-small cover on right side only.   B-B-chimney centre-line for saturated engines: superheated engine shewn.   C-spare lamp irons on left side only.
D-wood block to raise running-plate to tender level.   E-brake rigging outside wheels.   F-left-hand sand-box omitted, so as to shew splashers and running-plate.   G-Wheel treads and
flanges drawn to scale: allowances must be made for out-of-scale wheels.   Dimensions in feet (full size) and in millimetres to nearest half m'metre for Gauge O.

Beyer-Peacock & Co. made many engines for the Great Western and as well as those on *Page 69* perhaps the most successful was the '322' class of standard goods engines. Their origin goes right back to 1864, when Gooch ordered twenty 0-6-0 tender engines and left the design completely to the manufacturers. Two years later a further ten similar locomotives were commissioned by Joseph Armstrong, and this then constituted the '322' or 'Beyer' class, the oldest of which lasted until 1934. As would be expected with a class of engine which worked for seventy years, many were the rebuilds and boiler changes, and six engines were rebuilt as saddle tanks *(see page 85)*. The photographs show the engines as they were finally rebuilt, with the B4 type boiler and firebox. They could always be identified by the curved framing over the outside cranks, and those so slender coupling rods. Swindon *Diagram A1* is shown in *Figure 181* illustrating the Belpaire boiler of 1911, and the Templer drawing in *Figure 182* shows the final period with short chimney and Churchward tender. Note the official drawing does not show sandboxes, but they were fitted around 1883.

Some of the cab footsteps were staggered, some were straight.

These locomotives were numbered 322-359. Wheels were 5' 0", coupled wheelbase 8' 0" and 8' 3", totalling 16' 3". *Figure 183* illustrates No. 358 (with straight footsteps) and *Figure 184* shows No. 337 (with curved steps).

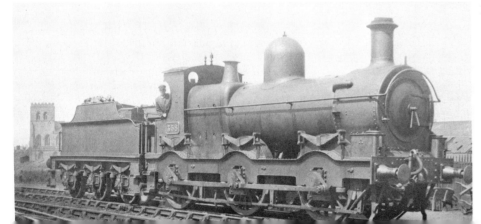

Figure 183

Figure 184

'Standard Goods' is the term usually applied to the '2301' class of 0-6-0 tender engines, but in fact referred to the 'Armstrong Goods' engines described on the next three pages, and briefly mentioned on *page 69.*

The first Lot was known as the '9th Goods' and was built in the years 1866-67. Running numbers allotted were 388-406. As traffic increased rapidly, so did the need for freight engines, and in the ten years between 1866 and 1876 three hundred and ten Joseph Armstrong 0-6-0 goods engines were constructed.

Figure 185

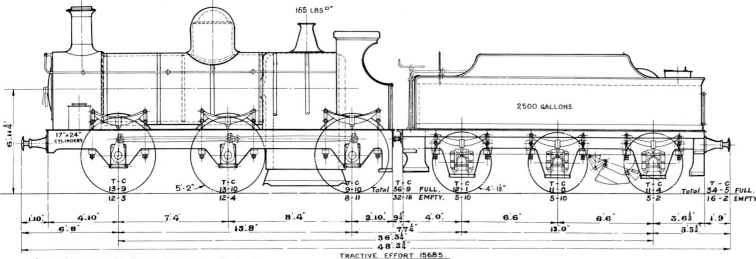

Figure 187

Figure 186

Over the years this large class naturally had many of its locomotives rebuilt, some at Swindon and others at Wolverhampton, so that, fitted with various types of boilers and parts, the class soon became far from uniform.

The earliest photograph is that shown in *Figure 187* of No. 794. This engine was built in 1873, and is seen with the S4 type of boiler, with the round-topped firebox. Note the filled-in coal rails on the tender, and also note the engine is still following the practice of carrying a lifting jack on the running plate.

*Figure 185* of No. 788 is dated 1902 and shows the fitting of the B2 boiler and firebox with the dome on the front ring. The official diagram in *Figure 186* is the Swindon *A9* and illustrates the class, fitted with superheater and B4 boiler, also with the Churchward tender.

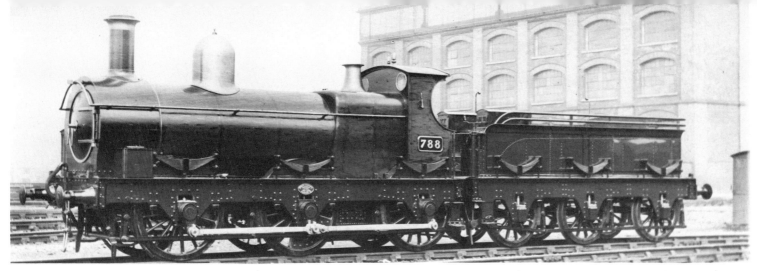

Figure 188

Another picture of No. 788 is shown in *Figure 188* also in 1902, but showing a three-quarter view which gives slightly more detail of the front end. It is of interest to note that the water gauge 'shut-off' lever was still being mounted outside the cab, and that the communication cord stanchions were erected on the tender, meaning of course that some of this class of 'goods' engine were being used for passenger services.

*Figure 190* is of No. 700 at Shrewsbury shed, coupled to a later type of tender, with the open-slotted frames and coal sides in place of rails. As the records show No. 700 to have received her B4 boiler in July 1904, this picture would be dated around that period.

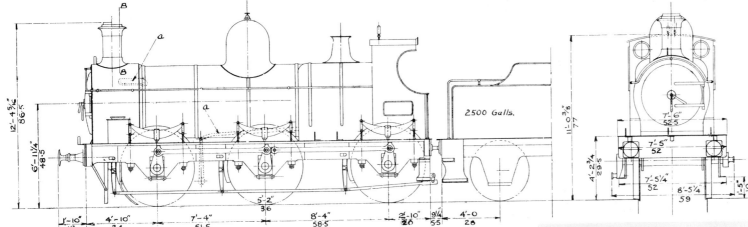

2500 Galls.

Figure 189

*PAGE 73*

The drawing in *Figure 189* is one of Col. Templer's reductions from Swindon diagrams, and illustrates several features not shown on the official drawings, namely the whistle placings, the dome lubricator mounting, brake and guard iron positions, and lamp brackets, etc. The drawing is 4mm scale, with measurements in feet and in millimetres.

Figure 190

Figure 191

Two more pictures and another drawing of the '388' class adorn this page, still showing minor variations. At the top in *Figure 191,* we see No. 1110 resplendent in her glossy green livery, straight out of shops in 1913. Notice how it is possible to see the reflections of the splasher tops in the boiler sides! Also these three illustrations show three different types of tender. No. 1195 in *Figure 193* is seen in her final form in the 1930s; in fact, she was the last of the series, being finally withdrawn in 1934 after 58 years service, after running over a million miles!

Mr. Maskelyne's lovely drawing of No. 27 shows the engine with the round-topped firebox, with a brass dome and copper-topped chimney.

Many were the duties of these ubiquitous locomotives, more often than not, working the stopping goods, but were also seen working passenger trains across the old Severn Bridge on Sunday duty. Mr. Maskelyne records No. 424 and No. 1202 bringing in the 'Cornish Riviera' after a failure in 1907!, and also No. 700 (illustrated) diagrammed to work the 9.35 p.m. ex Chester for Shrewsbury with an express train, complete with dining car, on a daily timetable in 1918.

Figure 192

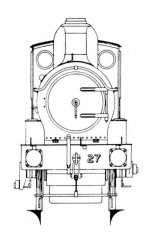

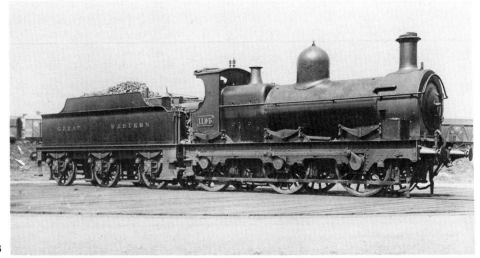

Figure 193

Figure 194

Figure 195

Figure 196

These three pictures show No. 1089 just before the engine was withdrawn after nearly sixty years' service! She was originally built in 1870 at Swindon and was reboilered at Wolverhampton in 1889 with a W3 type boiler. This lasted until 1909 when the engine received an R2 boiler. Finally in 1919 a B4 design boiler was installed, and in December of 1922 this engine was one of the few in the class to be superheated.

*Figure 196* shows the complete right-hand side of No. 1089 and gives some idea of the smokebox door and boiler front. *Figure 195* clearly shows in closer detail on the front end, the strengthening plates which have been added to the outside framing around the hornplates. The large sandbox can be seen with its operating lever, running away behind the leading splasher. *Figure 194* illustrates the back end of the 'Armstrong Goods' and gives a clear impression of the slender coupling rods and the rather short cab.

At first glance, the numbering on these engines would seem to place them in the 'Dean Goods' class, but this is not so. These twenty 0-6-0 goods engines were built in 1885-86 under *Lot 67* and were different in that they had double frames, but the springs were underhung, and outside the driving wheels. Numbers ran from 2361 to 2380 and the two illustrated on this page are Nos. 2364 and 2377.

*Figure 198* shows the class as built, with the dome on the front ring of the boiler, which was a special long boiler, classified as S2B, being 10′ 6″ long instead of the more usual 10′ 3″. Several points of interest in the picture include the water feed pipe entering the side of the firebox, the lubricator just behind the chimney, and the continuing use of the communication gong on the tender side (see *Figure 205*) The tender itself is unusual, in that it has no side rails, and would appear to be fitted with two rectangular fillers at the rear, one on each side!

*Figure 197* shows No. 2377 in 1904, equipped with the standard Great Western Railway snow plough. The engine is seen fitted with the S4 type of boiler, which was of the 10′ 3″ length standard. Note the safety valve control passing through the cab spectacle plate, and protuding through the cab roof. The snow ploughs were kept at many locomotive sheds throughout the system, and were fitted on to a particular engine like this during the winter months.

Figure 197

Figure 198

Figure 199

Figure 200

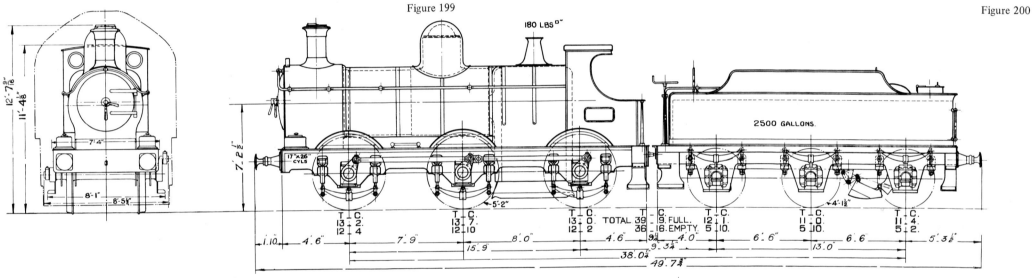

Figure 201

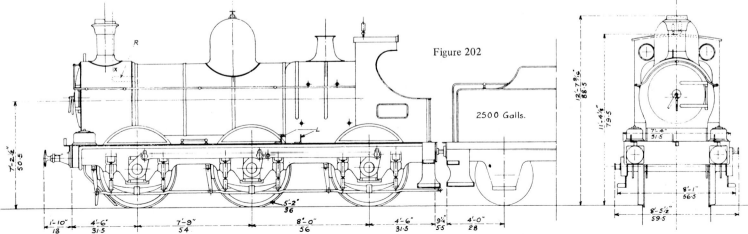

Figure 202

*Figure 199* shows No. 2370 in the last state of rebuild, whereas *Figure 200* shows No. 2361 as constructed in 1885. One can see the differences in the boilers fitted. No. 2361 having the special S2B. boiler, and No. 2370 carrying the final form of boiler used being the Belpaire B4, superheated. The two drawings are of the same class, but *Figure 202,* from the pen of Col. Templer, shows the non-superheated boiler and *Figure 201* is the weight diagram from Swindon dating 1922 to *A12,* which shows the extra length of the superheated design. Note the slight difference in cab roof height, and the chimney and safety valve bonnet on the Templer drawing.

Figure 203

Figure 204

C.W.R.

TYPE OF GONG IN USE ON THE
**GREAT WESTERN RAILWAY**
AS A MEANS OF COMMUNICATION
BETWEEN PASSENGERS AND ENGINEMEN
PRIOR TO THE YEAR 1880

Figure 205

More close-up details are shown on this page of the '2361' class. *Figure 203* shows the shape of the smokebox and door, and the position of the hinged lid over the cylinder heads. In the lower photograph the left-hand side front is seen, which gives a clear picture of the underhung spring anchorages in the outside frame plates. Note the small footstep on the smokebox side and the shallow sandboxes. The 2″ pipe running along the framing is the vacuum pipe, taken along the side in this fashion to avoid the motion.

*Figure 205* shows an example of the warning gong which was fixed on the driver's side of the tender and operated by means of a chain for use by any passenger wishing to stop the train in an emergency. As can be seen in *Figure 198,* these engines were originally equipped with this form of communication.

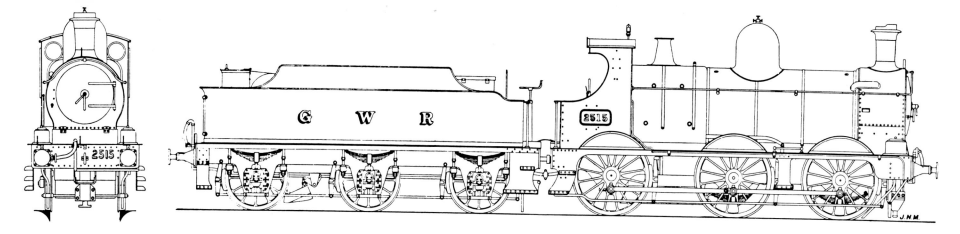

Figure 206

We come now to that classic of 0-6-0 tender engines known as the 'Dean Goods'. First designed and built by William Dean in 1883, no less than two hundred and sixty of this class were constructed between then and 1899.

These engines were of the inside frame style, and slightly shorter than their predecessors, the 'Armstrong Goods', the wheelbase being 15′ 6″ compared to the 15′ 8″ of the '388' series.

The first twenty had domeless boilers as can be seen in *Figure 207*, having smokeboxes flush with boiler diameter and feed water clacks in the firebox sides.

Numbers ran from 2301 to 2580 consecutively, except for the small batch of twenty numbered 2361-80 already described on *pages 77* and *78*.

In *Figure 206* No. 2515 drawn by J.N. Maskelyne is reproduced here to 4mm scale. It is shown in the final condition with the Belpaire firebox and modern boiler, and fitted with the tapered chimney.

The class was very long lived indeed, this particular engine surviving until 1953.

No. 2463 in the same design as the drawing is shown in *Figure 208*, illustrating the left-hand side. Note that the safety valve bonnet appears higher in the photograph than in the drawing.

Figure 207

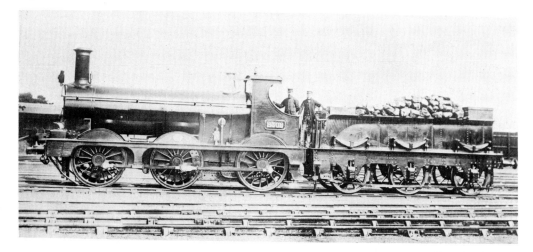

Figure 208

Figure 209

Figure 210

Two interesting pictures depicting part of the history of the 'Dean Goods'. In *Figure 209* No. 2537 is seen in 1908, at Drayton Green fitted with the S4 boiler, polished dome and copper-topped chimney. Note that the early boiler having a lower height than the Belpaire type meant that the windows in the spectacle plate were consequently larger. The other engine in the photograph is an old 'Armstrong Goods'. In *Figure 210* No. 2382 stands at the head of a farm removal train in 1934. The location is Llanwrda on the Vale of Towey Joint line (LNW & GW) between Builth Road and Llandilo. The engine has the Belpaire firebox B4 of the last pattern, and the chimney is of the taper pattern with capuchon as per the drawing on the previous page. It is interesting to note that this engine carries a class 'C' red lamp headcode.

Two early shed scenes on the next two pages are included to illustrate how very clean the engines were kept in 1906. *Figure 212* is of Worcester shed and amongst the saddle tanks can be seen Dean Goods Nos. 2328, 2335 and 2345 plus one other unidentifiable engine, all carrying the S2 type of boiler with polished narrow dome on the front ring. Also in the picture can be seen three Armstrong Goods, and a '517' class tank. *Figure 211* is an enlargement of a 'Dean Goods' cab and details of the fittings from left to right are as follows: On the extreme left can be seen the boiler feed clack box, then the water gauge glass cut-off lever and test cocks. Next, the steam heating gauge and then the regulator is show in full open position. The three wheel valves under the regulator, are, top blower valve, bottom left, injector steam supply, left-hand injector, bottom right and the same for the right-hand injector. Next, the brake handle with centre position, for running, and moved left to apply brake and moved right to release. (This was steam and vacuum combined brake system.) Alongside, can be seen right-hand clack box, and adjacent to this the sight feed lubricator. Finally extreme right, the top of reversing lever, with A.T.C. control above.

Figure 212

Figure 211

In contrast to the shed with a goods engine flavour, *Figure 213* depicts Exeter with many passenger engines. The single on the left is *St. George,* and the 'County' is No. 3825. Four 'Dean Goods' are visible, three with domed boilers and one domeless, also a curved frame 'Bulldog' and a small '517' class locomotive can be seen.

There are many interesting features in this photograph of 1905 from the massive yard lamp with the lattice column, which was a real landmark of Exeter, to the sand drier at the extreme left. Also the lifting shop, depot offices, the four road shed, cattle sidings in the middle distance, the goods shed top right, and finally, the station wall-rear on the extreme right.

Figure 213

Figure 214

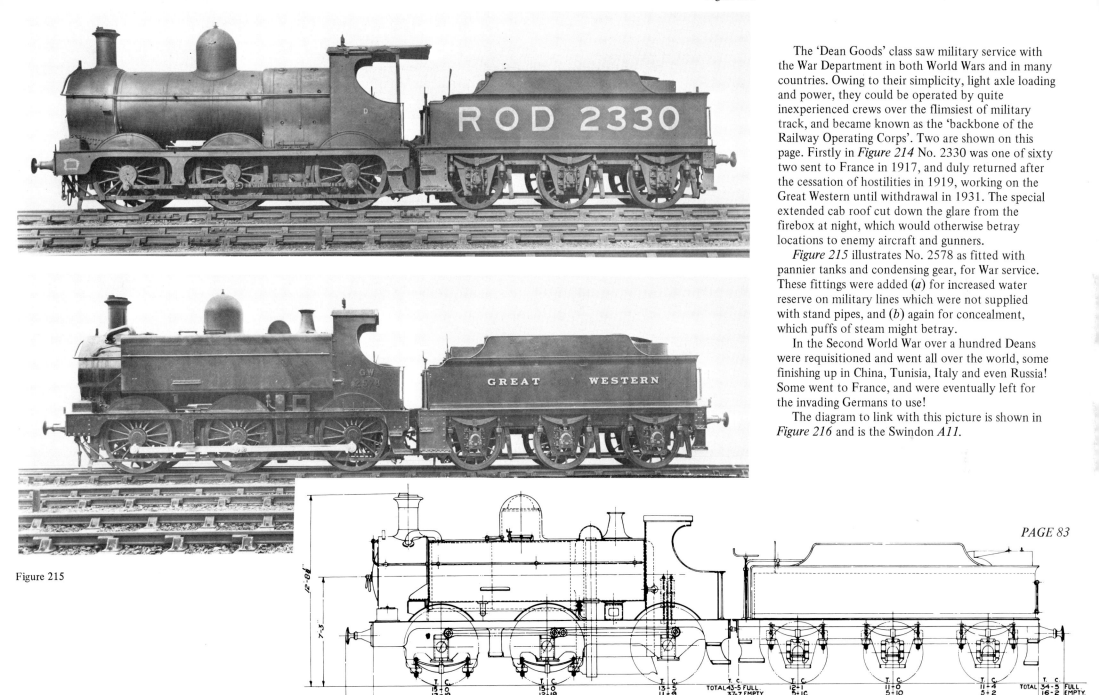

The 'Dean Goods' class saw military service with the War Department in both World Wars and in many countries. Owing to their simplicity, light axle loading and power, they could be operated by quite inexperienced crews over the flimsiest of military track, and became known as the 'backbone of the Railway Operating Corps'. Two are shown on this page. Firstly in *Figure 214* No. 2330 was one of sixty two sent to France in 1917, and duly returned after the cessation of hostilities in 1919, working on the Great Western until withdrawal in 1931. The special extended cab roof cut down the glare from the firebox at night, which would otherwise betray locations to enemy aircraft and gunners.

*Figure 215* illustrates No. 2578 as fitted with pannier tanks and condensing gear, for War service. These fittings were added (*a*) for increased water reserve on military lines which were not supplied with stand pipes, and (*b*) again for concealment, which puffs of steam might betray.

In the Second World War over a hundred Deans were requisitioned and went all over the world, some finishing up in China, Tunisia, Italy and even Russia! Some went to France, and were eventually left for the invading Germans to use!

The diagram to link with this picture is shown in *Figure 216* and is the Swindon *A11*.

*PAGE 83*

Figure 215

Figure 216

Figure 217

Figure 218

Figure 219

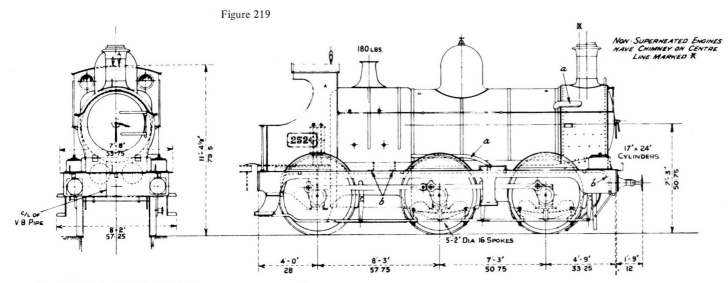

180 LBS.

NON-SUPERHEATED ENGINES
HAVE CHIMNEY ON CENTRE
LINE MARKED ✕

2524

17' x 24'
CYLINDERS

11-4⅜'
79·5

7-3'
50·75

c/L OF
V. B PIPE

7-8'
53·75

8-2'
57·25

5-2' DIA 16 SPOKES.

4'-0'
28

8'-3'
57·75

7'-3'
50·75

4'-9'
33·25

1'-9'
12

ALL DETAILS ON R.H. SIDE MARKED 'a'

No. 2408 was, for many years, the snow plough engine at Banbury loco shed, and is seen as such in *Figures 217* and *218,* the two pictures showing both sides. Built in November of 1891 with an S2 boiler, she was reboilered with S4 type in 1905, converted back to an S2 boiler in 1909 and given the Belpaire B4 in 1911, being finally superheated in 1921. This engine was one of two that were loaned to the L.N.W. Railway in the years 1915-17. The snow plough was fixed to this type of locomotive because the design of plough was such that it had to be an engine with a straight up and down front as the attachment points were to the brackets seen on the front of the framing, the coupling hook and the smokebox front.

The drawing in *Figure 219* is another of Col. Templer's scale diagrams to 4mm and complements the photographs well. Note the parallel-sided chimney. How pleasant to record that 'Dean Goods' No. 2516 has been preserved and can be seen at Swindon Museum today.

Figure 220

Figure 221

A page of comparisons. *Figure 220* although looking remarkably like a 'Dean Goods' is in fact a 'Cambrian' 0-6-0, No. 892 seen here at Barmouth in 1939. Originally built by R. Stephenson in 1903, she was reboilered at Swindon in 1930 and given Diagram *A.28*.

*Figure 221* shows No. 2578 (see *Figure 215*) in Tyseley shed in 1950 alongside an L.M.S. 0-6-0 No. 43712. *Figure 222* is the official weight diagram of the '844' class reduced to 4mm scale. The Cambrian numbers were 15, 29, 42, 89, 100 and 101, Great Western numbers being 844, 49, 73, 87, 94 and 95.

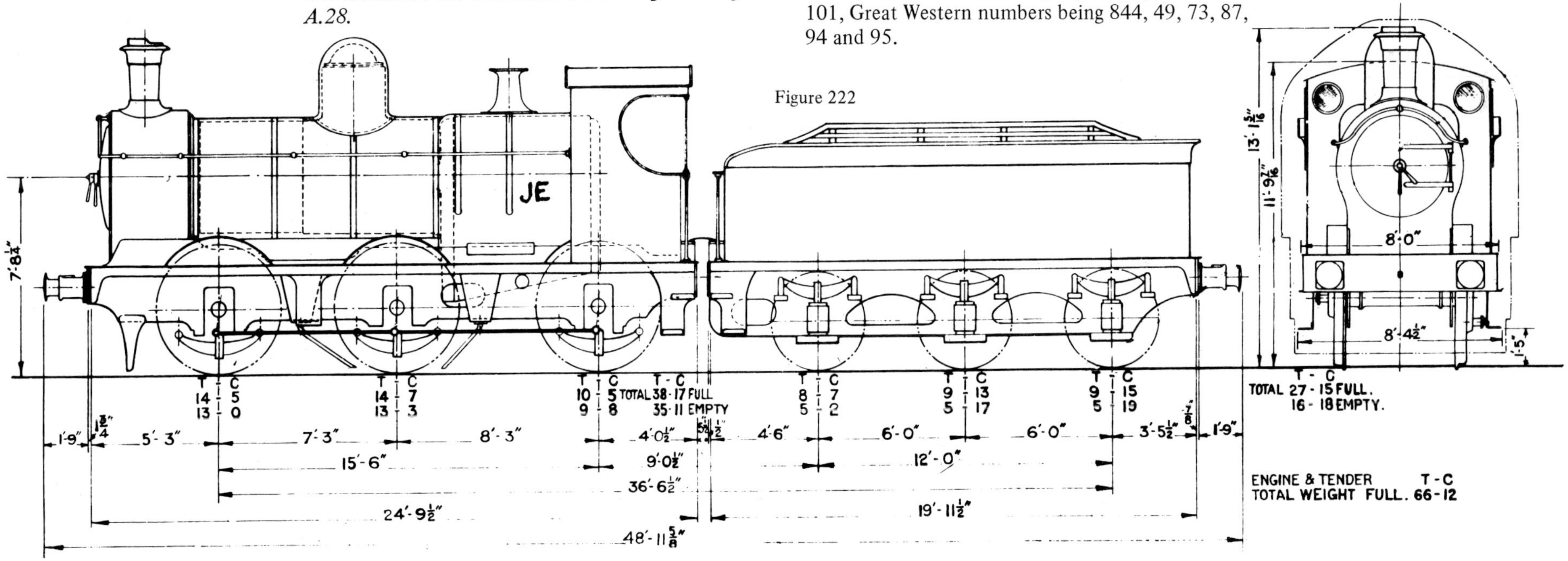

Figure 222

Figure 225

*PAGE 86*

The penultimate page of 'Dean Goods' is of two particular engines. *Figures 225* and *225A* show No. 2407 at Cardiff loco shed in 1949. Many features can be seen clearly in this picture.

No. 2516 the 'Dean' which J.N. Maskelyne did so much to get preserved, was photographed at Swindon in the course of being restored, and in the lower picture the cab details can be seen just as the engine was taken out of service. In *Figure 223* the same cab can be seen with all the copper and brass fittings polished, almost ready for the static show-piece she is today. Note that several fittings have been changed.

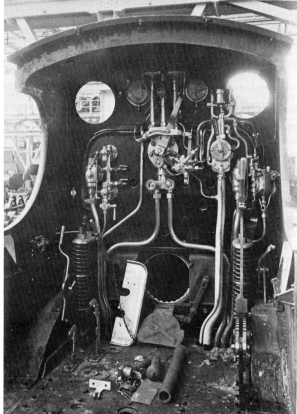

Figure 223

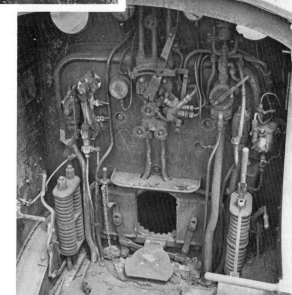

Figure 224

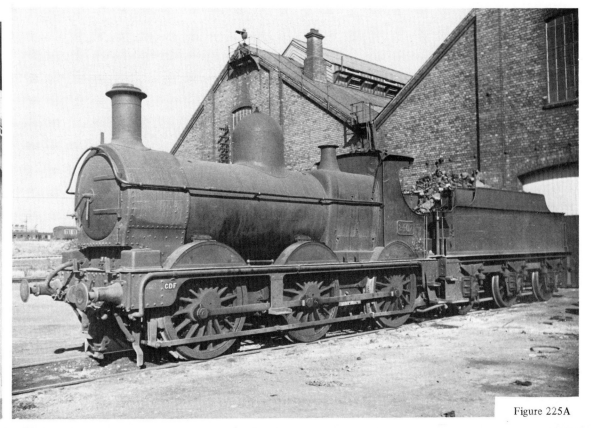

Figure 225A

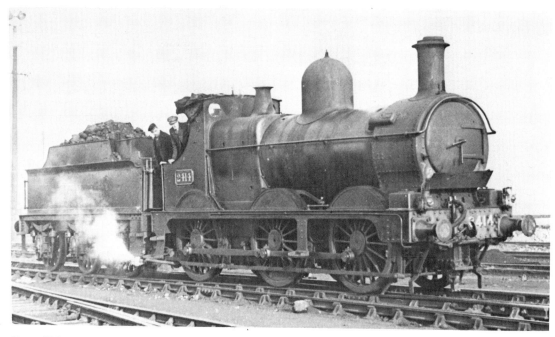

Figure 226

The last pictures of the 'Dean Goods' shows this class operating various duties! No. 2414 is seen carrying 'A' express passenger headlights at Bristol, prior to running Sunday only top link trains from Temple Meads to Cardiff, via the old Severn Bridge. In *Figure 227,* again at Bristol, No. 2444 is being coaled by means of steam crane and grab. Note the different tenders and chimney on these two engines.

Figure 227

Figure 228

150 LB/□″

1052 GALLONS.

CYLINDERS 17″ × 24″

TRACTIVE EFFORT 15935 LB.

Figure 229

The next few pages are devoted to the 0-6-0 tanks of which the Great Western Railway built no less than 1,109! between the years of 1870 and 1905.

It is so easy to just lump all the pannier tanks together and call them 'G.W. Matchboxes' but not one of this batch started life as a locomotive with these 'panniers'. All of them had either side tanks, that is, tanks that came right down on to the framing, or saddle tanks, tanks which followed the curve of the boiler, and straddled across the tops of both boiler and firebox.

The whole series can be divided into three parts for convenience:

(*a*) Those built at Swindon between 1870 and 1901, consisting of 10 classes with numbers starting as detailed below:- 1076 class, 727, 1134, 1813, 1661, 1854, 905, 2721, 2779, and 2796 classes respectively.

(*b*) The large Wolverhampton tanks built at Stafford Road between 1864 and 1897 consisted of eight classes with numbers starting 302, 1016, 633, 645, 1501, 119, 322 and 655.

(*c*) The smaller tanks also built at Wolverhampton whose class numbers commenced 850, 1901, 2021 and 2101 were all constructed between the years 1874 and 1905.

From here on, the classes that I can illustrate will be in the order shown, and referred to be these initial numbers.

Figure 230

The first example is she in Figure 229 and is the *Diagram B* for the '1076' class of *Lot 22*. The drawing shows the rebuilt state with the saddle tank on the S2 boiler. As originally built, these engines had side tanks and no cab, but then they were fitted with cabs and after this modification were stripped of their side tanks and equipped with saddle tanks as shown in the drawing. *Figure 230* shows one of the same class, No. 1601 in 1902 with the S2 boiler and different cab shape that these engines carried from here on. Note the marine type bearing on the driving crankpin coupling rod. *Figure 228* shows the class much later with pannier tank and spark arresting chimney. This is the official *Diagram A 53*.

Figure 232

Figure 231

*Figure 231* illustrates another of the same class as on the previous page, namely the '1076' or 'Buffalo' class. No. 1176 is portrayed in the 1910 condition with the long saddle tanks and polished dome and safety valve bonnet. The picture ties up nicely with the 4mm drawing by J.N. Maskelyne in *Figure 233*, in which No. 1564 is seen in side elevation with two ends elevations plus the different radii of the saddle tank itself.

The right-hand picture of No. 1232 is an interesting engine in that she was one of those fifty convertibles, which ran on the broad gauge. Nos. 1228-1237 worked on the 7' track from 1876 until 1892, and No. 1232 was the only one to be rebuilt whilst still on the broad gauge. She received pannier tanks in 1923 and was withdrawn in 1930. Note the position of the water filler, and the dome on the front ring of the boiler, *Figure 232*.

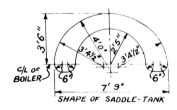

SHAPE OF SADDLE-TANK

Figure 233

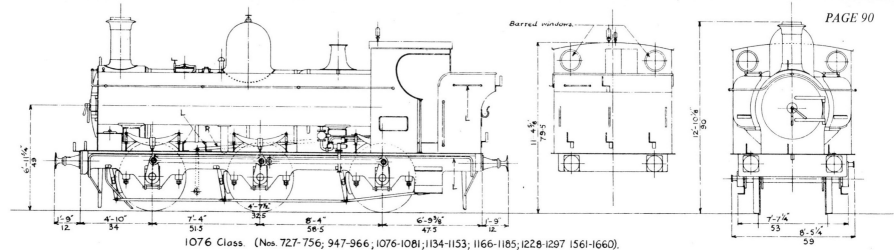

Figure 234

1076 Class. (Nos. 727-756; 947-966; 1076-1081; 1134-1153; 1166-1185; 1228-1297 1561-1660).

_NOTES._ Details marked "L" are on left side only; those marked "R" on right side only. Wheel treads and flanges drawn to scale; allowance must be made for out-of-scale wheels. Dimensions in feet (full size), and in millimetres to the nearest half-millimetre for Gauge "O".

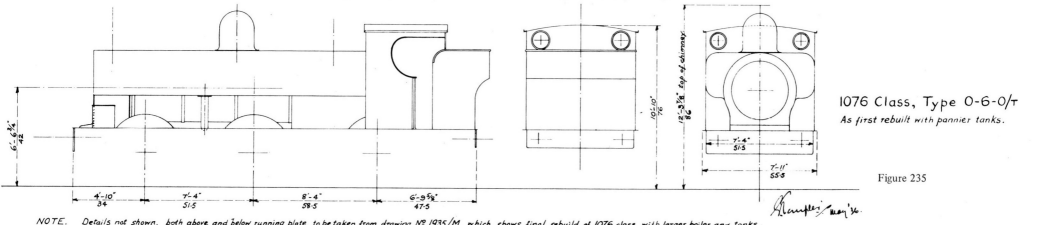

1076 Class, Type 0-6-0/T
_As first rebuilt with pannier tanks._

Figure 235

NOTE. Details not shown, both above and below running plate, to be taken from drawing Nº 1935/M, which shows final rebuild of 1076 class with larger boiler and tanks.

Pannier tanks replaced the saddle tanks on the '1076-1134' class gradually over many years, commencing in 1911, but as these tanks were tailored to fit the boiler on to which they were hung, so they altered in shape and size as the engines were rebuilt with different boilers. These two drawings of Colonel Templer's illustrate the point well. In *Figure 234* one of the class '1076' locomotives shown with the large boiler and tanks which made the engines considerable taller than when fitted with the smaller boiler as per *Figure 235*. Note the different size of spectacle plate and boiler fittings.

The photograph in *Figure 236* shows No. 1172 fitted with one of the early style of panniers, with open cab and small bunker. Just to give an idea of the extent of rebuilding these engines endured. No. 1172 was built in 1875 with its first boiler change in 1892, the second in 1903, the third in 1920, the fourth in 1924, and its final change in 1928. She was finally withdrawn in April 1930.

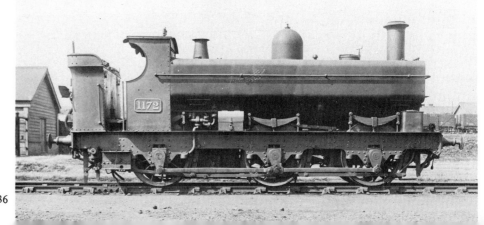

Figure 236

Figure 237

Figure 238

It is not generally known that some of the early pannier tanks had rectangular cab windows in the front only. But this was so with this '1134' class, and *Figure 237* proves this fact. Amongst the engines so fitted were No. 738, 1167, 1234/5/52/65/69/71/84, 1567/70/1600. Also twenty of the class were equipped with gear for working with auto-car trailers, No. 1600 being so fitted in 1917. To help with passenger traffic working many were fitted with screw reversing gear in place of the usual lever.

*Figure 238* is a very clearly detailed picture of No. 1169 taken at Swindon in 1926, when the engine was straight out of shops after a major overhaul. Only eight years later she was finally withdrawn, after fifty nine years' service in one form or another. It is apparent in these two pictures that these engines were so obviously the tank versions of the 'Standard Goods' 0-6-0 tender engines, already described.

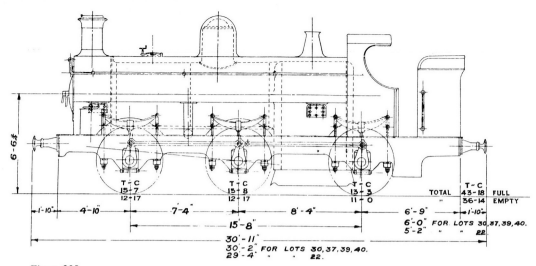

Figure 239

Figure 241

Two diagrams and two pictures are shown on this page, still dealing with the '1076' class. In *Figure 241* engine No. 738 is seen as another example of the rectangular front window style, with the closed cab, whereas in *Figure 242*, No. 1282 has the round windows and the open small-bunkered cab. The two diagrams, both official, show the class at two different stages of rebuild. In *Figure 239* we see *Diagram A.17* (1911 version) with pannier tanks and a 'Q' class boiler, of the B4 classification. *Figure 240* shows *Diagram B.23* of 1925 fitted with a 'P' class boiler still of the B4 pattern. Note the different size and shape of the panniers and boiler fittings.

Figure 242

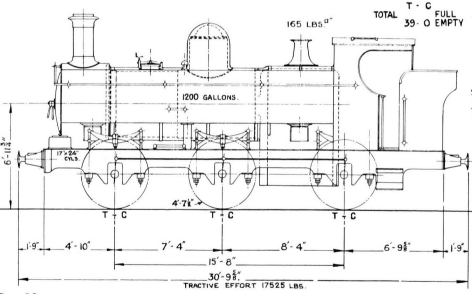

Figure 240

*Page 93*

This page shows 4 diagrams of the '1076' class in various conditions and at different periods. Plus one '27xx' class.

*Figure 243* shows diagrams for No. 1287 with enlarged bunker.

*Figure 244* shows *Diagram B.24* pannier tanks with B4 boiler class P.

*Figure 245* shows *Diagram A.22.* pannier tanks with S4 boiler class Q.

*Figure 246A* shows *Diagram A.54* saddle tank with S4 boiler class O.

*Figure 246B* shows *Diagram A.61* pannier tank with B4 boiler class O.

*Figure 246C* shows *Diagram B.47* pannier tank with B4 ('2721' class).

The last has been included to show how similar were the designs.

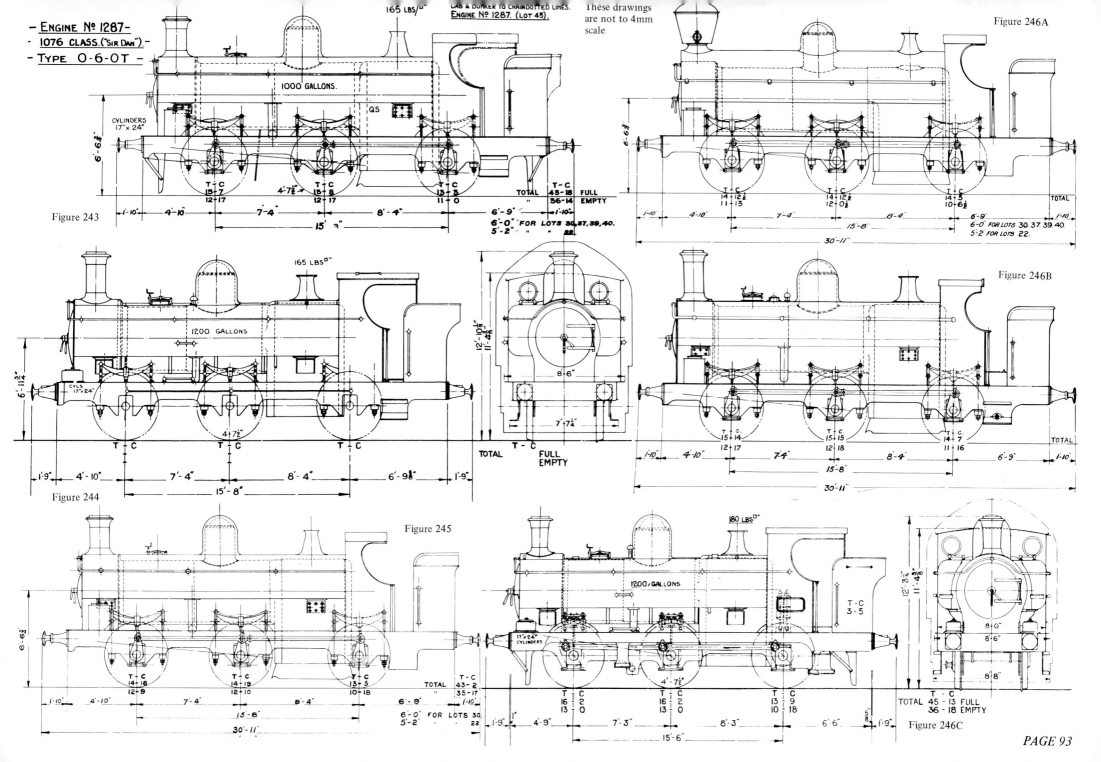

ENGINE № 1287
1076 CLASS. ("SIR DAN")
TYPE O-6-OT

CAB & BUNKER TO CHAINDOTTED LINES.
Engine № 1287. (Lot 45).

165 LBS/□

These drawings are not to 4mm scale

Figure 246A

1000 GALLONS.

QS

CYLINDERS 17"x 24"

6'-6¾"

T-C 15-7    4'-7½"    T-C 15-8    T-C 13-3    TOTAL    T-C 43-18    FULL
12-17    12-17    11-0    36-14    EMPTY
1'-10"    4'-10"    7'-4"    8'-4"    6'-9"    1'-10"
15'-9"    6'-0" FOR LOTS 30,37,39,40.
5'-2"  "  "  22.

Figure 243

6'-6¾"

T-C 14-12½    T-C 14-12½    T-C 14-5
11-13    12-0½    10-6½
1'-10"    4'-10"    7'-4"    8'-4"    6'-9"    TOTAL
15'-8"    6'-0" FOR LOTS 30.37.39.40.
5'-2 FOR LOTS 22.
30'-11"

165 LBS□

1200 GALLONS

CYLS. 17"x24"

6'-11¼"

T-C    4'-7½"    T-C    T-C
1'-9"    4'-10"    7'-4"    8'-4"    6'-9⅝"    1'-9"
15'-8"

Figure 244

12'-10½"
11'-4⅝"

8'-6"

7'-7¼"

TOTAL    FULL    EMPTY

Figure 246B

T-C 15-14    T-C 15-15    T-C 14-7
12-17    12-18    11-16
1'-10"    4'-10"    7'-4"    8'-4"    6'-9"    TOTAL
15'-8"    1'-10"
30'-11"

Figure 245

6'-6¾"

T-C 14-18    T-C 14-19    T-C 13-5    TOTAL    T-C 43-2
12-9    12-10    10-18    35-17
1'-10"    4'-10"    7'-4"    8'-4"    6'-9"    1'-10"
15'-8"    6'-0" FOR LOTS 30.
5'-2"  "  "  22.
30'-11"

180 LBS□

1200 GALLONS

T-C 3-5

17"x24" CYLINDERS

4'-7½"

12'-3⁵⁄₁₆"
11'-4⅜"

8'-0"

8'-6"

8'-8"

T-C 16-2    T-C 16-2    T-C 13-9
13-0    13-0    10-18
1'-9"    4'-9"    7'-3"    8'-3"    6'-6"    ⁵⁄₈"    1'-9"
15'-6"    TOTAL 45-13 FULL
36-18 EMPTY
Figure 246C

PAGE 93

*Figure 247* illustrates No. 1282 again at a later date, this time fitted with a spark arresting chimney for working towards the end of her days in the Didcot Ordnance Depot. The official photograph of No. 1635 taken in 1911, shows this engine at the height of her career with pannier tanks, polished safety valve bonnet, and smokebox door rim, with the water tanks decorated with the full insignia of the period, copper-topped chimney and being immaculately clean of course. She was one of *Lot 55* built in 1880, with saddle tanks, rebuilt with panniers in 1911 and finally condemned in 1932.

Figure 247

A list of the 'Buffalo' class from 1870 to 1881 is as under:

| Nos. 1076-1081 | *Lot 22* | of | 1870 |
|---|---|---|---|
| Nos. 727-756 | *Lot 30* | of | 1872-73 |
| Nos. 947-966 | *Lot 37* | of | 1874 |
| Nos. 1134-1153 | *Lot 39* | of | 1874-75 |
| Nos. 1166-1185 | *Lot 40* | of | 1875 |
| Nos. 1228-1247 | *Lot 43* | of | 1876-77 |
| Nos. 1248-1267 | *Lot 44* | of | 1877 |
| Nos. 1268-1297 | *Lot 45* | of | 1877-78 |
| Nos. 1561-1580 | *Lot 48* | of | 1878-79 |
| Nos. 1581-1600 | *Lot 49* | of | 1879 |
| Nos. 1601-1620 | *Lot 50* | of | 1879-80 |
| Nos. 1621-1640 | *Lot 52* | of | 1880 |
| Nos. 1641-1660 | *Lot 55* | of | 1880-81 |

Figure 248

Figure 249

Figure 250

Figure 252

When first built, these '119' class engines had tenders, and were renewed in this tank form in 1878-83. Note the painted coupling rods and typical Wolverhampton rolled top chimney, also the trailing sandbox on the running plate and open sandwich frames. Engines were numbered in this series Nos. 119-121 and 123-130 of renewal *Lots 4* and *5*.

Another Wolverhampton built tank of a later date and different class is seen in *Figure 253*. This is No. 1744, one of the '655' series. These engines which were built under three lots between 1892-97 were the last 'large' tanks to be constructed at Stafford Road, and the class was comparatively small. The numbers were 655-767 of *Lot A.3.*, Nos. 1741-50, 1771-90 of *Lot B.3.* and Nos. 2701-20 of *Lot E.3.* It should be noted that these last twenty locomotives although numbered in the '27XX' series, did not belong to the Swindon built '27XX' class. When built, they had saddle tanks and rolled top chimneys similar to *Figure 251*, but all but No. 1778 received pannier tanks and Swindon-style boiler fittings.

A page of contrasting tank locomotives consisting of four engines of four different classes, two of Swindon origin and two built at Wolverhampton. *Figures 249* and *250* show No. 1850 as built at Swindon in 1883 with a domeless boiler and side tanks, with 'Charlie Chaplin' on the footplate! and later in 1912, fitted with long pannier tanks standing by the weighbridge at Swindon. Notice the coat-of-arms transfer used on the tank sides, the polished safety valve bonnet and the copper-topped tall chimney.

*Figure 252* is another Swindon engine of the same class as those on *page 92*. One of the '727' class seen here as running in the 1920's. No. 740 was built in 1873, received its pannier tanks in October 1914 and was withdrawn in the condition shown here, in October 1929.

An early Wolverhampton built engine, No. 126 in *Figure 251*, is seen depicted with saddle tanks.

Figure 251

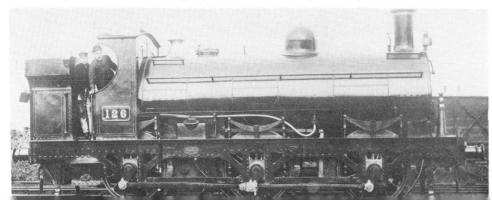

Figure 253

*PAGE 95*

Figure 254                    PAGE 96

The '1813' class of 0-6-0 tank engines were interesting, being the first in a long series of inside-framed tanks, which finally culminated in 1948, with the building of the 94XX class. These engines were the first to be designed with single inside frames and underhung springs, and when first built had long side tanks as seen in *Figure 249.* All except two were rebuilt with saddle tanks, and all except No. 1829 carried pannier tanks. Some were fitted with this pattern as early as 1903, and were amongst the earliest engines to be so equipped. The first of the class, No. 1813, was sold to the Pembroke & Tenby Railway between 1883 and 1896 and carried the name *Holmwood* which it kept until withdrawal in 1928.

*Figures 254* and *255* are both official Swindon photographs of No. 1819 taken at the Works in 1924 when this engine had just been fitted with its pannier tanks. Two special points distinguish this '1813' class from other 0-6-0 tanks:

(*a*) The coupling rods were jointed with an upright swivel pin in front of the centre crank pin, and

(*b*) The step for access to the motion was small and of unusual shape.

Numbers of these locomotives ran from 1813 to 1853 inclusive except for No. 1833 which is not in this class. Lots Nos. were *59 and 60,* and dated 1882-84. No. 1819 was withdrawn in January 1938.

Figure 255

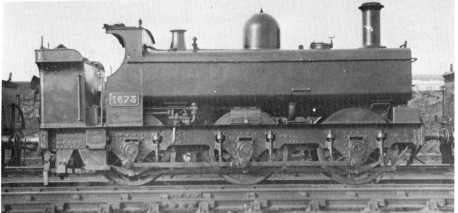

Figure 256

Figure 257

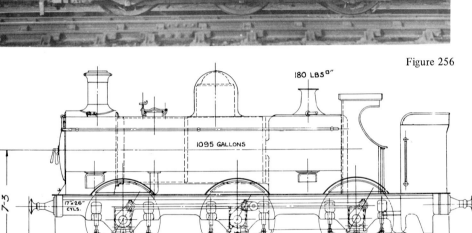

There were forty engines in this the '1661' class. Built at Swindon between 1886-87, the frames were originally intended for 0-6-0 tender locomotives of the '2361' class, but with the success of the 'Buffalo' class of tanks on the coal runs from South Wales to Swindon, it was decided to build them as tanks.

Nos. 1661-1680 were built in 1886 under *Lot 69*, and Nos. 1681-1700 in 1886-87 on *Lot 71* originally *Diagram D*.

As can be seen in *Figure 256*, the outside frames were of the same pattern as the '3201', '3501' and '2361' class with underhung springs and anchorages in the frames. *Figure 257* of No. 1644 is added to show the difference between the '1661' class, and the '1134' series to which No. 1644 belonged.

The two drawings are both of the '1661' class. *Figure 258* is the official Swindon Diagram A.29 showing pannier tanks and B4 boiler, and *Figure 259* is a Templer drawing of the class, illustrating the closed cab and taller chimney.

Figure 258

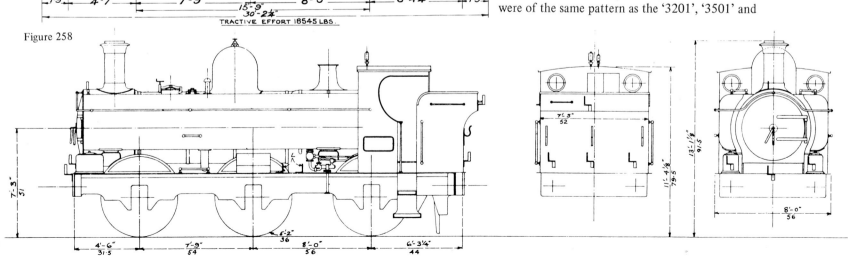

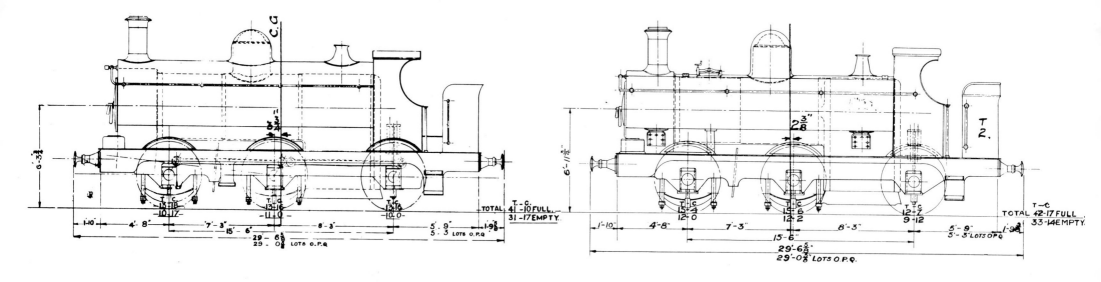

Figure 260

Figure 262

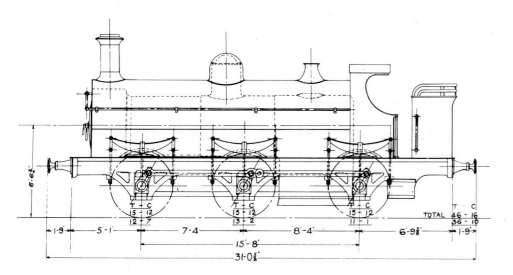

Figure 261

Here are three official drawings of 0-6-0 tanks of various vintages. *Figure 260* shows the '645' class of Wolverhampton-built engines as first constructed in 1872 *(Diagram K)*. *Figure 262* shows the same class in 1923, when fitted with B4 boilers and pannier tanks, and this drawing is of the *Diagram A.35*. The third drawing is of the '119' class, built to *Lots 4* and *5* as renewals at Wolverhampton in 1878-83. The diagram is *A*, showing this particular state of rebuild. Running numbers were 119-130 *(Figure 261)*.

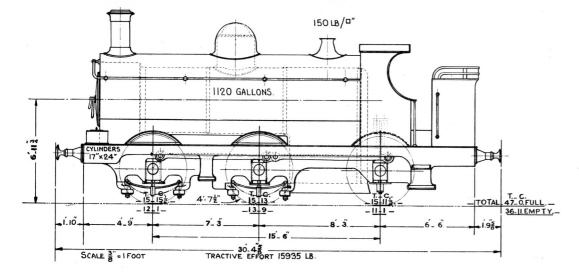

150 LB/□"

1120 GALLONS.

CYLINDERS 17" × 24"

SCALE 3/8" = 1 FOOT    TRACTIVE EFFORT 15935 LB.

Figure 263

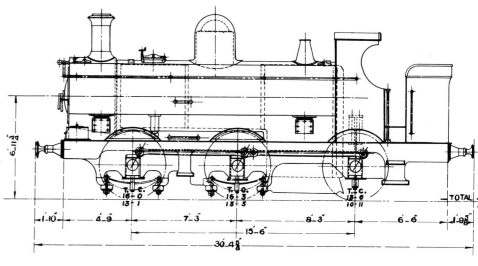

Figure 264

### 1701 CLASS
### TYPE 0-6-0T

Next in line of progression of the Swindon 0-6-0 tanks came the '1701' class, which itself was part of the '1854' series. One hundred engines were built over five years, as follows:

| Nos. 1854-73 | in | 1890 | to | *Lot 79* |
|---|---|---|---|---|
| Nos. 1874-93 | in | 1890-91 | to | *Lot 83* |
| Nos. 1701-20 | in | 1891 | to | *Lot 85* |
| Nos. 1721-40 | in | 1892 | to | *Lot 88* |
| Nos. 1751-70 | in | 1892-93 | to | *Lot 89* |
| Nos. 905-907 | in | 1895 | to | *Lot 98* |
| Nos. 1791-1800 | in | 1895 | to | *Lot 98* |
| Nos. 1894-1900 | in | 1895 | to | *Lot 98* |

*Figure 265* is an official photograph of No. 1752 as built in 1892 with the dome on the front ring of the boiler, and tall safety valve bonnet. The Swindon diagram in *Figure 263* is lettered *E* and shows the class as first rebuilt with the S4 boiler and smaller dome and valve bonnet. No. 1752 received pannier tanks in 1922, was superheated for a spell in 1927, and finally withdrawn in March 1950. *Figure 264* shows the class with pannier tanks as *Diagram A.19.*

Figure 265

Still with the '1701' class, two drawings are shown on this page. *Figure 266* inscribed as '1701' type 0-6-0T, and *Figure 267* as '1501' series, although very little difference can be detected between the two locomotives. However, there are some details which are visible on one which is not shown on the other. Note, for instance the firebox, front guard irons and springs, etc. This shows the similarity of the Swindon and Wolverhampton designs.

No. 1860 with the open cab, is seen in *Figure 268* towards the end of her days, being withdrawn in December 1934. No. 1731 fitted with closed cab, is seen at Bristol Temple Meads in the 1920's. She was not scrapped until 1949. Wheels on this class were 4′ 6″ diameter and wheelbase 7′ 3″ x 8′ 3″ as shown in drawings *Figure 266*. No. 1860 was of the '1854' class of Swindon built origin.

Figure 266

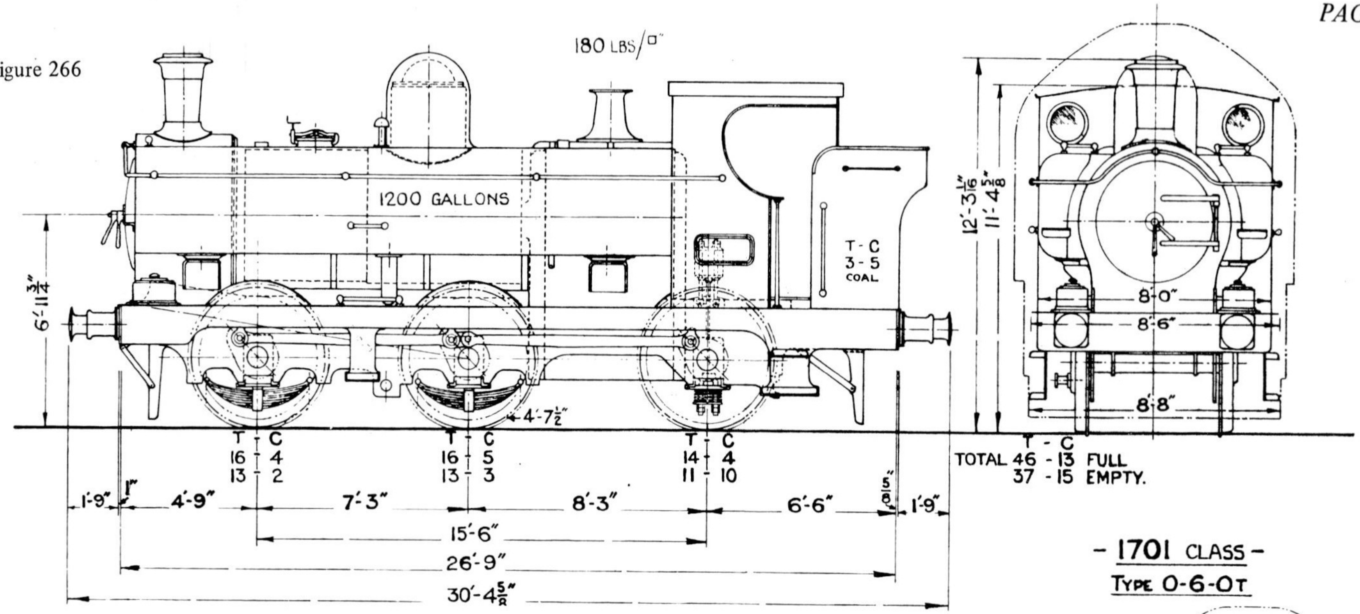

180 LBS/◻″

1200 GALLONS

T · C
3 - 5
COAL

12′-3 3/16″
11′-4 5/8″

8′-0″
8′-6″

8′-8″

TOTAL 46 - 13 FULL
37 - 15 EMPTY.

6′-11 3/4″

| T - C | T - C | T - C |
|---|---|---|
| 16 4 | 16 5 | 14 4 |
| 13 2 | 13 3 | 11 10 |

4′-7 1/2″

1′-9″   4′-9″      7′-3″         8′-3″         6′-6″    1′-9″

15′-6″

26′-9″

30′-4 5/8″

- 1701 CLASS -
TYPE 0-6-0T

Figure 267

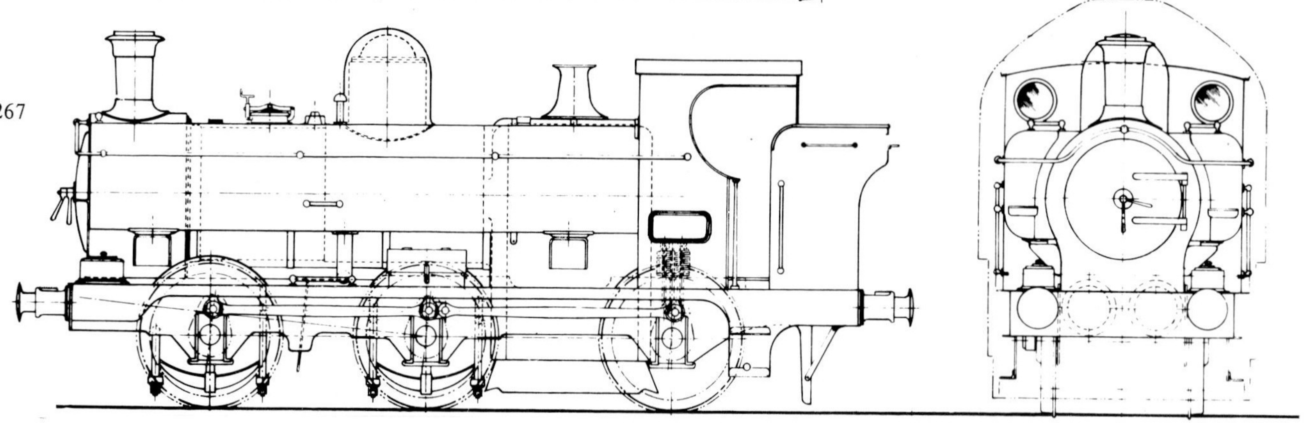

Figure 268

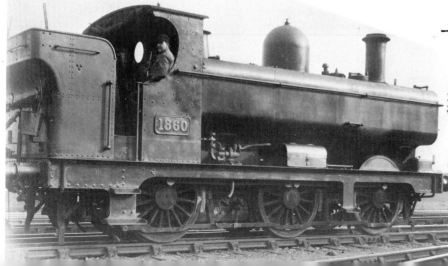

1860

Figure 269

batch of eighty 0-6-0 tanks to be constructed at Swindon to the following numbers and Lots:

| | | | |
|---|---|---|---|
| Nos. 2721-40 | in 1897-98 | to | *Lot 112* |
| Nos. 2741-60 | in 1899 | to | *Lot 115* |
| Nos. 2761-80 | in 1900 | to | *Lot 122* |
| Nos. 2781-2800 | in 1901 | to | *Lot 129* |

(No. 2800 was renumbered 2700 in 1912, when that number was required for the 2-8-0 tender engines.)

This '2721' series were slightly different to the '1701' class in that the wheels were 4' 7½" instead of 4' 6". They had sets of coil springs on all wheels when built, but later retained these only on the trailing drivers. The coupling rods fitted were of the fluted type similar to the tender engines of the '2301' class.

*Figure 270* shows No. 2734 as built and *Figure 271* illustrates No. 2725 with pannier tanks and tall chimney. The three diagrams in sequence of rebuild are *F, A.11* plus B.74. (Note that this B.74 diagram is slightly different being of the later 57XX class.)

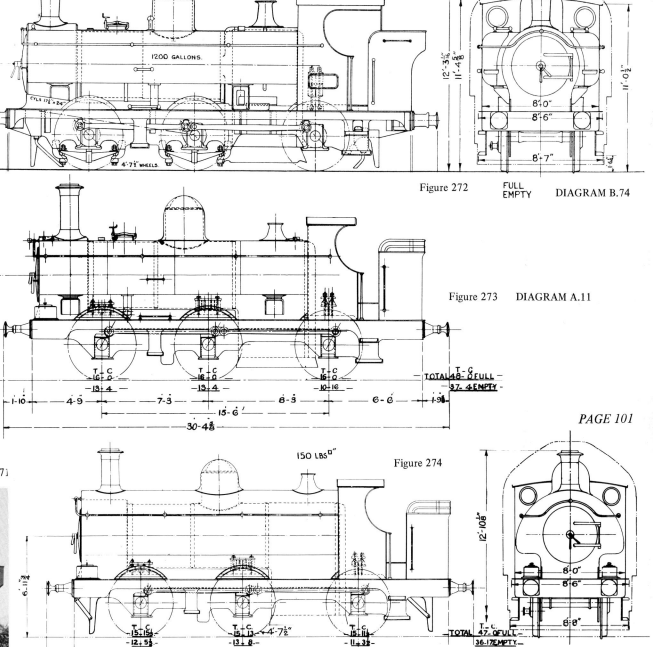

Figure 272        FULL
                  EMPTY        DIAGRAM B.74

Figure 270

Figure 273        DIAGRAM A.11

*PAGE 101*

Figure 274

DIAGRAM F

**2700 CLASS.**
**TYPE 0-6-0T.**

TRACTIVE EFFORT 15935 LBS.

Figure 271

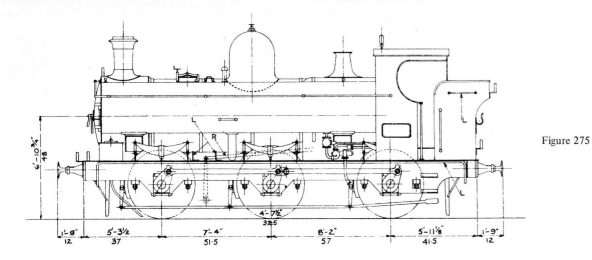

Figure 275

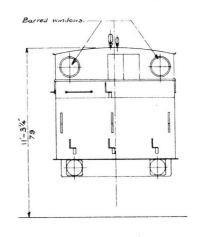

Barred windows.

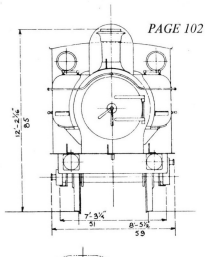

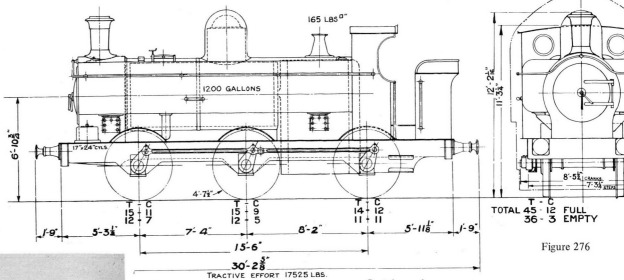

165 LBS
1200 GALLONS

17"×24" CYLS.

TRACTIVE EFFORT 17525 LBS.

| | T - C |
|---|---|
| TOTAL | 45 - 12 FULL |
| | 36 - 3 EMPTY |

Figure 276

1016 CLASS

TYPE $\frac{0 \cdot 6 \cdot 0}{T}$

Having covered the 0-6-0 tanks at Swindon up to the turn of the century, we now go back to Wolverhampton, and the first of the type described is the '1016' class. This class was started in 1867, and between then and 1871, sixty were built.

*Figure 277* is an early photograph of the class as first rebuilt, and shows the small saddle tank, outside frames and long low boiler well. Notice the painted coupling rods and the lighter springs on the centre drivers.

As built the driving wheels were 4′ 6″, but with thicker tyres the measurement became 4′ 7½″.

Serial numbers were:

| Nos. 1016-27 | Lot B | built | 1867 |
|---|---|---|---|
| Nos. 1028-39 | Lot C | built | 1867-68 |
| Nos. 1040-51 | Lot J | built | 1870 |
| Nos. 1052-63 | Lot K | built | 1870-71 |
| Nos. 1064-75 | Lot L | built | 1871 |

*Figure 276* is the official *Diagram B.17* showing the class with pannier tanks on the B4 boilers which were fitted in the mid-twenties. *Figure 275* is another Templer drawing of the '1016' class, as running in the 1930s, with closed cab and many other details and measurements. Note the different position of the balance water pipe, and that items marked 'L' are on the left side of the engine only, and 'R' on the right.

Figure 277

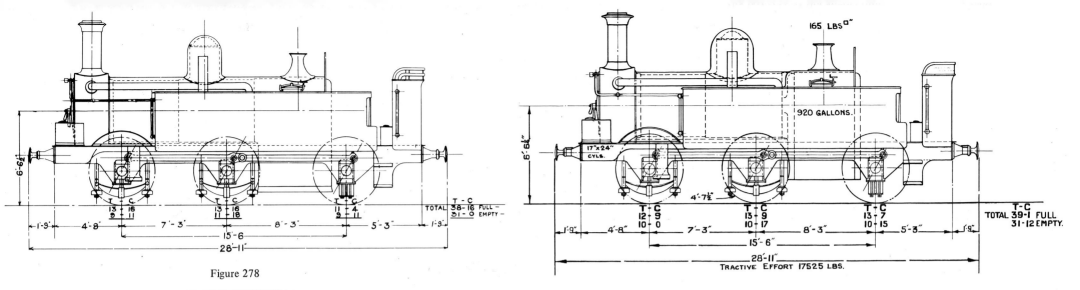

Figure 278

165 LBS □"

920 GALLONS.

17"x24"
CYLS.

6'-6¾"

4'-7½"

TOTAL 38-16 FULL
31-0 EMPTY

TOTAL 39-1 FULL
31-12 EMPTY.

TRACTIVE EFFORT 17525 LBS.

Figure 279

Twelve tank engines of the 0-6-0 classification were built at Wolverhampton between 1871-72 under *Lot M,* and fitted with fairly small side tanks of 980 gallons' capacity. This class carried these tanks until withdrawal in the mid-thirties and so were unusual in that they were never fitted with either saddle or pannier tanks.

The serial numbers ran consecutively from 633 to 644 and so henceforward they were known as the '633' class. Several engines were fitted with condensing apparatus for working over the Metropolitan line, and locomotives known to have carried this gear included numbers 633, 634, 641, 642 and 643. When first built they had the W3 boiler of Wolverhampton and bell-mouthed chimneys, but were rebuilt between 1887 and 1899 with the S4 and S2 boiler, all eventually finishing up with the B4 Belpaire boiler. The official *Diagram A.62* in *Figure 279* shows this last rebuild, and the photograph in *Figure 280* is of No. 642 with the S4 boiler and polished dome.

All the condensing engines remained cabless until withdrawn in 1933-34. *Figure 278* is the official Swindon *Diagram J* which shows the round topped firebox.

Figure 280

Figure 281

Figure 282

Figure 283

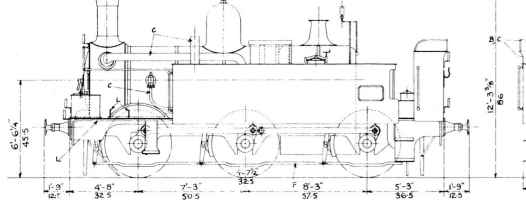

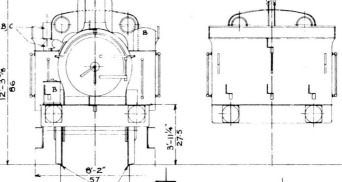

This page shows both sides of the '633' condensing tanks. *Figures 281* and *282* depict No. 643 and No. 633 at Old Oak Common in the 1930's, and a slight difference can be seen in the motion step shape.

*Figure 283* is another Templer drawing, which has been reduced to 4mm scale and supplements the two pictures.

Note the bucket hanging on the whistles in *Figure 281. Diagram A.59* is seen in *Figure 284* and shows the class with sides to the cab.

Figure 284

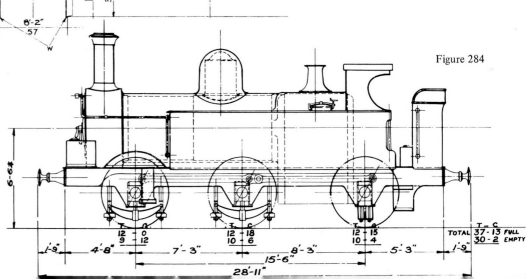

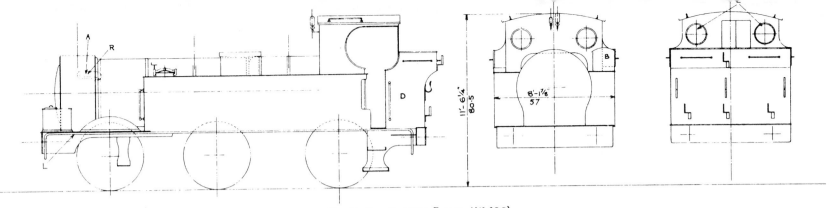

Fig 2. Non-condensing Engine. (Nº 635).

NOTES. All details not shown in fig 2 are as in fig 1, except those marked C, which are special to condensing engines. A. Also on condensing engines. B. On both sides, but only shown on one side in end view. D. Enlarged bunker also fitted to certain condensing engines. E. Barred windows. F. Brake rigging outside wheels. L. On left side only. R. On right side only. W. Wheel treads & flanges drawn to scale: allowances must be made for out-of-scale wheels. Dimensions in feet (full size), and in millimetres, to the nearest half m'metre for 'Gauge "O".

Figure 285

# G. W. R.  633 Class. Type 0-6-0/T.

The drawing in *Figure 285* is supplementary to that on page 104, and illustrates the difference between those engines fitted with condensing gear and spectacle plates, and those without the gear, and having closed cabs. For other details, see *Figure 283*.

*Figures 286* and *287* again show both sides of the non-condensing '633' class with No. 635 on the left and No. 644 on the right. No. 644's claim to fame is that she was withdrawn in June, 1930, but came out again for two more years service, painted unlined black. No. 638 was fitted with a spark arresting chimney for several years. Note that the two photographs on this page show the side clack-boxes have been removed, with water feed probably entering on the back plate via injectors.

Figure 286          Figure 287

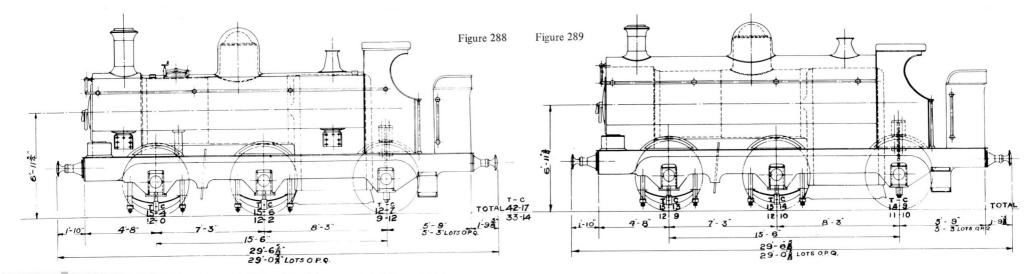

Figure 288    Figure 289

Figure 290

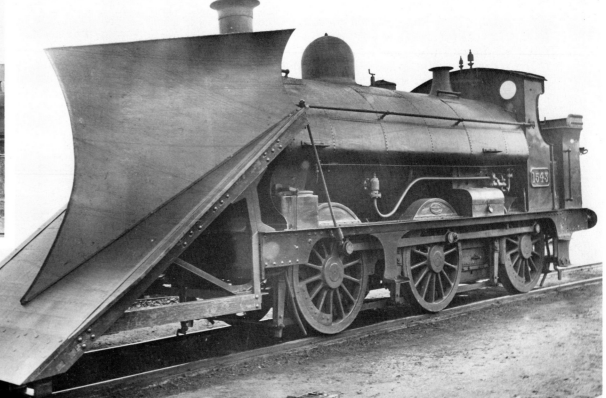

Figure 291

Another class built at Wolverhampton in the 1878-81 period was the '1501' class, which was part of an earlier series – the '645' class of 1872. Numbers ran from 1501 to 1560 with a further twelve numbered 1801-12 in 1881. When built they carried the Wolverhampton W3 boiler and long saddle tanks, but between 1913 and 1930 were gradually fitted with pannier tanks.

The photograph in *Figure 291* is of No. 1543 in 1907, fitted with a semi-permanent snow plough. The engine is shown at the second rebuilt stage, carrying the R2 boiler and saddle tanks. *Figure 290* shows No. 1511 of the class, with pannier tanks and open cab, and the drawing is of *Diagram A.35* with open cab and B4 boiler of class 'P'. The saddle tank diagram is the Swindon *A.40* also fitted with the B4 boiler *(see Figure 289).*

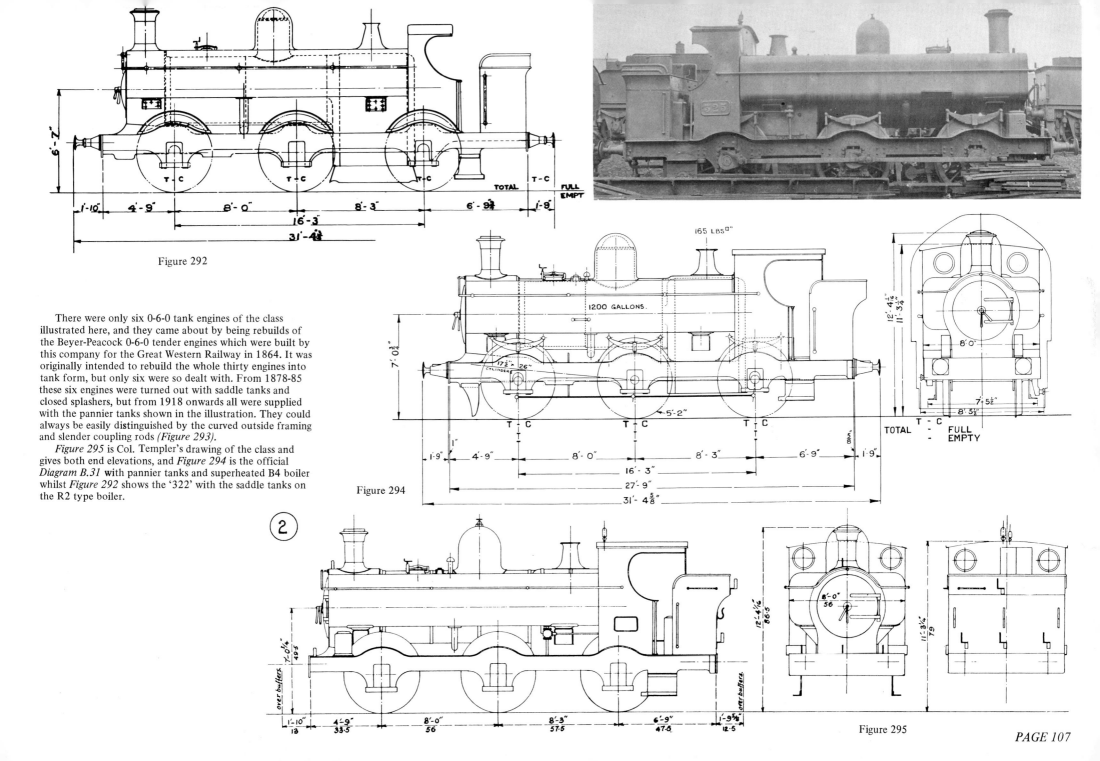

Figure 292

There were only six 0-6-0 tank engines of the class illustrated here, and they came about by being rebuilds of the Beyer-Peacock 0-6-0 tender engines which were built by this company for the Great Western Railway in 1864. It was originally intended to rebuild the whole thirty engines into tank form, but only six were so dealt with. From 1878-85 these six engines were turned out with saddle tanks and closed splashers, but from 1918 onwards all were supplied with the pannier tanks shown in the illustration. They could always be easily distinguished by the curved outside framing and slender coupling rods *(Figure 293)*.

*Figure 295* is Col. Templer's drawing of the class and gives both end elevations, and *Figure 294* is the official *Diagram B.31* with pannier tanks and superheated B4 boiler whilst *Figure 292* shows the '322' with the saddle tanks on the R2 type boiler.

Figure 294

Figure 295

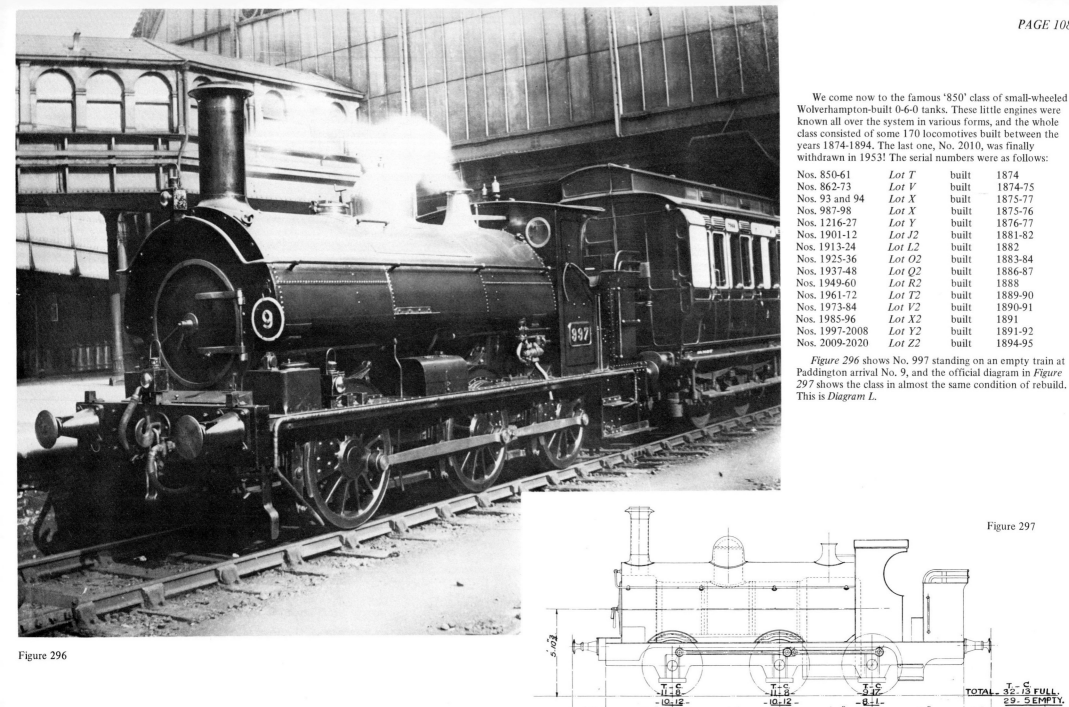

We come now to the famous '850' class of small-wheeled Wolverhampton-built 0-6-0 tanks. These little engines were known all over the system in various forms, and the whole class consisted of some 170 locomotives built between the years 1874-1894. The last one, No. 2010, was finally withdrawn in 1953! The serial numbers were as follows:

| Nos. 850-61 | Lot T | built | 1874 |
|---|---|---|---|
| Nos. 862-73 | Lot V | built | 1874-75 |
| Nos. 93 and 94 | Lot X | built | 1875-77 |
| Nos. 987-98 | Lot X | built | 1875-76 |
| Nos. 1216-27 | Lot Y | built | 1876-77 |
| Nos. 1901-12 | Lot J2 | built | 1881-82 |
| Nos. 1913-24 | Lot L2 | built | 1882 |
| Nos. 1925-36 | Lot O2 | built | 1883-84 |
| Nos. 1937-48 | Lot Q2 | built | 1886-87 |
| Nos. 1949-60 | Lot R2 | built | 1888 |
| Nos. 1961-72 | Lot T2 | built | 1889-90 |
| Nos. 1973-84 | Lot V2 | built | 1890-91 |
| Nos. 1985-96 | Lot X2 | built | 1891 |
| Nos. 1997-2008 | Lot Y2 | built | 1891-92 |
| Nos. 2009-2020 | Lot Z2 | built | 1894-95 |

*Figure 296* shows No. 997 standing on an empty train at Paddington arrival No. 9, and the official diagram in *Figure 297* shows the class in almost the same condition of rebuild. This is *Diagram L.*

Figure 297

Figure 296

Figure 298

Two pictures show the little Wolverhampton tank No. 1941 seen at Swindon in 1896 (according to the date on the register) in the Works undercoat paint. Shown in side and three-quarter view many details are revealed, such as the 'H' section spokes with which many of these tanks' wheels were fitted, the lubricator behind the chimney, the sand-box operating rods, and even the small pipe from the saddle tank to rail head for lubricating the flanges with water! Notice also the square coupling rod brasses and retaining cotter.

Figure 299

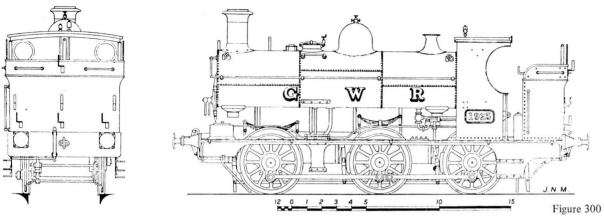

Only two of the '850' class survived with the saddle tank into British Railways days, No. 2007 and No. 1925 seen in the Maskelyne drawing in *Figure 300*. As drawn, with the G.W.R. initials on the tank sides, this was a special condition which applied only for the making of a film in 1947, and was not standard practice. In fact, there appears to be no record of any other of these saddle tanks carrying the Company's letters or initials.

*Figure 301* shows a tank top view of another of the class at Exeter St. David's locomotive depot in 1914. An interesting picture this, as although these were the 'clean engine' days – as one can see by the polished valve bonnet and dome – there is still a lump of dirty waste alongside the lifting ring. The hooks on the cab roof were for anchoring the wet weather sheet, and note that this engine has the tall Dean chimney, unlike No. 2007 which sported the short squat type. To add interest, the passenger brake van seen is No. 939, and the Horse Box is No. 620.

Figure 300

Figure 301

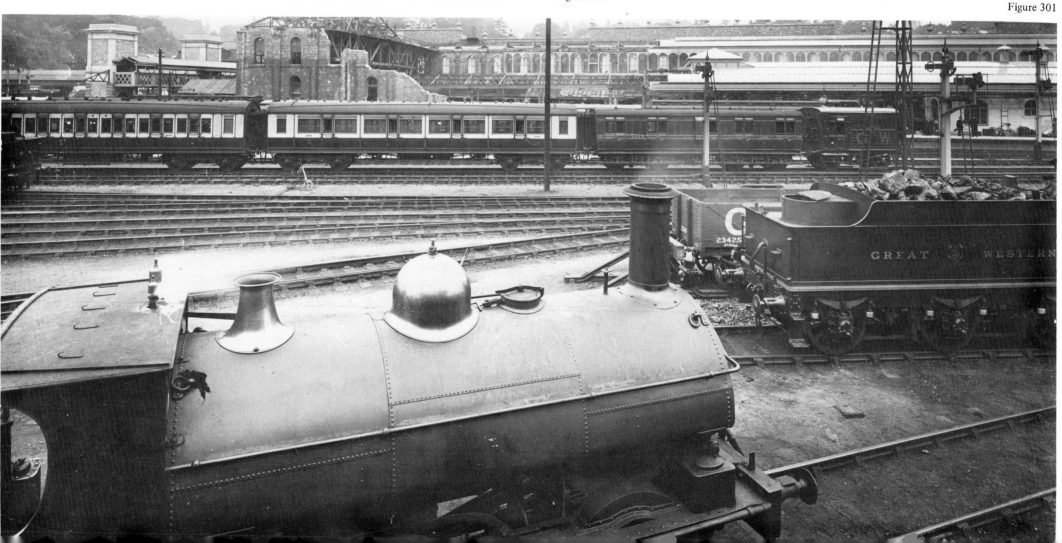

Figure 302

Figure 304

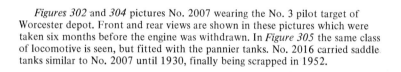

Figure 303

*Figures 302* and *304* pictures No. 2007 wearing the No. 3 pilot target of Worcester depot. Front and rear views are shown in these pictures which were taken six months before the engine was withdrawn. In *Figure 305* the same class of locomotive is seen, but fitted with the pannier tanks. No. 2016 carried saddle tanks similar to No. 2007 until 1930, finally being scrapped in 1952.

Figure 305

Figure 307

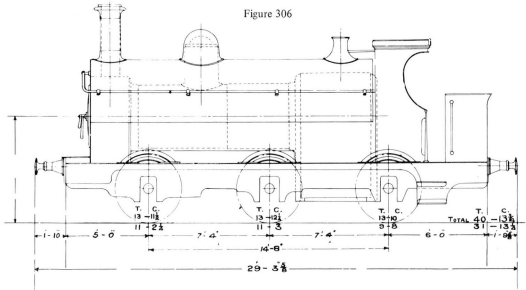

Figure 306

Figure 308

*Figure 307* shows an '850' class 'undressed', and illustrates what was hidden under No. 2008's tanks!

No. 1227, seen in *Figure 308,* is unusual in that the engine has the flat-sided enlarged bunker, and has had the frames extended to accommodate this increased size. Also fitted with the 'H' section cast spokes, it should be noted that these wheels did not carry balance weights in the usual style. This engine was withdrawn in 1938. The diagram in *Figure 306* is the *N* of the succeeding class, the '2021' series and is very similar but just a little larger all round.

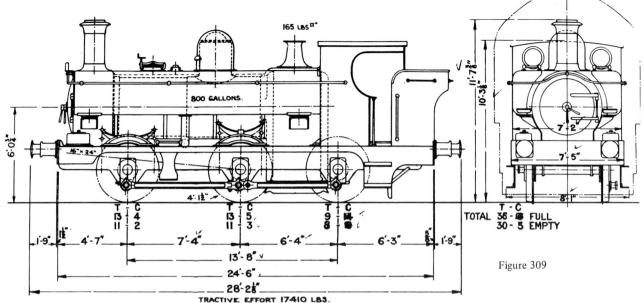

165 LBS □"

800 GALLONS.

15" × 24"

TRACTIVE EFFORT 17410 LBS.

TOTAL 36 - 16 FULL
30 - 5 EMPTY

Figure 309

Figure 311

Three more examples of the '850' or perhaps more correctly the '1901' class, and a diagram of the later in final condition. First, *Figure 310* shows No. 1961 with the saddle tank as running in 1925. The engine was fitted with pannier tanks in 1927 and finally withdrawn in 1936.

*Figure 311* is of No. 1921 equipped with pannier tanks and tall chimney. The photograph was taken in 1930, five years before the engine was scrapped. No. 1907, seen in *Figure 312*, was converted to pannier tanks in 1911, and carried them right through into British Railways days, finally being cut up in 1950. The diagram shown in *Figure 309* is the *B.51*; the last issued for this class of locomotive, B4 boiler and pannier tanks.

Figure 310

Figure 312

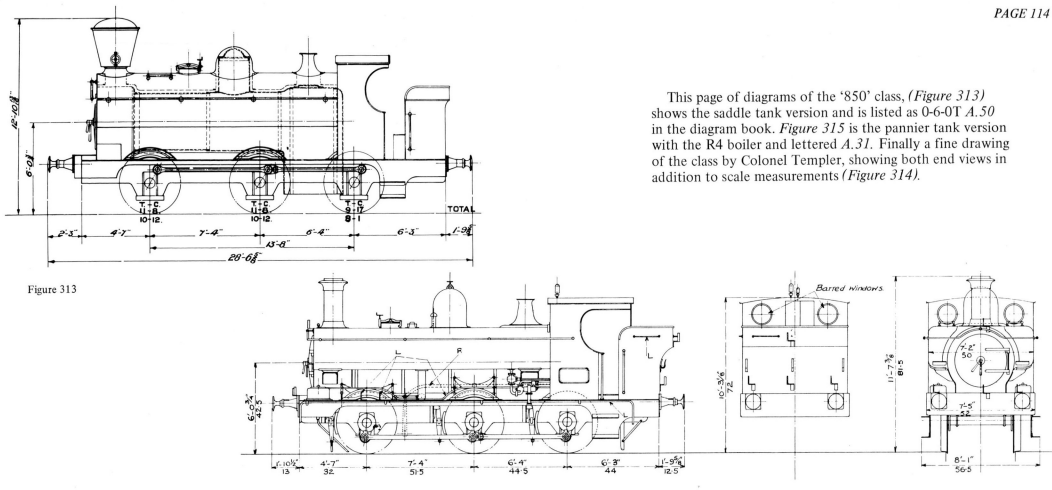

This page of diagrams of the '850' class, *(Figure 313)* shows the saddle tank version and is listed as 0-6-0T *A.50* in the diagram book. *Figure 315* is the pannier tank version with the R4 boiler and lettered *A.31.* Finally a fine drawing of the class by Colonel Templer, showing both end views in addition to scale measurements *(Figure 314).*

Figure 313

*Barred Windows.*

*Fig. 1. 850 Class.*

Figure 314

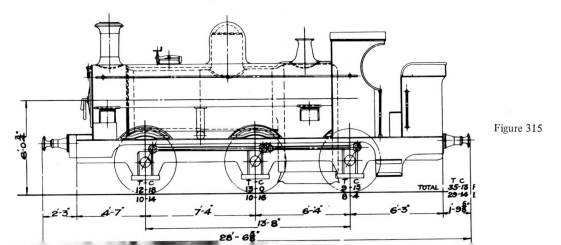

Figure 315

Two photographs of No. 1923 at Swindon immediately after a major overhaul and the fitting of its pannier tanks in 1924. Painted in works grey and black, the gold transfers have been affixed to the tanks especially for the pictures. No. 1923 was built in 1882, had two boiler changes in 1910 and 1924 and was finally sold to the Ocean Coal Company of Blaengarw in 1939. Later she went to N.C.B. Newlands Colliery, then to Maesteg, and finally to Penllwyngwent.

Figure 316

Figure 317

Figure 318

*Figure 319* shows the final form of livery used on the '1901' class before nationalisation. This official photograph taken straight out of the paint shop in 1946 of No. 1967, shows the plain green with initial transfers of gold and red shading. The dome and safety valve bonnet are painted green, the chimney, smokebox front and frames black, the buffer beams and buffer shanks in post office red, and the small letters LLY indicated the engine was allocated to Llanelly depot.

*Figure 318* is a head-on picture of No. 1966, taken in 1935.

Figure 319

The final batch of small Wolverhampton 0-6-0 tanks to be illustrated at this point, are the '2021' class. These engines were slightly bigger in dimensions and were in effect an updated version of the '850' series just described.

They can be divided into two groups, namely Nos. 2021 to 2100, and 2101 to 2160. Building dates and Lot numbers were as follows:

| | | | | | |
|---|---|---|---|---|---|
| 2021 | to | 2030 | *Lot D.3* | built | 1897 |
| 2031 | to | 2040 | *Lot F.3* | built | 1897-98 |
| 2041 | to | 2060 | *Lot G.3* | built | 1898-99 |
| 2061 | to | 2080 | *Lot H.3* | built | 1899-1900 |
| 2081 | to | 2100 | *Lot J.3* | built | 1900-1901 |
| 2101 | to | 2120 | *Lot K.3* | built | 1902-1903 |
| 2121 | to | 2140 | *Lot L.3* | built | 1903-1904 |
| 2141 | to | 2160 | *Lot M.3* | built | 1904-1905 |

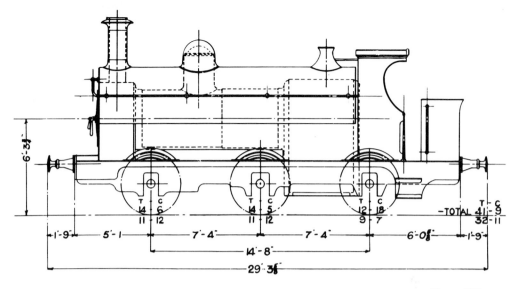

Figure 320

Figure 321

When built the '2021' class were fitted with round-topped raised fireboxes with the dome on the front boiler ring, whereas the '2101' series started life with the Belpaire firebox and domeless boilers.

*Figure 321* shows No. 2050 as built in 1898 with the three-section saddle tanks and the very small bunker. Note the wing plates at the smokebox front. Wheels were the same diameter as those used on the '850' class, but the wheelbase at the trailing end, was one foot longer than the earlier engines, this extra being necessary to allow for the larger firebox fitted.

The *Diagram O* in *Figure 320* shows the class as in 1898, fitted with saddle tanks, R2/3 boiler and small bunker. Many of these locomotives lasted right into the 1950s.

Three variations of the original theme are depicted here, with a weight diagram for comparison as the final rebuild. Firstly *Figure 323* illustrates one of the '1901' series No. 2005, with the saddle tanks she carried until 1937. The shorter trailing wheelbase can clearly be seen here, when compared with No. 2048 in *Figure 324*. The picture shows this particular engine as fitted with domeless boiler and saddle tanks, and strangely enough, she was not fitted with pannier tanks until 1948, being withdrawn four years later in 1952.

*Figure 325* depicts No. 2112 as built in 1902, with the long Dean chimney and domeless boiler. She was fitted with the pannier tanks in 1916, being withdrawn in 1954.

In these three pictures, note the different bunkers used, and varying boiler fittings.

The drawing is the official Swindon *Diagram B.52* which shows the extended frames.

Figure 324

Figure 322

Figure 323

Figure 325

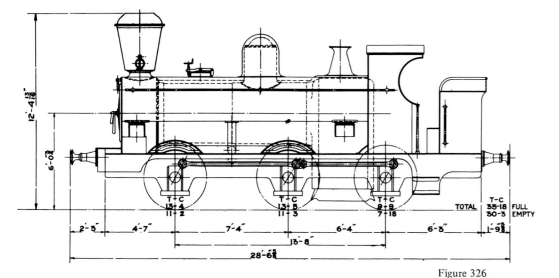

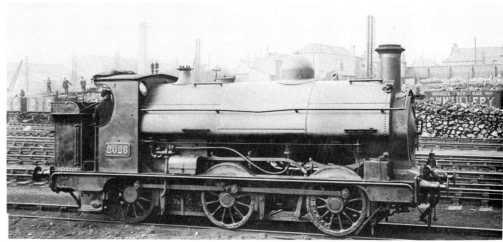

Figure 329

Figure 326

Figure 327

Three stages in the history of the '2021' class. *Figure 329* is an unusual picture in showing the original saddle tank and small bunker, but with extended smokebox. *Figure 328* is of No. 2090 fitted with pannier tanks, enlarged bunker and warning bell for use on Birkenhead Docks. Finally, No. 2047 is shown in *Figure 330* in its final stage, with closed cab, and relates well with the 4mm scale drawing by Col. Templer in *Figure 327*.

Although very similar to the '850' class, no evidence can be found that any of the '2021' series were fitted with the 'H' section spoked wheels. Many were used on 'auto' work, in fact, two engines numbered 2120 and 2140 were modified specially in 1906, and emerged from Swindon works with a dummy coach shell to harmonise with the trailer cars (see Volume two). Also, No. 1080 was used as a prototype in 1930 for the '5400' class and temporarily fitted with 5' 2″ wheels (see Volume two). All but 20 lasted into British Railways stock. *Figure 326* shows one of the '850' class with spark arresting chimney, built to *Diagram A.57.*

Figure 328

Figure 330

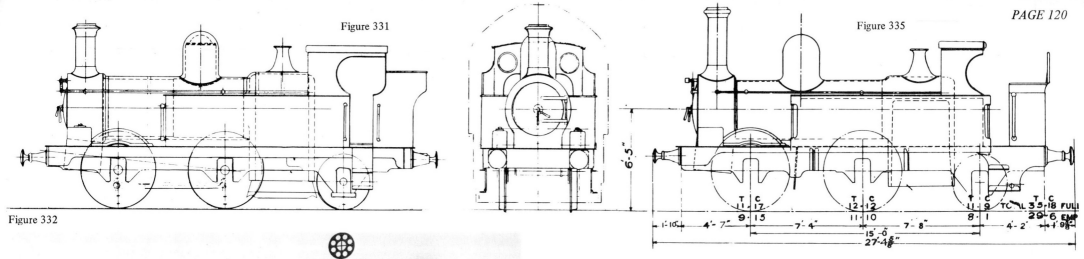

Figure 331

Figure 335

Figure 332

Figure 334

Figure 333

Having dealt with the 0-6-0 tanks in reasonable depth, it is fitting now to consider the contemporary small front-coupled engines of the 0-4-2T classification, namely the famous '517' class. These delightful little engines were built progressively over the years from 1868 to 1885 at Wolverhampton, for use on branch lines and where light axle loading was essential. There were many variations within the class, but the main differences can be roughly divided into three. Firstly, as built, those numbered 517-576 had a short wheelbase of 13' 7" made up of 7' 4" and 6' 3", and with the exception of Nos. 571-76 were fitted with the small saddle tanks as seen in *Figure 332*. Some of the engines had inside axleboxes to the trailing wheels, but outside bearings were gradually adopted. The second group which consisted of all the series except Nos. 1483-88, were of the side tank variety, and had a longer wheelbase, being 15' in total, 17 inches longer than the first batch. The final six were even longer, having wheelbases 7' 4" + 8' 2", a total of 15' 6".

*Figure 333* illustrates No. 1440 in the 1920s, after having the frames lengthened, and fitted with Belpaire boiler. Note the shape of the bunker and polished dome. In similar condition in 1930, but with closed cab and whistles mounted on the spectacle plate, No. 571 is shown in *Figure 334* shortly before withdrawal in 1936. The official drawing in *Figure 331* is the Swindon *Diagram L* which gives the state of rebuild as shown in the photograph in *Figure 334*.

The early diagram in *Figure 335* shows the tall chimney and round topped firebox version lettered 'A'.

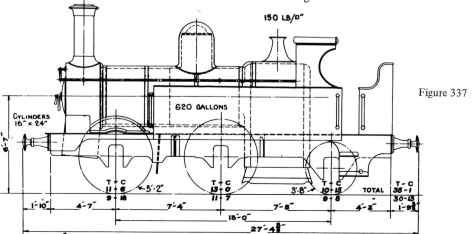

Figure 336

This picture of No. 539 was dated 1910 and shows the '517' class with the round-topped R4 boiler and firebox and with the frames lengthened. This engine was built in 1869 with small saddle tanks, and in 1881 was rebuilt with side tanks, and the short wheelbase of 13' 7" was changed to 15'. She saw many other changes and survived until 1933.

A list of the '517' series with Lot numbers and dates follows below:

| Nos. 517 | to 528 | built in 1868 | to Lot D |
|---|---|---|---|
| Nos. 529 | to 540 | built in 1868-69 | to Lot E |
| Nos. 541 | to 552 | built in 1869 | to Lot F |
| Nos. 553 | to 564 | built in 1869 | to Lot G |
| Nos. 565 | to 576 | built in 1869-70 | to Lot H |
| Nos. 826 | to 836 | built in 1873-74 | to Lot R |
| Nos. 838 | to 849 | built in 1874-75 | to Lot S |
| Nos. 1154 | to 1165 | built in 1875-76 | to Lot W |
| Nos. 202-05, 215-222 | | built in 1876 | to Lot Z |
| Nos. 1421 | to 1432 | built in 1877 | to Lot I |
| Nos. 1433 | to 1444 | built in 1877-78 | to Lot C.2 |
| Nos. 1465 | to 1476 | built in 1883 | to Lot M.2 |
| Nos. 1477 | to 1488 | built in 1884-85 | to Lot P.2 |

In *Figure 338*, No. 1162 is seen at Exeter prior to withdrawal in 1934 with BR4 boiler. *Figure 337* is the official *Diagram B* which shows the '517' class as a 15' 6" wheelbase with outside bearing to the trailing wheels and termed a 'Swindon rebuild'.

Figure 337

150 LB/□"

620 GALLONS

CYLINDERS 16" x 24"

6'-7"

T+C 11+6 / 9+18    ←5'-2"→
T+C 13+0 / 11+7
3'-8"→ 10+15 / 9+8
TOTAL T+C 36+1 / 30+13

1'-10"  4'-7"  7'-4"  7'-8"  4'-2"  1'-9½"

15'-0"

27'-4⅞"

3"

GREAT WESTERN 1162

Figure 338

Figure 339

Engine No. 555 was rebuilt at Wolverhampton in 1886 with side tanks and also had the wheelbase lengthened at the same time. Later in 1902 she was fitted a new R2/3 boiler with round-topped firebox, and given an extended smokebox with wing plates, which can be clearly seen in *Figure 339.* Note the lubricator behind the chimney and the clack box into the boiler side. *Figure 340* shows No. 1485 at Swindon in 1929 after a major overhaul and is interesting to note the design of the trailing axlebox and spring gear fitted. This engine was one of the final six to be built with the longer 15′ 6″ wheelbase. She was finally withdrawn in 1936.

Figure 340

Figure 341

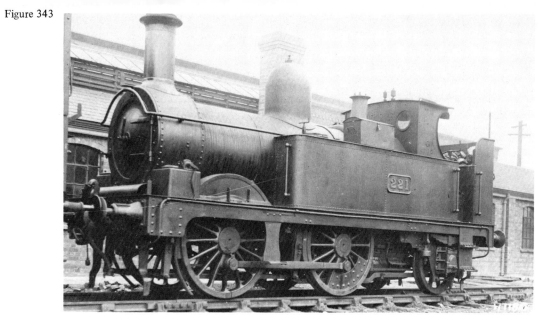

Figure 343

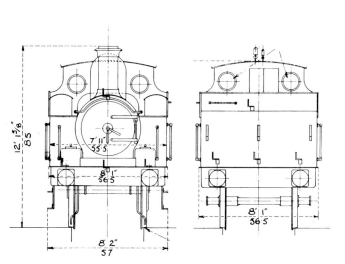

Figure 342

Figure 344

Three different variations of the '517's are shown here. In *Figure 343* is No. 221 seen with the round-topped firebox, open cab, and tall straight-sided bunker. This engine did not receive the Belpaire type boiler and firebox and was scrapped in 1929. *Figure 341* shows also a '517' class locomotive with the round-topped firebox. This is No. 518 pictured in 1912 coupled to trailer car No. 86 which incidentally is painted in crimson lake livery. This engine lasted until 1928, having a life of sixty years! No. 835 in *Figure 344* was one of the few engines of the class which kept her shorter wheelbase until withdrawn, also as can be seen, she was not rebuilt with outside bearings to the trailing wheels. One feature of doubtful placing was the rear sandboxes, which were set right in the cab entrance! The drawing by Col. Templer of the '517' class in *Figure 342*, gives many leading dimensions in feet and inches, and in millimetres. Note that the closed cab has the bunker doors offset.

Figure 345

Figure 346

Figure 347

Ten engines similar to the '517' class were built between 1895 and 1897 at Wolverhampton, and received numbers 3571-80. Although their design followed the earlier 0-4-2T style closely, they could always be identified by the unusual extended valance at the trailing end which covered the springs and hangers of the trailing truck. Engine number 1477 of the '517' series was used as a prototype for developing this class, and in *Figure 347* one can see the single slot which had to be cut in the outside framing to give access for oiling on this engine. In the 3571 class, two smaller holes were arranged for this purpose instead of the single large aperture. *Figure 345* shows No. 3580 as fitted with Belpaire firebox and boiler, but still retaining early bunker and rear spectacle plate. *Figure 346* shows the left-hand side of No. 3574 at Worcester in 1947, and the official drawing is *Diagram D* giving the R4 boiler, in *Figure 348*. The same diagram but with shorter rear overhang is seen in *Figure 349, Diagram C*.

Figure 348      Figure 349

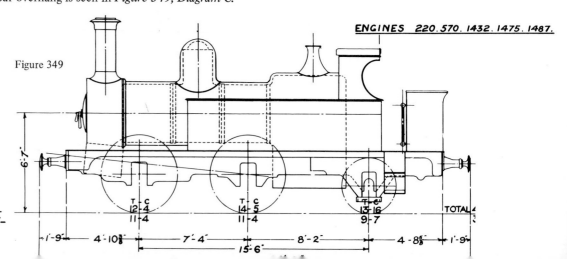

Figure 350

*Figure 352* shows engine No. 3574 at Worcester. Many details are clear. The large Swindon coal bunker has been fitted, and parallel buffers, but apart from these features the engine is seen in the same condition as the final rebuild of 1927. When photographed she was lettered G.W.R. on the tank sides with the number plate in between letters. *Figure 350* shows No. 564 in an early stage of rebuild at Newnham station on a Forest of Dean train, and *Figure 351* shows yet another, No. 1425 at Wood Green tunnel. The reduced works drawing in *Figure 353* is the Swindon plan of the rear end alteration carried out on the '540' class in 1885.

Figure 352

Figure 351

Figure 353

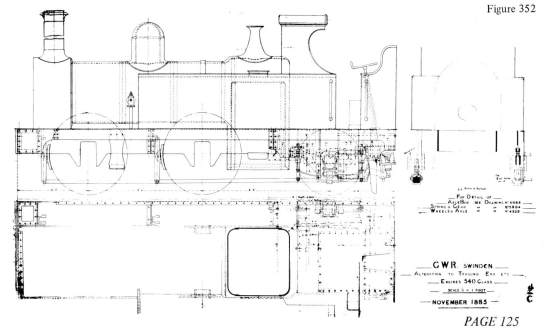

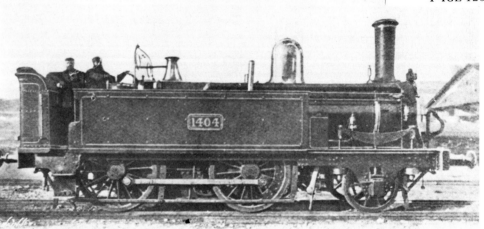

Figure 354

Figure 355

It always seemed rather strange to me that the Wolverhampton-built small four-coupled tanks were nearly always 0-4-2T's, whereas their contemporaries built at Swindon in the same period were 2-4-0T's. From the engineman's point of view, the 2-4-0T's were stronger, perhaps because the weight was distributed more over the drivers than the front wheels. Nevertheless, the latter were the better riders, the 0-4-2T's jumping about considerably when at speed. However, a word of their history. They were always known as the 'Metro' tanks owing to many of the early engines working over the Metropolitan Railway system, and being fitted with condensing gear for that purpose. Built over a period of thirty years from 1869 to 1899, there were three variations, those with small side tanks, those with medium tanks, and others with really large tanks. As built the 'Metro' class looked like *Figure 354,* with inside bearings on the front wheels and the dropped platforms (note the headlamps). *Figure 355* shows the design as at 1874 with straight framing and outside bearings, which gradually developed into the style seen in *Figure 354A* of No. 469. J.N. Maskelyne's drawing illustrates this feature well *(Figure 356).*

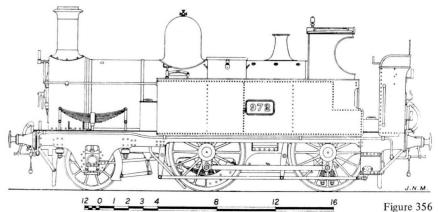

Figure 356

A list of numbers and dates of the 'Metro' tanks as below:

| 455-470, 3-6 | built | 1869 | Swindon | to | *Lot 18* |
|---|---|---|---|---|---|
| 613-632 | " | 1871 | " | " | " *25* |
| 967-986 | " | 1874 | " | " | " *38* |
| 1401-1420 | " | 1878 | " | " | " *47* |
| 1445-1464 | " | 1881-2 | " | " | " *57* |
| 1491-1500 | " | 1892 | " | " | " *91* |
| 3561-3570 | " | 1894 | " | " | " *96* |
| 3581-3590 | " | 1899 | " | " | " *117* |
| 3591-9, 3500 | " | 1899 | " | " | " *119* |

Although twenty years elapsed between the building of the two engines illustrated here, these two show the design as at the turn of the century. No. 968 is seen at Paddington in 1903 when on the Middle

Figure 357

Circle route, namely from 'Underground' Addison Road, Bishops Road to Moorgate Street and Bishopsgate Street to Oldgate. Fitted with condensing gear, note the polished dome, hooks on smokebox door for route indicator and the depot plaque holder on the tool box side. No. 3565 seen in *Figure 358* is straight out of Swindon shops in works undercoat and the photograph is dated 1896. She was refitted with one of the large 1080 gallon tanks in 1898, two years later.

Figure 358

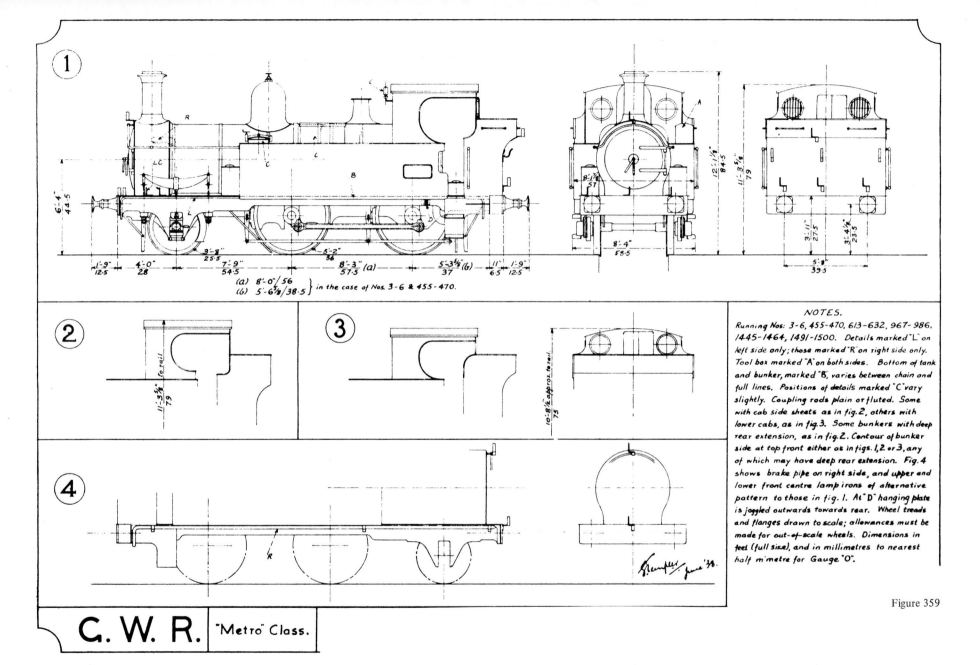

Figure 359

**NOTES.**
Running Nos: 3-6, 455-470, 613-632, 967-986, 1445-1464, 1491-1500. Details marked "L" on left side only; those marked "R" on right side only. Tool box marked "A" on both sides. Bottom of tank and bunker, marked "B", varies between chain and full lines. Positions of details marked "C" vary slightly. Coupling rods plain or fluted. Some with cab side sheets as in fig.2, others with lower cabs, as in fig.3. Some bunkers with deep rear extension, as in fig.2. Contour of bunker side at top front either as in figs. 1, 2 or 3, any of which may have deep rear extension. Fig.4 shows brake pipe on right side, and upper and lower front centre lamp irons of alternative pattern to those in fig. 1. At "D" hanging plate is joggled outwards towards rear. Wheel treads and flanges drawn to scale; allowances must be made for out-of-scale wheels. Dimensions in feet (full size), and in millimetres to nearest half m'metre for Gauge "O".

**G. W. R.** "Metro" Class.

The small tank 'Metro' class in the drawings of Col. Templer, reproduced to a scale of 4mm to 1 foot with the dimensions in feet, and with millimetres for 7mm scale modellers. The notes appended speak for themselves, and show the variations in cab shapes.

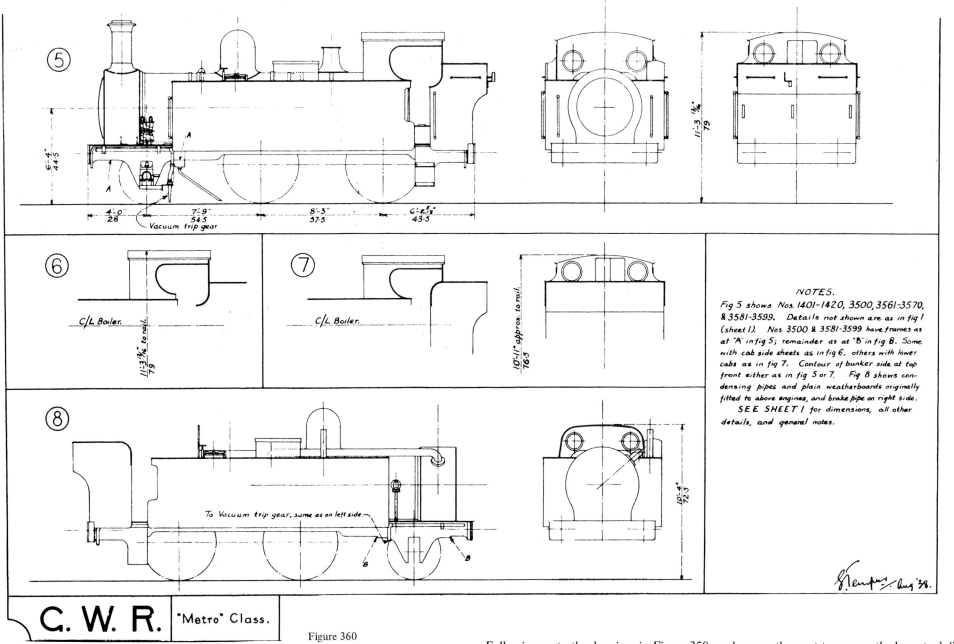

⑤

⑥ C/L Boiler.

⑦ C/L Boiler.

⑧ To Vacuum trip gear, same as on left side.

Vacuum trip gear

NOTES.
Fig 5 shows Nos. 1401-1420, 3500, 3561-3570,
& 3581-3599.   Details not shown are as in fig 1
(sheet 1).   Nos 3500 & 3581-3599 have frames as
at "A" in fig 5; remainder as at "B" in fig 8. Some
with cab side sheets as in fig 6, others with lower
cabs as in fig 7.   Contour of bunker side at top
front either as in fig 5 or 7.   Fig 8 shows condensing pipes and plain weatherboards originally
fitted to above engines, and brake pipe on right side.
    SEE SHEET 1 for dimensions, all other
details, and general notes.

G.W.R.  "Metro" Class.

Figure 360

Following on to the drawings in *Figure 359*, we have on the next two pages the large tank 'Metro' as drawn by both Col. Templer and J. N. Maskelyne. All the many differences in cab styles are shown, *Figures 360, 361*.

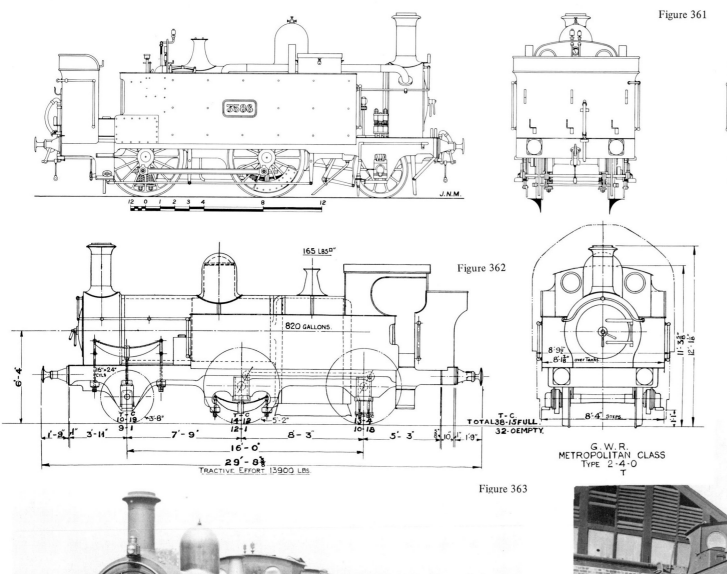

Figure 361

165 LBS.□″

820 GALLONS.

Figure 362

16″×24″ CYL⁹

6′·4″

T·C 10·19    3′·8″    T·C 14·12    5′·2″    T·C 13·4    10·18    T·C TOTAL 38·15 FULL 32·0 EMPTY.

1′·9″ 4″ 3′·11″ 9·1    7′·9″    12·1    8′·3″    5′·3″    10″4″ 1′·9″
16′·0″
29′·8⅜″
TRACTIVE EFFORT 13900 LBS.

8′·9½″
8·1⅞″ over Tanks

11′·3⅝″ 12′·1⅝″

8′·4″ STEPS

G.W.R.
METROPOLITAN CLASS
TYPE 2-4-0
T

Figure 364

Both sides of the small tank 'Metro's can be seen in *Figures 363* and *364*. On the right is No. 1492 photographed in 1925 when the number plates had been moved back from the tank centre to the position just under the cab sides. The little engine on the long train at Didcot seen in *Figure 363* is No. 976 which still has the number plates in the centre of the tank. This locomotive was withdrawn in November 1930.

The official drawing is the *Diagram I* of the Belpaire boilered engines of the 'Metro' series showing the 820 gallon tank and closed cab.

Figure 363

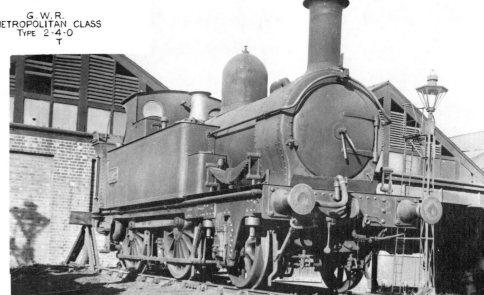

Figure 365

Figure 367

*Figures 367* and *368* show No. 5 at two different stages in her existence. The early one in *Figure 367* gives the number plate in the centre of the tank and whistles on top of a shallow cab, and in *Figure 368* the same engine has been fitted with parallel buffers, a spectacle plate on the bunker, and the number plate back in the cab position.

*Figure 365* illustrates No. 972 with small tank and open cab, and No. 457 in *Figure 366* in the twenties with closed cab and enlarged bunker (*see next page for drawing*).

Figure 366

Figure 368

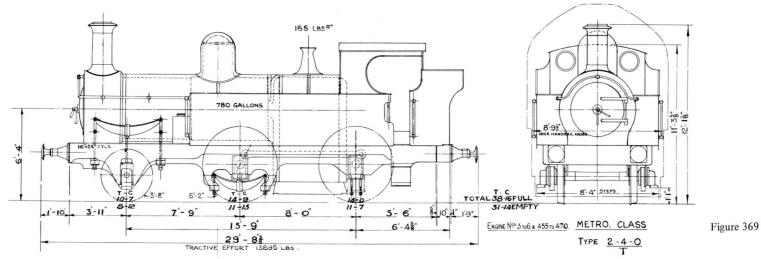

165 LBS□"

780 GALLONS

T.C
TOTAL 38·16 FULL
31·14 EMPTY

16"×24" CYLS.

T C
10·7
8·12

3'-8"

5'-2"

T G
14·9
11·13

T G
14·0
11·7

1'-10"    3'-11"    7'-9"    8'-0"    5'-6"    10"    1'-9"

15'-9"    6'-4⅝"

29'-8⅜"

TRACTIVE EFFORT 13895 LBS.

T.C

8'-9½"
OVER HANDRAIL KNOBS

8'-4" STEPS

11'-3⅝"    12'-1⅛"

1'-1"

ENGINE Nº³ 3 TO 6 & 455 TO 470.    METRO. CLASS

TYPE  2-4-0
      ——
       T

Figure 369

Figure 371

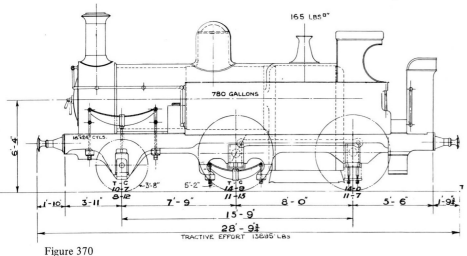

165 LBS□"

780 GALLONS

16"×24" CYLS.

6'-4"

T C
10·7
8·12

3'-8"

5'-2"

T G
14·9
11·13

11·7

1'-10"    3'-11"    7'-9"    8'-0"    5'-6"    1'-9½"

15'-9"

28'-9¾"

TRACTIVE EFFORT 13895 LBS.

Figure 370

Two official drawings of the 'Metro' class feature on this page, both to the *'K' diagram* of 2-4-0T, but with different cabs and bunkers. *Figure 370* has the small bunker and open cab, and *Figure 369* shows the extended frames to accommodate the enlarged coal capacity and the closed cab. Both drawings depict the 780 gallon side tanks.

*Figure 371* is an official photograph of No. 615 taken in 1908 resplendent with polished brass and seen with the S4 type boiler. She was later fitted with a Belpaire B4 in 1915 with closed cab, as can be seen in *Figure 375* on the next page.

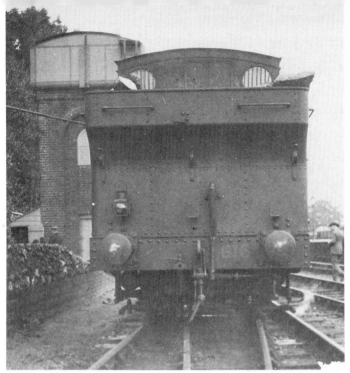

Figure 372    Figure 373

Figure 374

A set of detailed pictures appear on this page, all dealing with the small tank 'Metro' class. *Figure 375* shows No. 615 at Reading in 1925. Note again the offset doors in the rear spectacle plate and also the vacuum pipe on the right of the coupling hook. A close-up of the cab shape is seen in *Figure 376* and is an interesting comparison with the sister engine No. 616 in *Figure 374.* Not only is the bunker itself of different shape, but also the curve of the cab side is dissimilar. Full frontal shots are often useful to modellers and *Figure 372* gives this view of the front end of No. 616 *(Figure 373* shows rear end detail).

Figure 375

Figure 376

Figure 377

Figure 378

Figure 379        Figure 380

For more detail on the small 'Metro' class, *Figure 377* shows a side view of No. 1464 with yet another arc to the bunker side-plates. A detailed close-up of the leading wheels of No. 1464 is shown in *Figure 380,* and it is interesting to study the difference with that of No. 616 in *Figure 378* where strengthening plates have been added to the framing. No. 980 in *Figure 379* is seen with the side rods 'off' at Reading shed in 1932 just prior to withdrawal. Note the cranked vacuum pipe and the A.T.C. shoe under the rear buffer beam.

Figure 381

Figure 383

Figure 382

Before moving on to the large-tanked 'Metro' series, I thought you would like to see these two consecutive tanks, Nos. 1499 and 1500. Although the dates in the photographic register are given as 1892 for both, I personally think that this might apply to No. 1500, but would put No. 1499 as later, due to the more modern axle-box. However, the two pictures do show both sides well, and with different chimneys. Note also the unusual handrail on the cab of No. 1499.

*Figure 382* gives a good indication of the rebuilding which took place on these engines. No. 1500 is seen in 1935 fitted with Belpaire boiler and firebox, closed cab, and with the number plate moved back to the cab side position.

Figure 384                                                                 Figure 386                                            PAGE 136

Figure 388

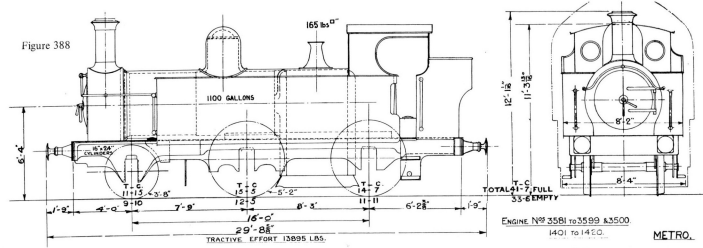

165 lbs □"

1100 GALLONS

16"x24" CYLINDERS

T C 11·15   3'-8"   9·10

T C 15·5   5'-2"

T C 14·7   11·11

1'-9"   4'-0"   7'-9"   12·5   8'-3"   6'-2⅜"   1'-9"

16'-0"

29'-8⅝"

TRACTIVE EFFORT 13895 LBS.

12'-1¹/₁₆"   11'-3¹³/₁₆"

8'-2"

T·C
TOTAL 41·7 FULL
33·6 EMPTY

8'-4"

ENGINE N°S 3581 TO 3599 & 3500.
1401 TO 1420.          METRO.

6'-4"

The next illustrations are of the large tank 'Metro' class. There were thirty one engines recorded as being fitted with these larger 1080 gallon side tanks, and this conversion was carried out between 1898-99. The length of these tanks meant that the laminated springs for the leading wheels would foul the end of the tank, and so a cluster of four volute springs was substituted.

*Figure 384* is of No. 3564 and was one of the engines which had top feed into the boiler and the tall deep bunker. No. 3583 seen in *Figure 386* has the enclosed cab with the large Collett cab of 1924. No. 3589 seen in *Figure 385* is another of the class which was shedded at Oxford in the 1940s and which I photographed at Morris Cowley in 1946. *Figure 387* illustrates the use of the roundel transfer on the large 'Metro' tanks, No. 3564 being pictured outside the Works in 1936. The official drawing is *Diagram H* of the class, seen in *Figure 388*.

Figure 387

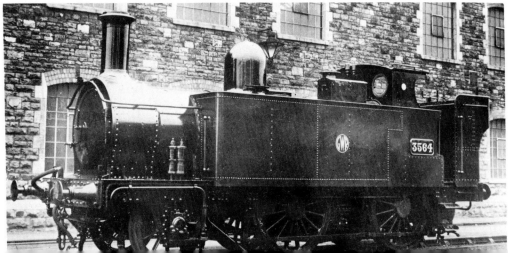

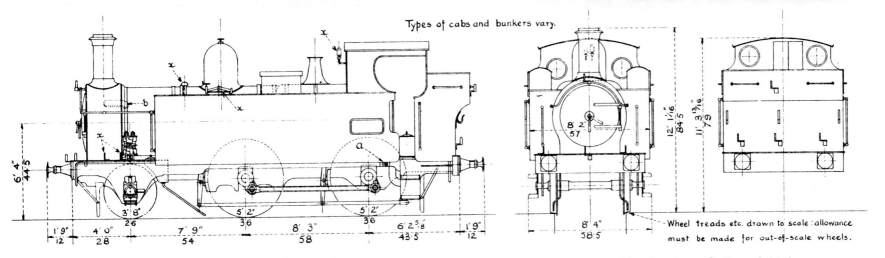

Types of cabs and bunkers vary.

NOTES. At "a" hanging plate widens towards rear. "b" is on right side only. Spare lamp irons on left side only. Position of details marked "x" varies. Coupling rods may be plain or fluted. Brake rigging outside wheels. Dimensions in feet (full size), and in millimetres to nearest half-m'metre for Gauge "O". Scale 7 m.m = 1 foot. Reduced from official drawings.

Wheel treads etc. drawn to scale: allowance must be made for out-of-scale wheels.

**G.W.R.** METRO. Class. Numbers:- 1401-1420, 3500, 3561-3570, 3581-3599.

Figure 390

This Templer drawing, reduced to 4mm scale, gives many dimensions of the large 'Metro' tanks, and shows the closed cab variety as in *Figure 386*. The photograph of No. 1415 in *Figure 389* was taken in 1925 just before the engine was fitted with auto gear in 1930. The engines which had the big tanks are listed below:-

1401-1420, 3500, 3561-3570, 1446, 1460 and 1462.

These engines kept their 1080-gallon tanks until being scrapped.

Figure 389

Figure 393

PAGE 138

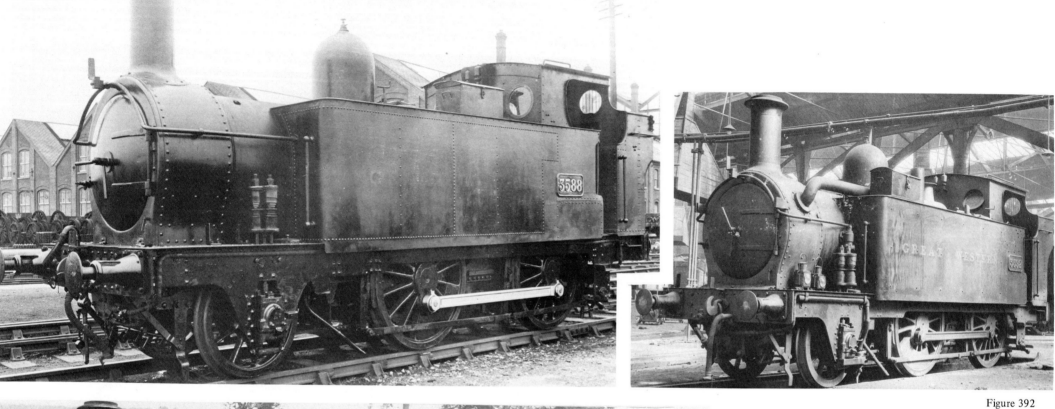

Figure 392

Three different styles of large 'Metro' tanks are seen in these photographs. The official picture in *Figure 393* is of No. 3588 seen outside 'A' erecting shop at Swindon in 1929, after a major overhaul. Although very clean, she has not been repainted as can be seen from the dull transfers on the tank sides.

No. 3592 in *Figure 392* photographed inside Old Oak Common loco shed is an example of the type with condensing gear and closed cab. Note the vacuum trip gear just to the rear of the leading wheels, and the clack-box going into the boiler side. Finally an excellent study of No. 3593 which was converted to a 2-4-2T form in 1905. This photograph by Maurice Earley was taken at Twyford in 1927 just before the locomotive was withdrawn *(Figure 391)*.

Figure 391

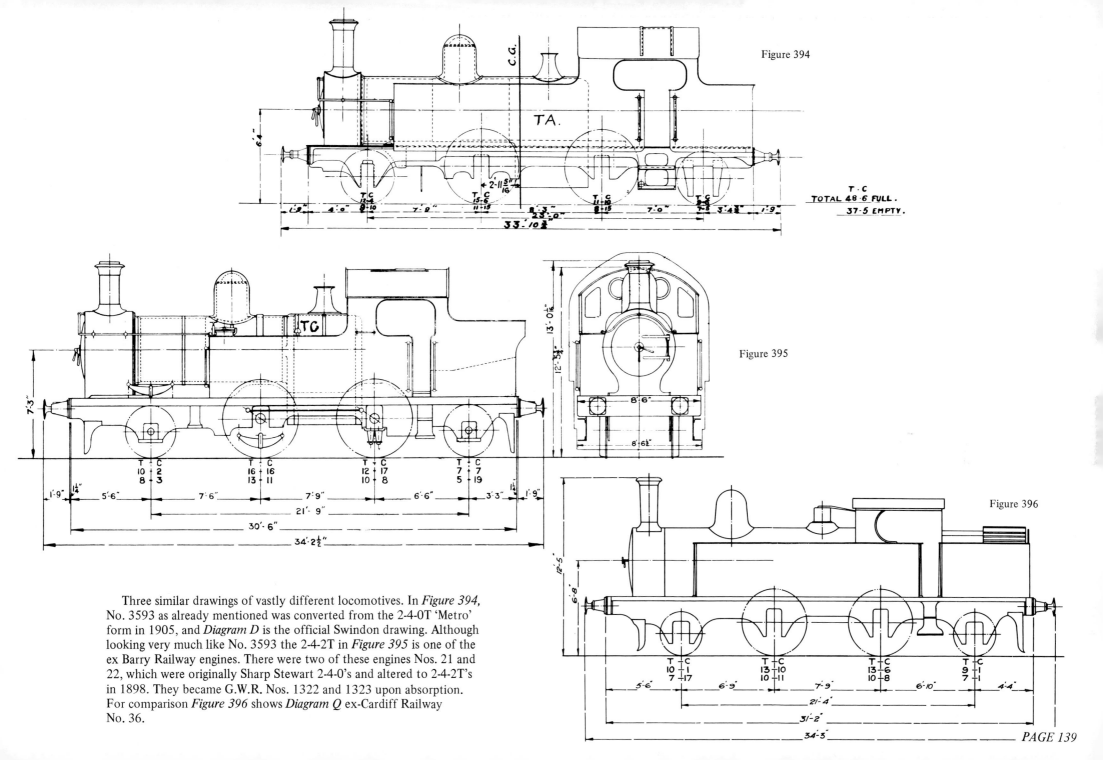

Figure 394

T·C
TOTAL 48·6 FULL.
37·5 EMPTY.

Figure 395

Figure 396

Three similar drawings of vastly different locomotives. In *Figure 394*, No. 3593 as already mentioned was converted from the 2-4-0T 'Metro' form in 1905, and *Diagram D* is the official Swindon drawing. Although looking very much like No. 3593 the 2-4-2T in *Figure 395* is one of the ex Barry Railway engines. There were two of these engines Nos. 21 and 22, which were originally Sharp Stewart 2-4-0's and altered to 2-4-2T's in 1898. They became G.W.R. Nos. 1322 and 1323 upon absorption. For comparison *Figure 396* shows *Diagram Q* ex-Cardiff Railway No. 36.

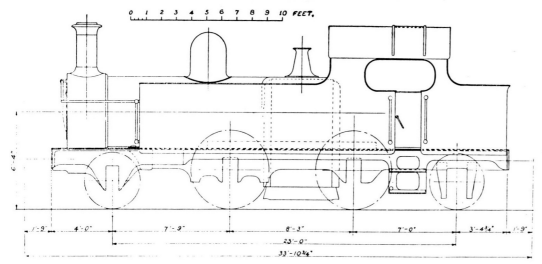

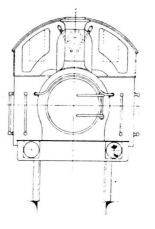

Figure 399

*Page 140*
No. 3593 being a one off job had two diamond shaped and one round window in the front spectacle plate whereas the two windows at the rear were completely different. Note also the angled whistles and the spaced rivets on the side tanks. There was also a sliding ventilator in the cab roof. (Fortunately J. N. Maskelyne sketched the bare bones of this steeple-cabbed engine in the thirties as in the drawing shown.)

Both sides of this engine are shown in *Figures 397* and *398*.

Figure 397

Figure 398

*Page 141*
Seven drawings of the little absorbed engines which were contained in the Great Western 'Small Engine' diagram book. They are all to the 4mm scale and pictures of each will be located in Part 3 of the R.C.T.S. books under the numbers quoted.

*Figure 401*, Nos. 1298 and 1300 were built by Ince Forge in 1878 for the South Devon Railway. One other, No. 1299, became a crane engine No. 1299 (photograph on page C146 in Part 3 of the R.C.T.S. book). (See also *Figure 407* next page.)

*Figure 403*, No. 1384, built by Sharp Stewart in 1876 for the Watlington and Princes Risborough Railway was No. 2. See photograph on page 142, *Figure 409*.

*Figure 402*, No. 1385, built by Fox, Walker & Co. for the Whitland and Cardigan Railway as No. 1. Photo on illustration C161, Part 3, R.C.T.S.

*Figure 406*, No. 1388, *Goonbarrow* built by Peckett & Co. in 1904 for Cornwall Minerals Railway. Photo on illustration C183, Part 3, R.C.T.S.

Figure 404 is of No. 45, an old Sharp Stewart of 1853, which belonged to the Shrewsbury and Birmingham Railway.

Figure 405 is of old No. 92 which started life as a 0-4-2T in 1857, and built by Beyer Peacock. It was altered to 0-4-0T in 1878 at Chester and rebuilt at Wolverhampton in 1893. In this condition she lasted until 1942 after 85 years on the Great Western books (see Figure 416).

Finally, No. 95 in Figure 400 was built by Sharp Stewart in 1857 for the Birkenhead Railway and lasted on the Great Western until 1924. Photo on page 145, Figure 419.

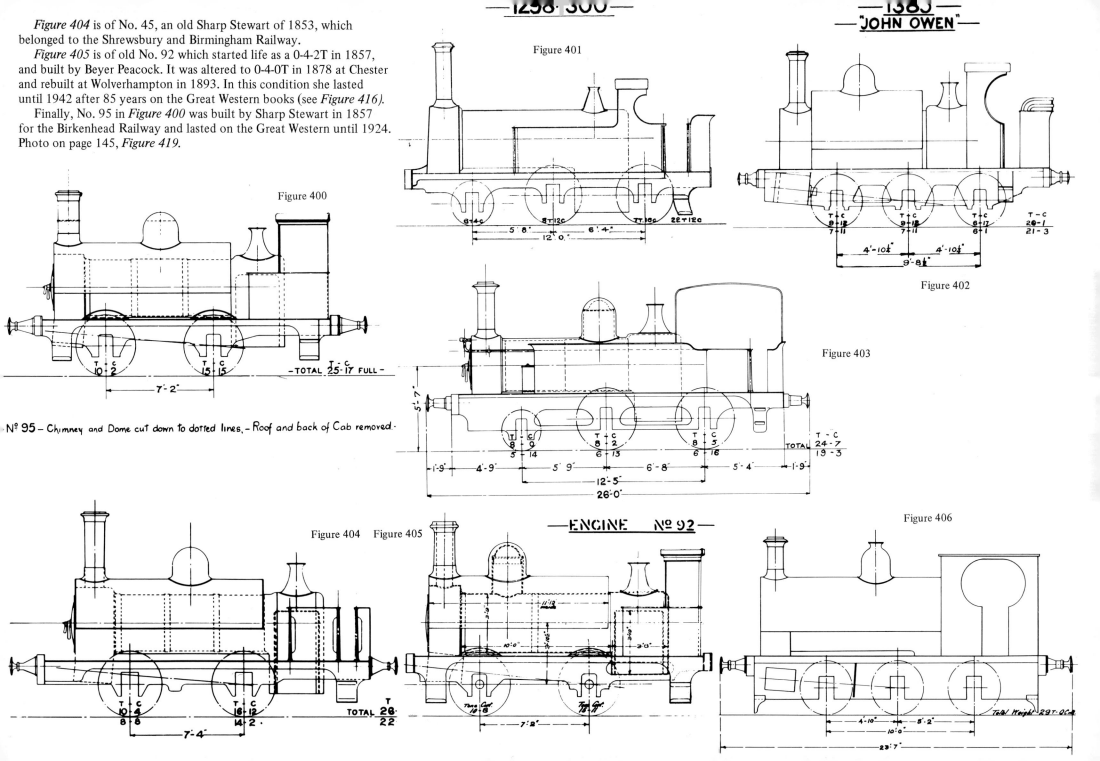

Figure 401

Figure 400

Figure 402

Figure 403

Nº 95 - Chimney and Dome cut down to dotted lines. - Roof and back of Cab removed.

Figure 404    Figure 405

Figure 406

ENGINE Nº 92

"JOHN OWEN"

Figure 407    Figure 408

PAGE 142

One other engine of the large 'Metro' series was also treated to a large high cab similar to No. 3593. This was No. 3596, but apart from the cab no other alteration took place, and she always remained a 2-4-0 tank. The vaulted cab was slightly different to that of No. 3593, not only in the length but in having no round window in the middle of the front spectacle plate. *Figure 408* shows this engine with the cab and bunker which was fitted in 1905, but in 1927 Mr. Collett rebuilt the back end with the more usual deeper standard type, and fitted the engine with vacuum trip apparatus for working over the Metropolitan lines.

Figure 409

Two small odd 2-4-0 tanks also feature on this page. No. 1300 seen at Exeter in 1928 started life on the South Devon Railway as *Mercury* and was under construction at Newton Abbot when the South Devon Railway was absorbed into the Great Western. She was finished at Swindon in 1878 and rebuilt there in 1905 as shown in the photograph. A sister engine, No. 1299, was transformed into a mobile crane in 1881 and can be seen in Volume Two. The drawing is on page 141.

*Figure 409* is portrayed in 1902 at Swindon. No. 1384 started life as No. 2 of the Watlington and Princes Risborough Railway, there only being two engines accorded to that Company. Built by Sharp Stewart in 1876, No. 2 came into Great Western hands in 1883 and was used on both the Bodmin and Lambourn branches. She was rebuilt to the condition seen in the picture, in 1899, and worked over both the Wrington Vale Light Railway and the Culm Valley branch before being withdrawn in 1911. After being sold to the Bute Works Supply Co., the little tank finally finished up on the Clevedon and Portishead Railway until being scrapped in 1937. The

Figure 410

Figure 411

This experimental one off job was most unusual as built, with a strange floating type of four-wheeled bogie under the front end, and almost full-length side tanks. However, this suspended leading bogie caused so much trouble in derailments that two years after completion, the design was altered to a 2-4-0T configuration with outside frames to all wheels and the side tanks shortened considerably.

In 1899 she was fitted with a 'Duke' type boiler S4, which placed the dome on the back ring, and finally in 1914 received the Belpaire design as shown in the illustrations. This engine was always a favourite with Mr. Maskelyne, and his drawing appears in *Figure 412* to 4mm scale with detailed measurements. She was finally withdrawn in 1924, after working in the Bristol and West Country divisions for many years, and even seeing service at Chester, working fast passenger trains to Birkenhead and Wolverhampton. J. N. Maskelyne reports that at the turn of the century this unique engine was fully lined out, including frames, and with polished dome, valve bonnet and beading with a handsome copper-topped chimney.

WORKING PRESSURE, 180 LB. PER SQ.IN.; TRACTIVE FORCE, 16,900 LB.; TOTAL LENGTH, 37' 9¾'. WEIGHT (FULL), (LEADING) 13 T. 12 C., (DRIVING) 16 T. 18 C., (TRAILING) 16 T. 8 C., TOTAL = 46 T. 18 C.

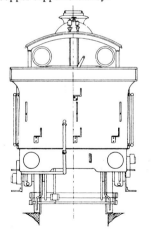

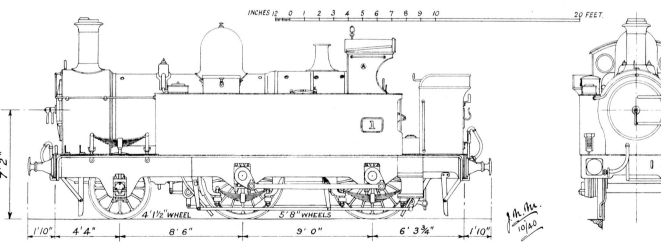

Figure 412

WIDTH OVER CAB SIDES = 6'0¼"; OVER TANKS = 7'8½"; OVER BUNKER (AT BOTTOM LEVEL) = 7'5"; OVER RUNNING-PLATE = 7'8"; OVER OUTSIDE FRAMES = 6'5"; OVER CRANKS = 7'9" AND OVER COUPLING-ROD PINS = 8'6½"; OVER LEADING SPRING CENTRES = 6'2"(?); OVER BUNKER COPING = 8'6"; OVER FOOTSTEPS = 7'10½".
HEIGHT TO RUNNING-PLATE = 4'2½"; TO LOWER FOOTSTEP = 1'4½"; TO BOILER CENTRE-LINE = 7'2"; TO CAB ROOF = 11'3½"; TO TOP OF CHIMNEY (OVER TOP OF CAPUCHON) = 13' 2¾"; OF TANKS (FOOTPLATE TO TOP OF BEADING) = 4'0"; OF HANDRAIL = 9" ABOVE BOILER C/L; OF BUNKER = 4'4" + 11" COPING.
DIAMETER OF SMOKEBOX WRAPPER, OUTSIDE = 5'3½"; OF BOILER CLEADING = 4'8½"; LENGTH OF SMOKEBOX = 3'3"; CHIMNEY C/L = 1'5½" FROM BACK EDGE OF WRAPPER-PLATE.
DIAMETER OF CHIMNEY = 1'4½"; OF DOME = 2'10½". LENGTHS OF SPRINGS = LEADING, 3'9"; DRIVING, 3'6"; TRAILING, 4'3". RADIUS OF CAB ROOF = 6'4".
RADII OF CAB-SIDE = 1'5", 1'0" + 1'5". PAINTING = STANDARD GREEN AND BLACK; NO CREST; NO TITLE; NO BRIGHT METAL-WORK, EXCEPTING COUPLING-RODS, BUFFER-HEADS AND DRAWHOOKS. "YELLOW A" ROUTE DESIGNATION. RED BUFFER-BEAMS, WITH YELLOW NUMBER, BLACK-SHADED ON EACH. LEADING SPRING HANGERS BLACK.
SPARE LAMP IRONS ON LEFT SIDE ONLY. LUBRICATOR-PIPE COVER ON RIGHT SIDE OF SMOKEBOX ONLY.

No. 1490's claim to fame is that she was the first engine on the Great Western Railway to be fitted with pannier tanks. To think that all the 0-6-0 'matchbox' tanks started from this experiment in 1898! We first see the hand of Churchward in this design with the unusual firebox and the large wide cab—surely all forerunners of the engines to come, like the 'Krugers', for instance. Outside bearings were used on all wheels, and the bogie wheels were of the

Figure 414

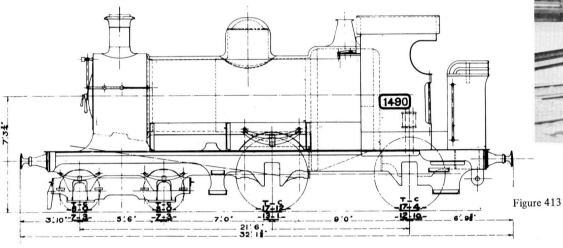

Figure 413

Figure 415

'Mansell' coach style. For her size the engine was very heavy, being 50 tons plus and therefore had a limited use. Although originally thought of as a successor to the 'Metro' tanks, this engine proved unsteady at speed, and was utilized at Bath and Swindon on shunting service. Sold by the Great Western to the Bute Works Supply, she worked at Pontypool for a spell, then on the Brecon & Merthyr Railway in 1908, and finished her days in Northumberland on colliery duties. She was finally broken up in 1929. The drawing in *Figure 413* is the official *Diagram B* of Lot 114, and is to 4mm scale.

The Great Western Railway tried out many experiments on locomotives over the years, and one of these was the use of oil fuel on Holden's principle in 1902. James Holden, known principally as the C.M.E. of the Great Eastern Railway, spent 20 years previously at Swindon, and his work on oil burning eventually culminated in 'Claud Hamilton'. Experimentally, the G.W.R. built a small 0-4-0 tank engine to give Holden's ideas an airing and the result was No. 101. However, the trials only lasted a year and in 1903 the engine was rebuilt with a Lentz boiler still retaining the oil burning system. Finally in 1905 she was converted to coal burning and ran until 1911 in the condition shown in *Figure 417*.

Figure 416          Figure 417

Figure 419

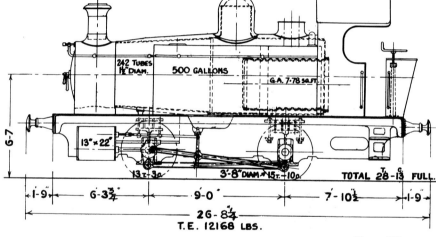

160 LBS/◻"

242 TUBES
1⅝" DIAM.          500 GALLONS                    G.A. 7·78 SQ.FT.

6-7

13" × 22"

13 T· 3ᴄ          3'-8"DIAM· 15 T·10ᴄ          TOTAL 28-13 FULL

1'-9"    6-3¾"          9-0"              7'-10½"    1'-9"

26-8¾"
T.E. 12168 LBS.

Figure 418

The tiny 0-4-0T engine in *Figure 416* was one of two built way back in 1857 by Beyer-Peacock for the honour of being the first shunting tanks to be provided for the standard gauge of the G.W.R. Originally of 0-4-2 saddle tank design, the two were knocked into one (No. 92) in 1878 as a 0-4-0ST. Then at Stafford Road Works in 1892 the engine was rebuilt again into the condition shown in the photograph. Strangely enough this little machine lasted until 1942, seeing 85 years of work!

No. 95, another 0-4-0 tank which was inherited by the G.W.R. when the Birkenhead Railway was absorbed, was built about 1857 by Sharp Stewarts. She was then called *Grasshopper* and numbered 6. Rebuilt in 1890 the height of the engine was reduced to enable her to work through a low tunnel at Croes Newydd, but the cab was eventually restored, and she worked in the condition seen in *Figure 419* until retirement came in 1924. In her time she worked in South Wales, Chester and Bristol areas. The drawing in *Figure 418* is the official *Diagram A* of the experimental No. 101 of *Lot 136*.

*PAGE 145*

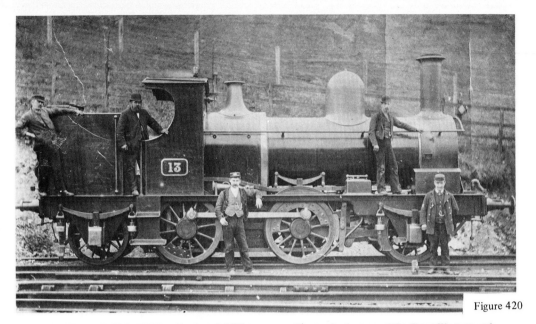

Figure 420

Figure 421

No. 13 was built in 1886 as the first 2-4-2T to run on the standard gauge of the Great Western and was odd in many respects. As can be seen from *Figure 420,* the driving wheels had inside bearings and the leading and trailing carrying wheels had outside axleboxes. The water supply was carried in a well tank and at the rear of the bunker, and she was the only locomotive built to this design. In this 2-4-2T condition the engine worked in the West Country on the St. Ives branch, and also saw service on the Abingdon line. Later in 1897 No. 13 was rebuilt as a 4-4-0T with a saddle tank and a shortened rear end. A bogie with 2′ 8″ wheels and outside bearings replaced the 3′ 6″ fixed carrying wheels and she was fitted with a new chimney, dome and bunker *(Figure 421).* After some use on the Highworth branch, the little No. '13' was moved to the Looe branch in Cornwall, and operated there from 1901 until 1922, working out her last four years as works shunter at Swindon.

Still with four coupled tank engines, mention must be made of the small class of twenty engines numbered 3521 to 3540. *Figure 422* shows one of the series as built in 1888 and it can be appreciated what a long wheelbase these outside framed tanks had, namely 7′ 0″ and 10′ 6″, total 17′ 6″. They were extremely unsteady and to try to overcome this, they were altered between 1891 and 1892 to 0-4-4ST, receiving a bogie in place of the rear-carrying wheels. However, even this did not cure the malady, and within ten years they were all given a 'volte-face', and turned into 4-4-0 tender engines. A further batch of twenty engines, numbers 3541 to 3560 were built in 1888/89, some with saddle tanks and all with broad gauge axles for use on the 7′ track. As the tanks proved unsteady they were later converted to the side tank design as seen in *Figure 423.* No. 3548 was one of the two 0-4-4 tanks to come off the road at Doublebois in 1895, the other being No. 3521. Like the rest of the class they had a long useful life when fitted with a tender.

Figure 422

Figure 423

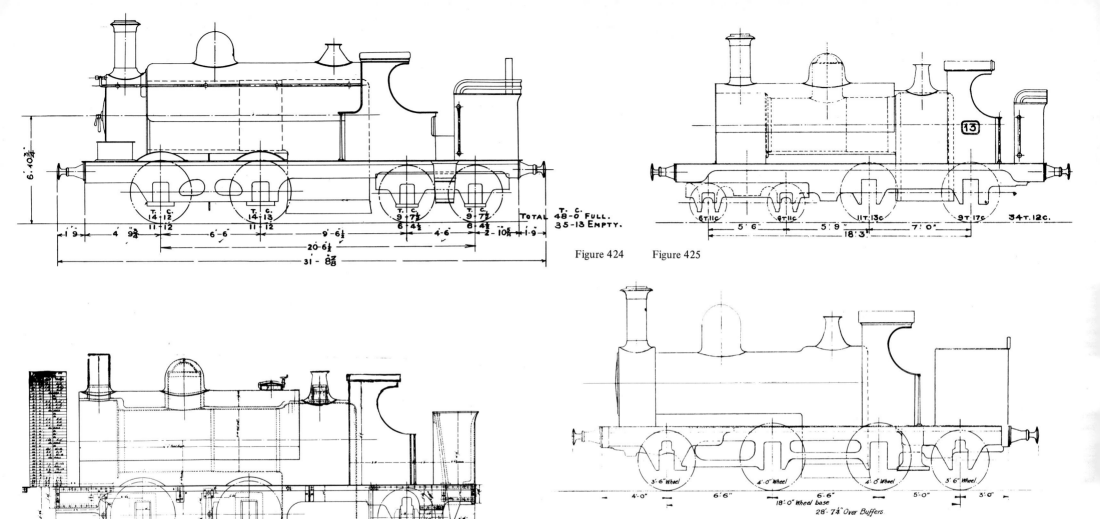

Figure 424    Figure 425

Figure 426    Figure 427

This page shows four official drawings, all to 4mm scale and three straight from the diagram book. *Figure 424* is of the 0-4-4T saddle class to *Diagram C,* the numbers being 1345 to 1352. *Figure 425* is to *Diagram A* and shows No. 13 which is the 4-4-0T as seen on the previous page (as last rebuild to the Lot No. 72). The sketch drawing is of the same engine No. 13 as originally built and complements *Figure 420* on page 146. The little 2-4-2T ran in this condition from 1886 until 1897. Finally, in *Figure 426* is shown the 0-4-2 saddle tank as a 'Frame Plan' drawing from Wolverhampton works.

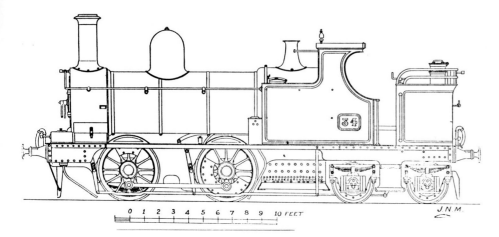

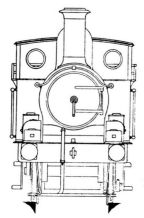

Figure 428

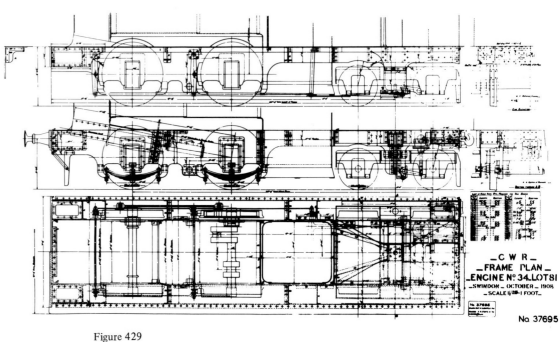

_C W R_
_FRAME PLAN_
_ENGINE № 34.LOT 81_
_SWINDON – OCTOBER – 1908_
_SCALE ¼ IN – 1 FOOT_

No. 37695

Figure 429

Figure 430

Two small 0-4-2T oddities were constructed at Swindon in 1890 and numbered 34 and 35. Designed by Dean specially for service on the Helston and St. Ives branches in Cornwall, which were both subjected to sharp curves and weight restrictions. When first built these engines had saddle tanks, but upon rebuilding as 0-4-4ST in 1895 the saddle tanks were removed and replaced by side tanks which were in one piece with the cab sides, and a well tank under the bunker. The bogie which was fitted had the small 2′ 8″ coach wheels, whilst the coupled drivers were 4′ diameter. *Figure 428* is the excellent drawing which Mr. Maskelyne produced, reduced to 4mm scale and it links up well with the official 1895 broadside photograph taken at Swindon Works in 1895.

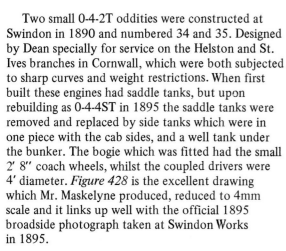

Figure 431

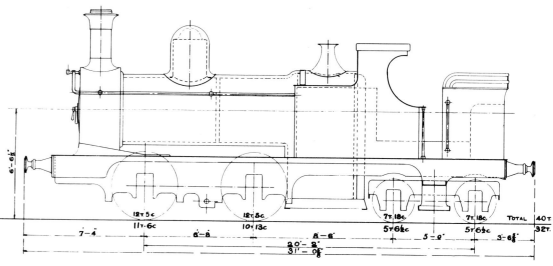

Figure 433

Figure 432

Two additional pictures of No. 34. *Figure 431* shows the right-hand side which had the reversing lever, and a three-quarter view in *Figure 432* which shows details of the front end. Incidentally, when these pictures were taken the engine was painted in the green and Indian red livery, with even the wheels lined out. They must have been very handsome little machines, with not only the copper-capped chimney, brass dome and safety valve bonnet, but also a wide-shaped brass rim around the front edge of the round-topped firebox. Reports have it that both engines went to the R.E. Depot at Longmoor around 1910, and No. 34 went to Swindon in 1921 for a general refit, but was found too far gone, so it is presumed she was scrapped at that date.

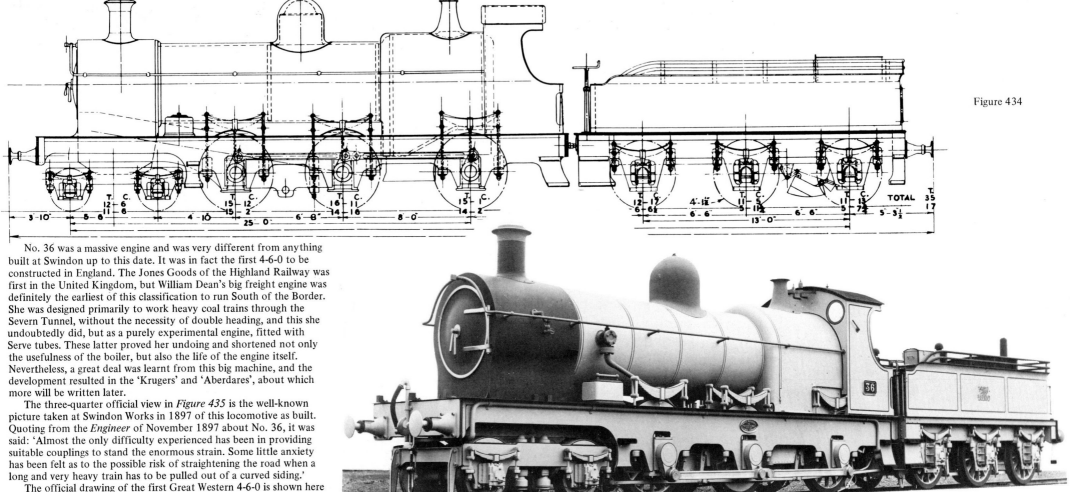

Figure 434

No. 36 was a massive engine and was very different from anything built at Swindon up to this date. It was in fact the first 4-6-0 to be constructed in England. The Jones Goods of the Highland Railway was first in the United Kingdom, but William Dean's big freight engine was definitely the earliest of this classification to run South of the Border. She was designed primarily to work heavy coal trains through the Severn Tunnel, without the necessity of double heading, and this she undoubtedly did, but as a purely experimental engine, fitted with Serve tubes. These latter proved her undoing and shortened not only the usefulness of the boiler, but also the life of the engine itself. Nevertheless, a great deal was learnt from this big machine, and the development resulted in the 'Krugers' and 'Aberdares', about which more will be written later.

The three-quarter official view in *Figure 435* is the well-known picture taken at Swindon Works in 1897 of this locomotive as built. Quoting from the *Engineer* of November 1897 about No. 36, it was said: 'Almost the only difficulty experienced has been in providing suitable couplings to stand the enormous strain. Some little anxiety has been felt as to the possible risk of straightening the road when a long and very heavy train has to be pulled out of a curved siding.'

The official drawing of the first Great Western 4-6-0 is shown here with the usual details that were always appended to these diagrams (*Figure 434*).

Figure 435

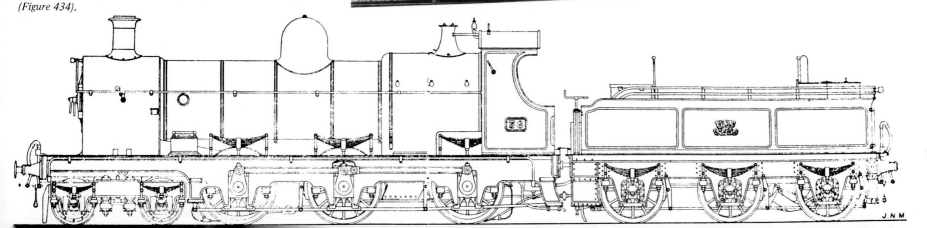

Figure 436

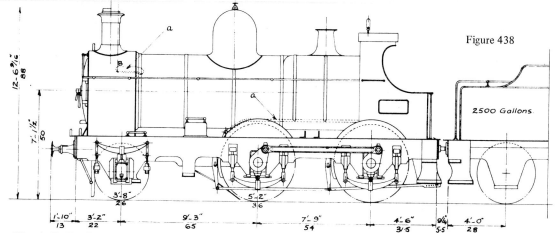

Figure 438

When built, No. 36 was equipped with crosshead pumps for boiler water supply, as well as one injector. The hoses at the bottom of the photograph are for water to and from the pumps, and one injector supply. The other smaller hose is the vacuum pipe, and as the engine never worked on passenger trains it had no steam pipe. Clack-boxes from the pumps entered in the boiler sides, and supply from the injector entered on the back plate, as can be seen on the left-hand side. A Salter-type spring was on the safety valve, and came into the cab, and a shut-off valve for the water gauge was carried on to the outside of the cab sheet. Two whistle valves were provided as usual just above the regulator, and two systems of brake were installed, vacuum and steam. The steam brake cylinders can be seen under the cab steps, in the same position as on the 0-6-0 Dean Goods. Reversing was by lever, and the small handle alongside the reversing rack was for applying sand. The two ring handles in the wooden floor were damper controls. The cab was large and spacious for the period but had no seats (Figure 437).

The idea of standardising, so successfully carried out by Churchward, was initially given a trial in 1884-87 by William Dean on a series of both tank and tender locomotives. This class was the '3201' series, or perhaps better known as the 'Stella' class. The first engine to be built in 1884, No. 3201 was, oddly enough, sold immediately to the Pembroke and Tenby Railway who numbered it '8', and gave her the name Stella, which the engine carried long after being reinstated into Great Western stock. The engines chosen to receive interchangeable cylinders, motion and double frames were Nos. 3201 to 3205 as seen in Figure 439, 3501 to 3520 which were tank engines, of which a narrow gauge example can be seen on page 39, Figure 99, 2361 to 2360 being goods engines of 0-6-0 classification, and tank engines 1661 to 1700. As the latter goods classes have already been illustrated, these pages only deal with the 3201s and 3501s. Ten of the tank series, Nos. 3501 to 3510 were fitted with 7' axles for use on the broad gauge as convertibles, and all the 35XX series were eventually converted to tender engines, so that when Stella was returned to the fold in 1896, there was a complete set of 25 engines numbering 3201 to 3205 and 3501 to 3520. Figure 438 is a Colonel Templer drawing of the class when later fitted with Belpaire B4 boiler, and the photograph shows Stella in 1902 before having her special nameplate removed.

Figure 437    Figure 439

Figure 440

On this page are two pictures of two similar engines, but in fact, No. 3504 has suffered major structural changes to finally emerge looking like her sister No. 3204. In *Figure 440*, No. 3204 is pictured in 1896, more or less as built in 1885, and just out of the Works after a major refit. Note the feed water clack-boxes entering into the side of the firebox. In the lower illustration, also dated 1896, is seen No. 3504, which when new in 1885 started life as a broad gauge tank engine with wheels outside the frames. Five of her sisters, Nos. 3501, 3502, 3505, 3507 and 3509, were changed to tender engines whilst still running on the 7' gauge track, and in 1892 all ten were converted to the standard gauge. Finally in 1894/95, all the remaining tanks were rebuilt as tender engines. Building dates etc. are as follows:

*Lot No. 64* Engine Nos. 3501 to 3520 built 1885
*Lot No. 65* " " 3201 to 3205 " 1884/85

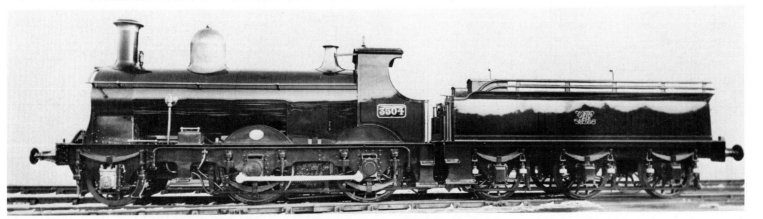

Figure 441

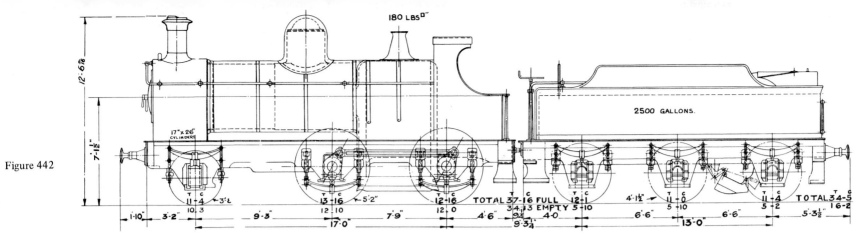

Figure 442

Figure 443

All the 'Stella's eventually received Belpaire boilers and fireboxes (B4) and the earliest to so do was No. 3202 seen in *Figure 443* at Taunton in 1910, having had the square firebox fitted in 1903. Strangely enough, the first engine to be built, being *Stella* herself, was the last to go, not being withdrawn until 1933.

The drawing at the top of the page is the official *Diagram O* which shows the engines with the non-superheated Belpaire boiler and firebox of 1910.

Figure 444

*Figure 444* is a Swindon photograph dated 1892, and shows No. 3510 immediately after being converted from a broad gauge tank engine. The boiler seen is the Swindon S2 type, with the polished dome on the front ring. Notice the smokebox wing plates which were removed when the engine was fitted with the S4 boiler seen in *Figure 446*. This would date the photograph in the 1904 period; the large dome has now come on to the middle ring of the boiler. The official drawing in *Figure 445* is *Diagram Y* which shows the superheated boiler of 1916. Incidentally, No. 3510 received a superheater in 1918 but reverted back to saturated steam before being scrapped in 1928. These engines worked the express passenger trains into the West Country from Newton Abbot until the 'Dukes' appeared on the scene in the late 1890's.

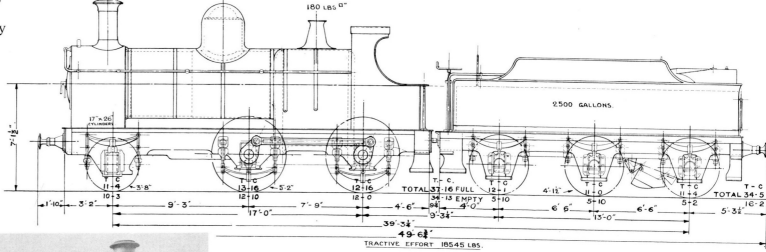

Figure 445

Figure 446

Seen here are the 35XX's, series of engines. In *Figure 447* we have an early picture (of poor quality but worth printing nevertheless) of No. 3511 as built in tank form, for the standard gauge in 1884. It is easy to see the standard frames and outside bearings to all wheels, plus the S2 boiler, with wing plates, and side clack-boxes.

*Figures 448* and *449* show these rebuilt tanks at the end of their days converted to tender engines, and fitted with the B4 boilers. Note the very short wheel-based tender on No. 3510 for use on the Cornish branches, which had restricted turntables.

Figure 447

Figure 448

Figure 449

Figure 450

Figure 451

Figure 452

This page of detail, on the 'Stella' class locomotive just prior to withdrawal in 1929 needs little explanation, as the pictures speak for themselves. However, that large leading axle box, surely derived from the big singles is intriguing *(Figure 450)*.

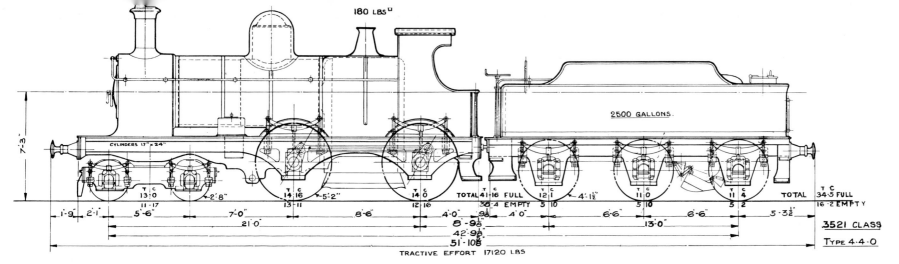

180 LBS

CYLINDERS 17" x 24"

2500 GALLONS.

7·3"

T C 13·0
11·17
1·9" 2·1" 5·6" 2·8"
7·0"
21·0"
T C 14·16
13·11
5·2"
8·6"
T C 14·0
12·16
4·0"
8·9⅜"
42·9⅜"
51·10⅝"
TOTAL 41·16 FULL
38·4 EMPTY
T C 12·1
9⅜"
5·10
4·0"
4·1½"
T C 11·0
5·10
6·6"
13·0"
6·6"
T C 11·4
5·2"
5·3¾"
TOTAL 34·5 FULL
16·2 EMPTY

3521 CLASS
TYPE 4·4·0

TRACTIVE EFFORT 17120 LBS

Figure 453

The '3521' class was not a new class as such, but they were rebuilds of the early ill-fated tanks referred to on page 146. Back in 1887, they were built originally as 0-4-2 side tanks, rebuilt in 1891 as 0-4-4 tanks (some as broad gauge and some as standard). Eventually they were completely reversed into the condition shown here, with cylinders and firebox changing ends, and became tender engines instead of tanks.

When first rebuilt, they had the S2 boiler with the dome on the front ring. Some were rebuilt with the S4 boiler, but all eventually ended up with the Belpaire type. *Figure 454* shows No. 3543 with the long chimney and large tender, and *Figure 455* illustrates No. 3529 with the shorter chimney and small tender.

Figure 454

Figure 455

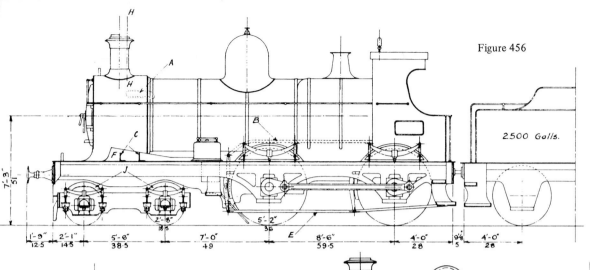

Figure 456

The two drawings are *Diagram A13* in *Figure 453* (previous page), and Colonel Templer's 4mm scale reduction in *Figure 456*. The notes are as follows:

A.    Small cover on right-hand side only.
B.    Reversing rod on right side only, passes behind firebox clothing plates.
C.    Spare lamp irons on left side only.
D.    Brake rigging, outside wheels.
F.    Inner frame flush with smoke box saddle.
H-H.  Chimney centre line for unsuperheated engines.
J.    Bogie splashers flush with frame.

Measurements in feet full size and millimetres for gauge 'O'.

2,500 Galls.

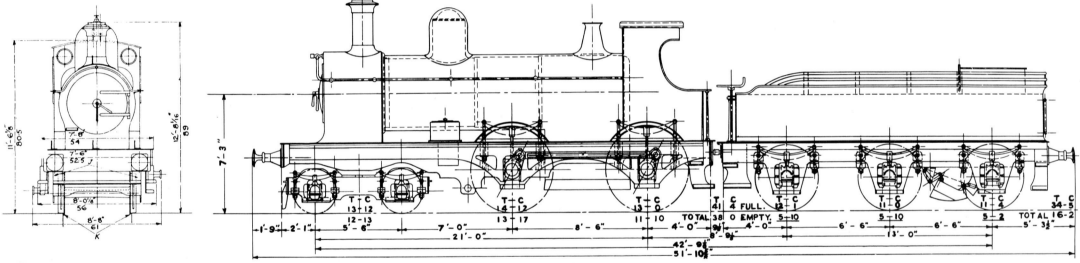

Figure 457

This delightful study of No. 3527 shows the class as first rebuilt with the round-topped firebox but with the dome on the second ring. Note the real short tender. The diagram in *Figure 457* is the Swindon 'B' and illustrates the S2 boiler. It is interesting to note the differing chimney positions with the varying boilers.

Figure 458

Figure 459

Following on from the '3521' class just mentioned, apart from those rebuilt with the S2 domed boiler, there were fourteen which received a more modern treatment. These were fitted with the standard No. 3 parallel boiler, plain cast-iron tapered chimney and with the safety valve on the second ring. Round drumhead smokeboxes were settled in made-up saddles and the large Belpaire firebox was used.

Figure 460

The two photographs shown here, illustrate both left and right hand sides of the engines in this 1900/01 condition and it can be seen that the frames are still those used in the early tank version of the 35XX series. A numerical list of these locomotives so rebuilt is given below:-

No. 3524 No. 3525 No. 3528 No. 3531
No. 3532 No. 3533 No. 3536 No. 3540
No. 3547 No. 3548 No. 3551 No. 3556
No. 3558 and No. 3559.

All these engines were later fitted with the D3 boiler, eleven were superheated, and many lasted until 1929 before being withdrawn.

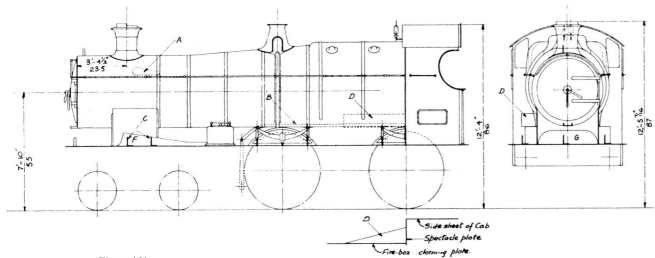

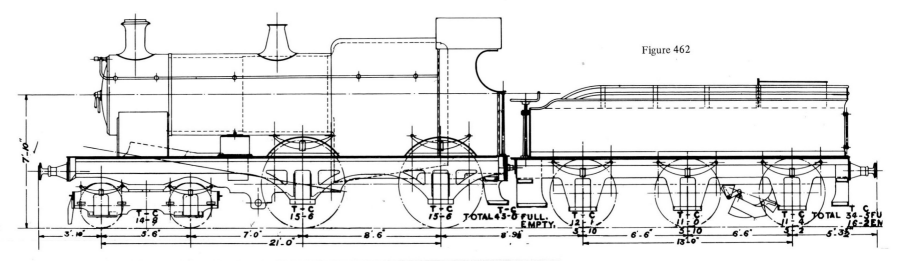

No. 3528 is seen again in *Figure 463*, in an official photograph taken at Swindon in 1912 when the engine was rebuilt with the coned D3 boiler, and fitted with superheater. Comparing this picture with that in *Figure 460* twelve years earlier, there are many changes. Not only has she the handsome copper-capped chimney, but also top feed and a modern tender. Also the bogie seems to have received some attention on the side bearing plates.

Colonel Templer's drawing in *Figure 461* gives many details of measurement (although the chimney shown should be treated with suspicion). The list of notes are useful for detecting which items were on which side of the locomotive. The official diagram is the Swindon, 4-4-0D.

Side sheet of Cab
Spectacle plate
Fire-box clothing plate.

Figure 461

Figure 462

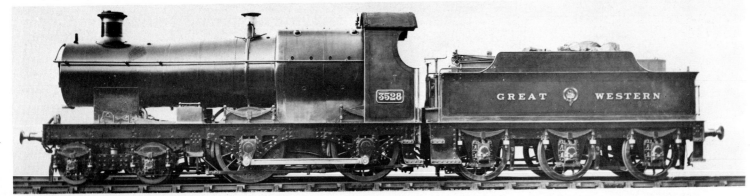

Figure 463

Figure 464    Figure 465

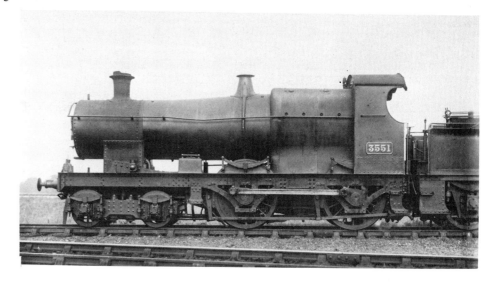

*Figure 464* shows No. 3524 at Gloucester in 1910 with the 'D' parallel boiler and a built up copper-capped chimney. Notice the unusual cover for the reverse rod out of the cab into the firebox cladding. This is shown in Colonel Templer's drawing in *Figure 461* on the previous page.

No. 3551 is seen in *Figure 465* (with taper boiler, top feed and cast iron chimney) just before withdrawal in 1929. Being the superheated version, the engine follows *Figure 466,* the official *Diagram A27* closely, with the exception of the chimney which is the built up type, minus capuchon, in the diagram.

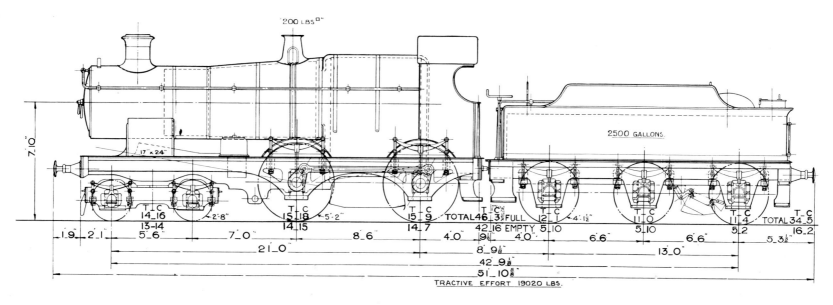

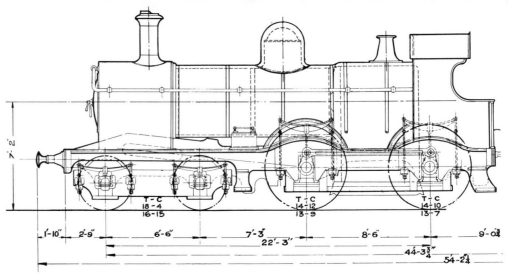

Figure 467

Figure 468

Coming to the close of William Dean's designs, and before moving on to the Churchward engines, the next class to be described and illustrated, is the famous 'Duke' series.

These engines were produced to take over where the bogie singles left off, for use on the severe banks and inclines west of Newton Abbot. Perhaps it would be sensible to begin with a list of engines and building dates:

| No. 3252-53 | Lot 97 | building | 1895 |
|---|---|---|---|
| No. 3254-61 | Lot 101 | " | 1895 |
| No. 3262-71 | Lot 102 | " | 1896 |
| No. 3272-91 | Lot 105 | " | 1896-97 |
| No. 3312-31 | Lot 113 | " | 1898-99 |

All these locomotives were allocated new numbers in 1912, when the re-numbering scheme came into being.

No. 3252 *Duke of Cornwall* was the first of the class to be built and it can be seen that these locomotives were comparatively large engines for the period with extended

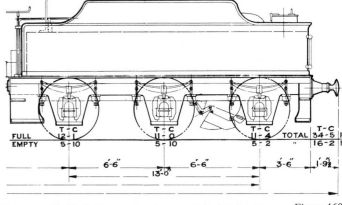

Figure 469

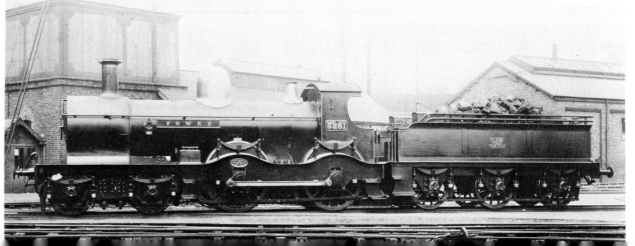

Figure 470

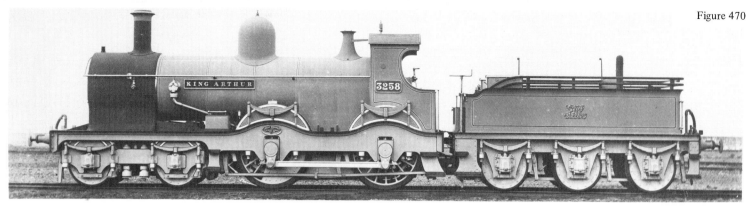

Three more official photographs of the early 'Duke' class, *King Arthur* being the seventh engine of the series to be built in September 1895. The straight nameplates with which the engines were originally fitted, were changed in 1905 for the more familiar curved type which followed the arc of the driving wheel. Incidentally, No. 3258 (afterwards becoming No. 3257) lost her name to avoid confusion in May of 1927 when the Collett 'King' class was introduced. The strange pock-marks on the dome and boiler in *Figure 471* unfortunately appear on the 77 year-old 12″ x 10″ glass negative, and is entirely due to age, and mildew. *Figure 472* is the full size official photograph of the prototype engine.

Figure 471

*continued from page 162*

smoke-boxes on the S4 flush round-topped boilers. The four-coupled driving wheels were 5′ 7½″ diameter, set at 8′ 6″ centres and the bogie and tender wheels were of the 'Mansell' pattern with wooden centres. *Figure 467* is the official *Diagram A29* which shows the flush Belpaire boiler, non-superheated, and in *Figure 469, Fowey* is seen as built, but in service.

The full cab details of *Duke of Cornwall* are seen in *Figure 468* and this makes a nice comparison with the cab of No. 36 on *page 151*. Note the narrower cab to allow for the overhung springs on the trailing drivers, and further restricted by the wheelboxes in the cab space. A screw reverse is fitted which also takes up valuable space. The cluster of water pipes at bottom left is the supply from the tender to the feed pump and return, the injectors, live and exhaust steam (right and left respectively). Notice the timber-lagged cab roof, and the coupling for the communication cord on the right-hand side of the cab roof valance. As far as can be seen in the actual photograph, this, via a chain and levers, operated on the brake whistle, so that passengers could from the carriage, call the attention of the driver. This emergency system followed that of the warning bell which used to be affixed on the tender side, and was, in its turn, superseded by the modern pattern, by which each vehicle could bleed air into the vacuum brake and so bring the train to a standstill automatically.

Figure 472

Figure 473

Figure 474

A trio of photographs of the early 'Duke' class, this time appearing in traffic, rather than the works grey livery. *Figure 475* shows No. 3270 *Trevithick* at Swindon in 1896 fully painted and lined out just prior to entering service. This engine was re-numbered in 1912 to No. 3264, and laboured on all over the Great Western system until final withdrawal in 1949.

No. 3260 seen in *Figure 473* was *Merlin,* and in this picture it will be noticed that the 'Mansell' wheels have been replaced by the spoked type, and the back feed water clack from the crosshead pumps have been changed for the lighter upright type of clackbox as used with an injector.

Another early picture of a 'Duke' in traffic, *Figure 474* illustrates No. 3322 *Mersey* with the nameplate moved back to the firebox side, but still in the straight format.

*Meteor* later was re-numbered to '3286' and lasted until 1936 before being scrapped.

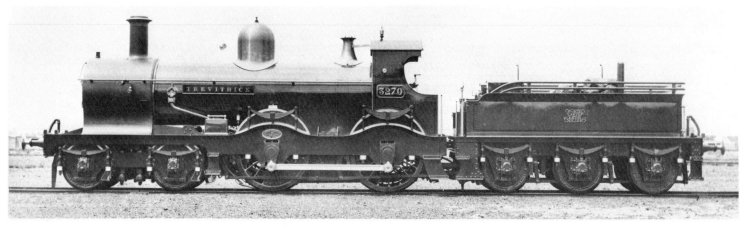

Figure 475

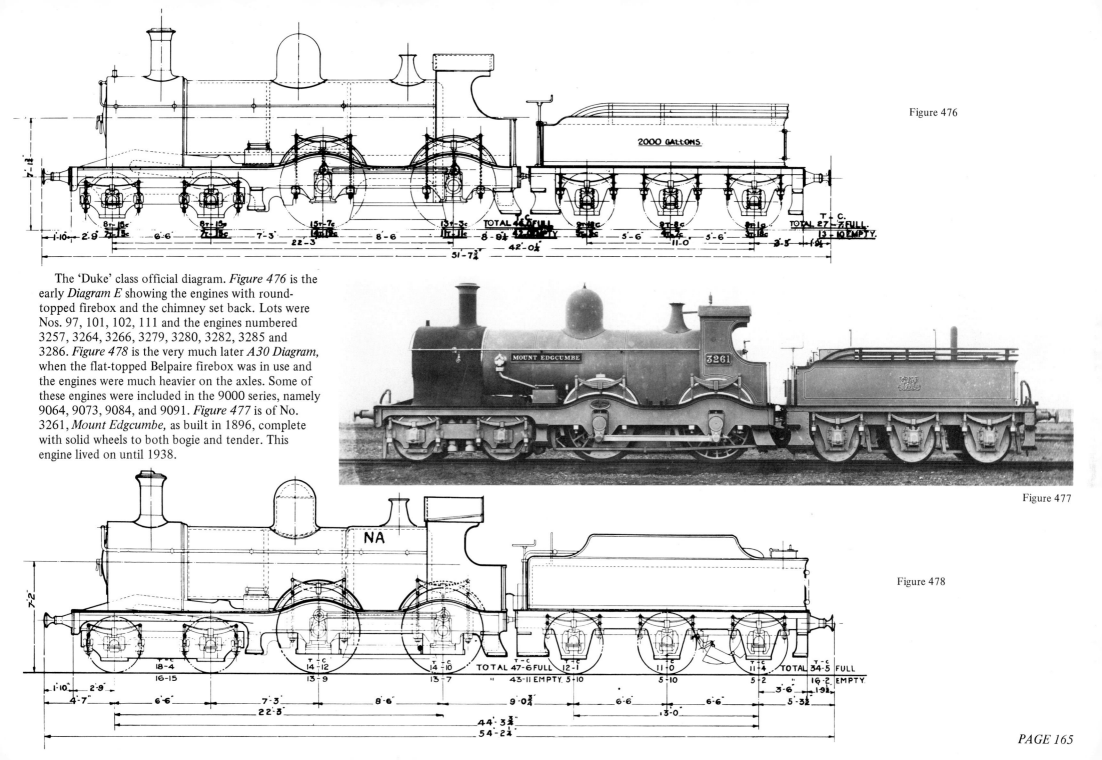

Figure 476

The 'Duke' class official diagram. *Figure 476* is the early *Diagram E* showing the engines with round-topped firebox and the chimney set back. Lots were Nos. 97, 101, 102, 111 and the engines numbered 3257, 3264, 3266, 3279, 3280, 3282, 3285 and 3286. *Figure 478* is the very much later *A30 Diagram,* when the flat-topped Belpaire firebox was in use and the engines were much heavier on the axles. Some of these engines were included in the 9000 series, namely 9064, 9073, 9084, and 9091. *Figure 477* is of No. 3261, *Mount Edgcumbe,* as built in 1896, complete with solid wheels to both bogie and tender. This engine lived on until 1938.

Figure 477

Figure 478

Figure 479

Figure 480

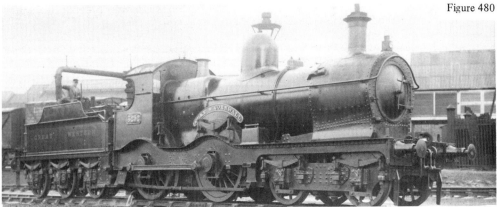

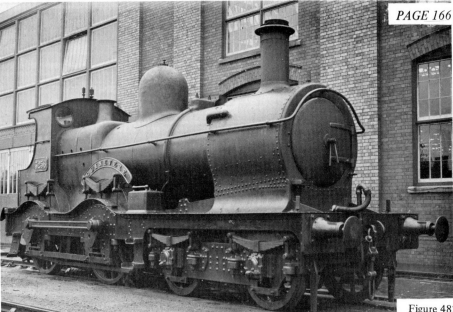

Figure 482

Figure 481

Five pictures are shown here and to illustrate the varying forms of rebuilding the 'Dukes' passed through. In *Figure 483*, *Cotswold* is seen with the rectangular nameplate fixed on the firebox and still with the rerailing jack carried on the running plate. *Maristowe* in *Figure 479*, started life as *Maristow* with straight nameplates, and when being fitted with curved nameplates the 'E' was added to the name thus in fact, spelling the name wrongly! Eventually this locomotive was rebuilt into the 'Bulldog' class in 1907, with the 'E' being dropped and correctly spelt again, when new plates were fitted in 1908. Note that '3282' has the feed water entry into the side of the firebox and the boiler side clacks, sealed off. *Figure 480* shows *Duke of Cornwall* again, at the last out-shopping, fitted with top feed and the wide cab which covered the trailing springs. Incidentally No. 3252 was the only one to keep her original number from building to withdrawal. No. 3256, *Guinevere* is seen in *Figure 482* outside Swindon 'A' erecting shop in the 1930's also with top feed, but retaining the narrow cab.

Photographed in 1935, No. 3277 *Isle of Tresco* is shown in *Figure 481*. Originally named *Tresco*, the nameplate was lengthened to accommodate its new name *Isle of Tresco* in 1904.

Figure 483

Figure 484

A typical Great Western Dean design seen here
almost at the end of the first part of this work, shows
both the early characteristic vintage locomotive of
the 1890s and the adaptation to the modern practice,
resulting in such a useful light locomotive, which was
employed in useful work right up to the late 1930s.
This design depicts the Great Western between the
Wars, and although *St. Ives* looks very 'Olde Worlde',
she could still run fast and haul a fair load. Note the
large deep window which was fitted to No. 3262,
*Figure 485*.

No. 3272, *Amyas* is illustrated in *Figure 484* still
with square-pegged headlamps, and with the early
numbering. She later became '3266' and lasted until
1938. (Note the old grounded coach body on the
right-hand side and the side plates added to the
tender rails.)

Figure 485

Figure 486

The last 'Dean' design – with a 'Duke' rebuild and lasting until 1949, was No. '9076' previously 3276 *St. Agnes,* and was shedded at Banbury for many years. Finally that lovely flowery crest, which so many of the engines in this section carried for years with honour.

This insignia used to be painted by hand on each tender by an expert in the paintshop, in gold leaf!

Figure 487

1897 was a year of special importance for the Great Western Railway. It was the year of the Diamond Jubilee of Queen Victoria and not only did the Company build a magnificent Royal Train for the occasion, but also, there was a massive development programme in the locomotive department. At long last, Churchward was able to exert his influence upon engine design and one of the first series to embody his theories on boiler proportions was the 'Badminton' class.

William Dean the Locomotive Superintendent made George Jackson Churchward his Chief Assistant in 1897, and whilst not being able to set to and design a locomotive completely from his own ideas, he could at least take a Dean engine, and try out some of the ideas which were formulating in his mind.

So, as trains were getting heavier, the engines which hauled them needed greater steaming capabilities, and to achieve this, Churchward went for the then new Belgian firebox with the flat top which we now know so well as the 'Belpaire'. Coupled to the

Figure 488

Figure 489

early parallel boiler, this first essay was known as the 'B.R.4' with the top of the firebox a clear 8½″ above the top of the boiler barrel. Thus we had an engine pure Dean in outline, but built now with the high standard 'square' firebox, which with modifications was to continue in use for fifty years hence. *Figure 489* shows No. 3292 as originally built in December 1897. She was then unnamed and carried the large cab with side windows and large-shaped windows in the spectacle plate. Five months later the engine received nameplates, which were fixed to the boiler side, but followed the arc of the leading driver and the name given to her was *Badminton*.

The next nineteen engines built in this class were all named as built, and were fitted with the narrow cab as seen in *Figure 488*. This engine was No. 3302 *Mortimer* which in the picture had the name blacked out. She was renamed *Charles Mortimer* in September of 1904.

Figure 490

Figure 491

Three 'Badmintons' are illustrated here, all 'as built'. In *Figure 490* we see No. 3295 *Bessborough* which was the fourth engine to be constructed in the series. She is seen standing outside the works, just after being used as a stand-in for the Royal Train. This can be seen from the brackets on the tender sides, which were affixed there to carry the Royal coat-of-arms (see *Figure 493)*.

A full broadside shot of No. 3300 *Hotspur* is shown in *Figure 491* and illustrates well the elegant proportions of these four coupled express engines. The driving wheels were of course the full 6′ 8″ and with steel centres, being another size and feature carried through to the 'Castles'.

Lower right, *Figure 492* is No. 3303 *Marlborough* in works undercoat. The small feature which personified all the 'Badmintons', namely the domed steam turret on top of the firebox, can clearly be seen. This turret was for obtaining dry steam for whistles, injectors, and other ancillary equipment, which had their supply emitting from this small dome.

Figure 492

Amongst the 'Badminton' class was No. 3297 named *Earl Cawdor*. This engine began with the illustrious duty of working the new Royal Train, and *Figure 493* shows the engine standing outside the drawing office carrying the coat-of-arms, the crown embellished headlamp and the three target discs which were always indicative of Royal Train working. Particular note should be paid to the adapted tender which was enlarged at the rear to carry more water and to enable the train to run non-stop on this particular journey to convey the Queen from Windsor to Folkestone.

In the 'Badminton' class of twenty engines there was one odd member, being No. 3310 *Waterford*. Underframe and running gear were similar to the other nineteen, but there the similarity ended. No. 3310 had a steel firebox and a boiler with a maximum outside diameter of 4′ 7½″ standing with its centre line 8′ 6″ above rail head level, nearly one foot higher than the rest of the class. A different cab

Figure 494

Figure 493

was fitted, wide, with no side windows, and a large non-standard oval name and number plate affixed to the locomotive. The boiler fittings were unusual, consisting of a short chimney and a 'Ramsbottom' valve, situated on the dome position. Here we see, surely, the prototype of the 'Atbara' class.

Two other points which should be mentioned about the 'Badmintons', are that the main and coupling rod cranks were unbalanced, being of the 'Stroudley' pattern with corresponding centres on the same side. This necessitated large crescent-shaped balance weights on the wheels. Also, this class of locomotive was fitted with steam sanding gear.

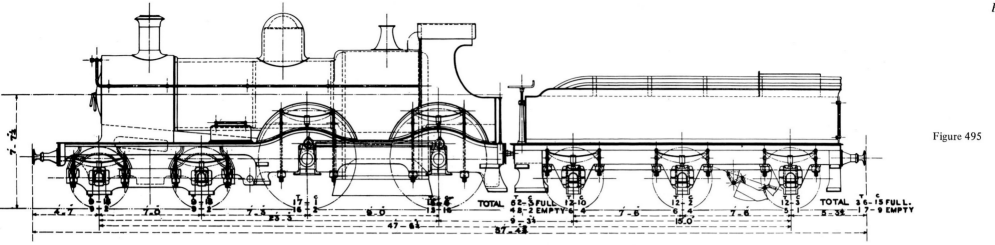

Figure 495

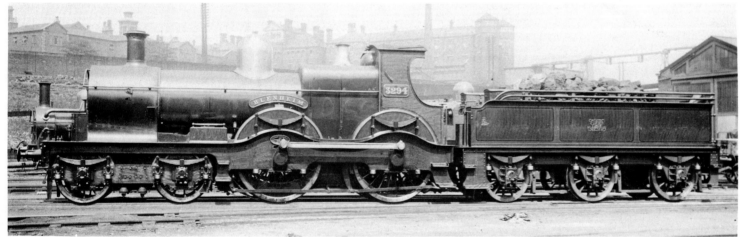

Figure 496

On this page is shown the official *Diagram J* of the 'Badminton' class, built under *Lot 109*. There were only twenty engines in the class, including *Waterford* and *Earl Cawdor*.

A complete list of names is given below:-

| | | | |
|---|---|---|---|
| 3292 (4100) | *Badminton* | 3293 (4101) | *Barrington* |
| 3294 (4102) | *Blenheim* | 3295 (4103) | *Bessborough* |
| 3296 (4104) | *Cambria* | 3297 (4105) | *Earl Cawdor* |
| 3298 (4106) | *Grosvenor* | 3299 (4107) | *Alexander* |
| 3300 (4108) | *Hotspur* | | *Hubbard* |
| 3301 (4109) | *Monarch* | 3302 (4110) | *Mortimer* |
| 3303 (4111) | *Marlborough* | 3304 (4112) | *Oxford* |
| 3305 (4113) | *Samson* | 3306 (4114) | *Shelburne* |
| 3307 (4115) | *Shrewsbury* | 3308 (4116) | *Savernake* |
| 3309 (4117) | *Shakespeare* | 3310 (4118) | *Waterford* |
| 3311 (4119) | *Wynnstay* | | |

*Figure 496* illustrates No. 3294 *Blenheim* as built and the upper diagram is a 4mm scale reduction of the special drawing Swindon made of this engine. *Figure 497* is the official diagram of No. 3310 *Waterford*.

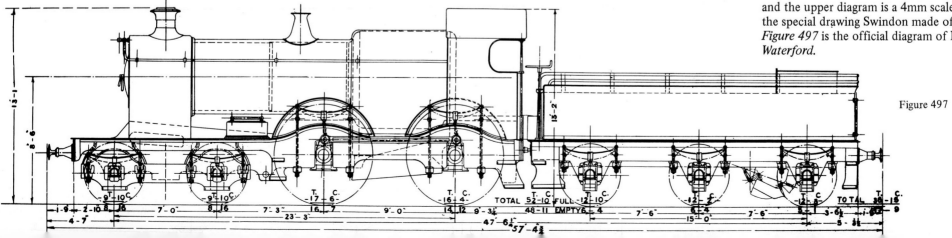

Figure 497

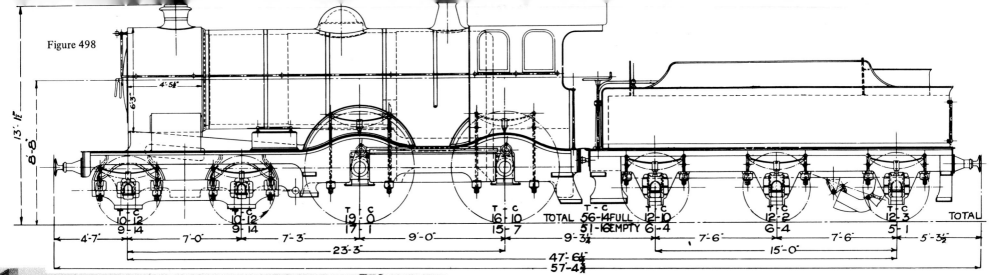

Figure 498

Figure 499

Figure 500

As mentioned previously *Earl Cawdor* was another experimental engine, starting out as a straightforward 'Badminton' class locomotive in 1903, but was eventually reconstructed in a completely new form. Always prepared to experiment, Churchward had been approached by his Chief Draughtsman, F. G. Wright, with an idea about a larger boiler with high reservoir capacity. Therefore, on to No. 3297 was erected the special round-topped firebox and boiler as seen in *Figure 501*. It was 11′6″ long and 5′5″ maximum diameter and its centre-line stood 8′8″ above rail level. The Swindon code for this special one-off boiler was S4X, and was so large that it required non-standard boiler fittings as can be seen by the chimney, dome and valve bonnet. There was a huge smoke box of 6′3″ diameter and a large roomy cab of Great Eastern Railway style. In fact, the engine was similar in many ways to *Claud Hamilton*.

Figure 501

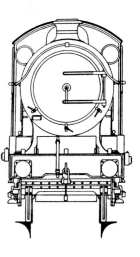

*Figure 501* shows the engine in 1903 as reconstructed, and *Figure 500* shows how a couple of years later the double window cab was removed and replaced with a standard wide cab. *Figure 499* shows No. 3309 *Shakespeare* as built, and the large balance weights can be seen clearly.

The Swindon diagram which was prepared for this engine is shown in *Figure 498* and is letter 'O'. It surely was a 'big' engine as was the Great Eastern *Claud*.

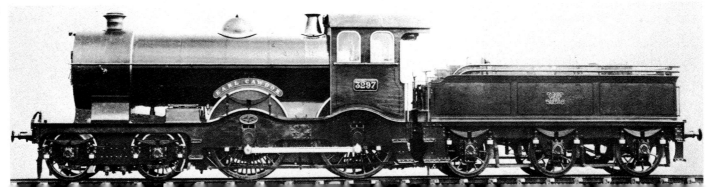

Figure 502

*Earl Cawdor* in the 1903 condition, is seen again in *Figure 502* but this time showing the right-hand side, *Figure 503* shows the final phase, when the engines were fitted with the tapered boilers and superheated, all being renumbered from No. 4100 to No. 4119 joining the 'Atbara' and 'Flower' classes.

The rebuilt 'Badmintons' could always be identified in later days, amongst the 'Atbaras' and 'Flowers' in that they were the only series with the curved frames in the 41XX numbering. *Figure 504* shows No. 4111 *Marlborough* as running in 1928 with a taper cast iron chimney, and the original engine *Badminton* at Swindon factory in 1927 with built up chimney *(Figure 505)*.

Figure 503

Figure 504

The drawing by Colonel Templer gives full-size measurements in feet, and dimensions in millimetres for 'O' gauge.

In *Figure 506* the chimney appears correct for the four rebuilt Armstrong 4-4-0's renumbered 4169-4172, but could be inaccurate for any others of the class.

Figure 505

Figure 506

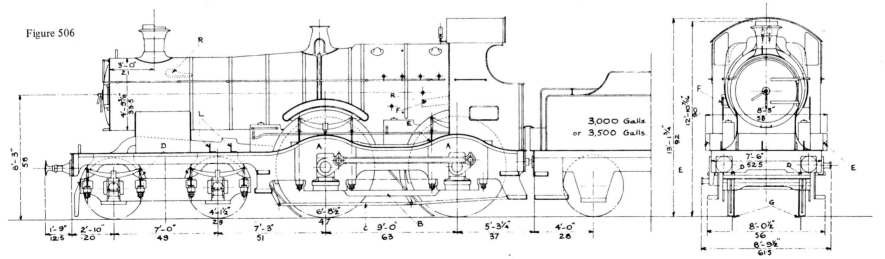

NOTES. *Details marked R on right side only, those marked L on left side only.   A, strengthening plates, separate, as shown, or as single long plate to chain line;*
*B, horn tie, omitted in some engines;   C, brake rigging outside wheels;   D, bogie splashers flush with frame;   E, point where running-plate widens towards*
*rear,  F, reverse rod cover;  G, wheel treads and flanges drawn to scale; allowances must be made for out-of-scale wheels. Dimensions in feet (full size) and*
*in millimetres, to the nearest half m'metre for Gauge "O".*

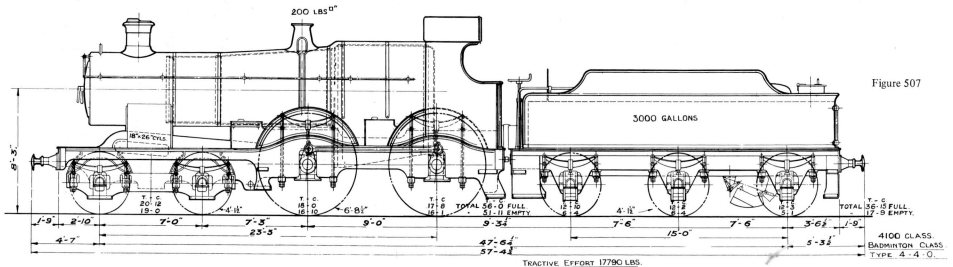

200 LBS□″

Figure 507

18″×26″CYLS.

3000 GALLONS

8′-3″

T. C. 20·12 / 19·0    4′-1½″    T. C. 18·0 / 16·10    6′-8½″    T. C. 17·8 / 16·1    TOTAL 56·0 FULL / 51·11 EMPTY    12·10 / 6·4    4′-1½″    12·2 / 6·4    12·3 / 5·1    TOTAL 36·15 FULL / 17·9 EMPTY.

1′-9″  2′-10″    7′-0″    7′-3″    9′-0″    9′-3¼″    7′-6″    15′-0″    7′-6″    3′-6½″  1′-9″

4′-7″    23′-5″    47′-6¼″    57′-4½″    5′-3½″

4100 CLASS.
BADMINTON CLASS.
TYPE 4-4-0.

TRACTIVE EFFORT 17790 LBS.

Figure 509

Figure 508

This official Swindon *Drawing A24,* gives a better idea of the built-up chimney, but the framing in relation to the motion steps seems to be slightly inaccurate in the drawing.

No. 4113 *Samson* is seen on the Swindon test plant in 1928, and is the final condition of the class, as she was withdrawn three years later in 1931, and in fact was the last to go *(Figure 508).* In the small photograph *Figure 509,* No. 4107 *Alexander Hubbard* is shown approaching Astrop in 1925 with a down Birmingham express.

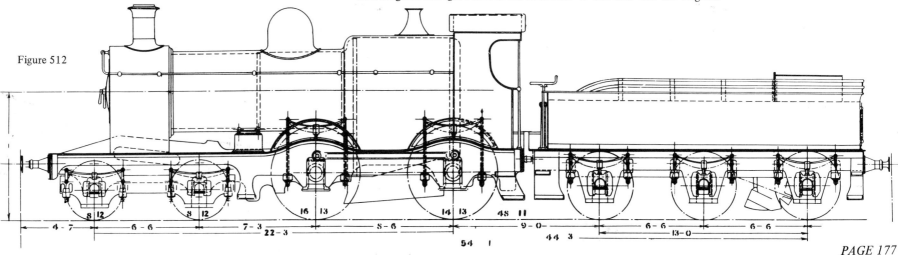

Figure 510

Figure 511

Having already mentioned the 'Duke' class previously, there was one engine which although ordered on the same Lot as the '3252' class, was nevertheless, an experimental engine, and became the first in a long line of small-wheeled light passenger locomotives known to all as the 'Bulldogs'.

As can be seen in these two early rather faded photographs, No. 3312 was below the underframe a 'Duke' but carried Churchward's standard No. 2 boiler, and an unusual cab design. There were pillars from the cab roof to the framing, and on the right-hand side, the contour had a cutaway forward, as well as aft, to cover the screw reversing gear. On the fireman's side a door opened out of the spectacle plate, and gave access to the running plate. The nameplate was of the straight type and fixed to the firebox side. This was changed to the normal curved type over the leading driver when the engine was rebuilt in 1906. At the renumbering the engine became No. 3311. This was an interesting and historical engine, linking as she did, the 'Duke' and the 'Bulldog' classes. The diagram in *Figure 512* is the *Swindon 'G'* for this 'one-off' engine.

Figure 512

Figure 513

Before moving on to the tender drawings, what better than to recap on the Great Western progress in locomotive design so far, by means of these three official photographs. *Figure 513* shows *Sylph* of 1846 with her proud crew and admirers, *Figure 514* illustrates the powerful *Dragon,* also with crew and admirers, and finally, as far as Volume I goes, an example of the pure 'Churchward' engine, No. 3386 *Pembroke,* one of the 'Atbara' class, shown as built in 1900, again with the faithful crew and admirer, *Figure 515.*

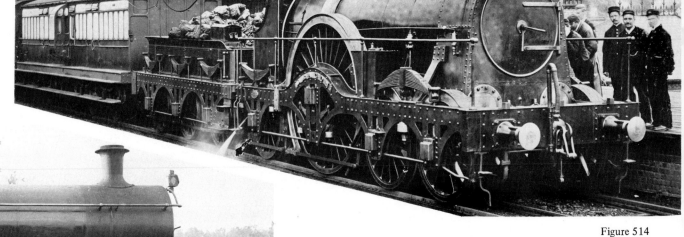

Figure 514

Figure 515

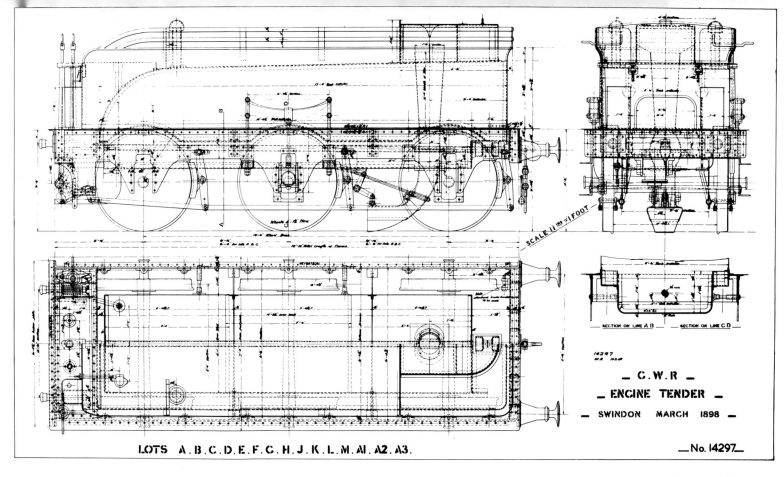

_ G.W.R _

_ ENGINE TENDER _

_ SWINDON    MARCH  1898 _

_No. 14297_

LOTS  A. B. C. D. E. F. G. H. J. K. L. M. A1. A2. A3.

Figure 516

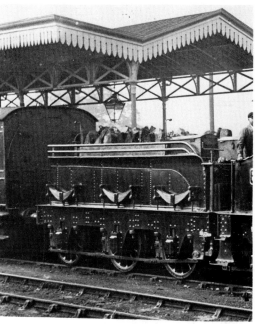

Figure 516A

To keep the collection as complete as possible, six works drawings of early Swindon tenders have been included, all of the narrow gauge. To enable dimensions to be readable, these six reproductions are to 7mm to 1′ scale (O gauge).

Photographic link-ups with these drawings can be found in these pages. The general arrangement drawing in *Figure 516* is of the early tenders, which when first constructed had a capacity of 1,800 gallons. The Lot letters and numbers can be read on the drawing and according to records, the building dates were between 1870 and 1877. This particular drawing was probably to show the fitting of water pick-up in 1898.

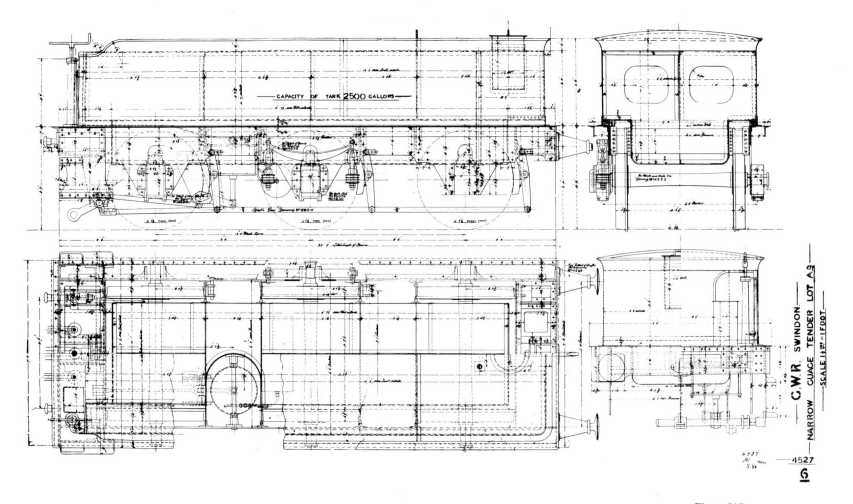

Figure 517

A larger tender with no coal rails or water pick-up is shown
in *Figure 517*. This is a 'general arrangement' drawing of the
Lot 'A9' built in 1887. There were only 10 built to this Lot,
with a water capacity of 2,500 gallons. For photograph see
pages 22 and 38.

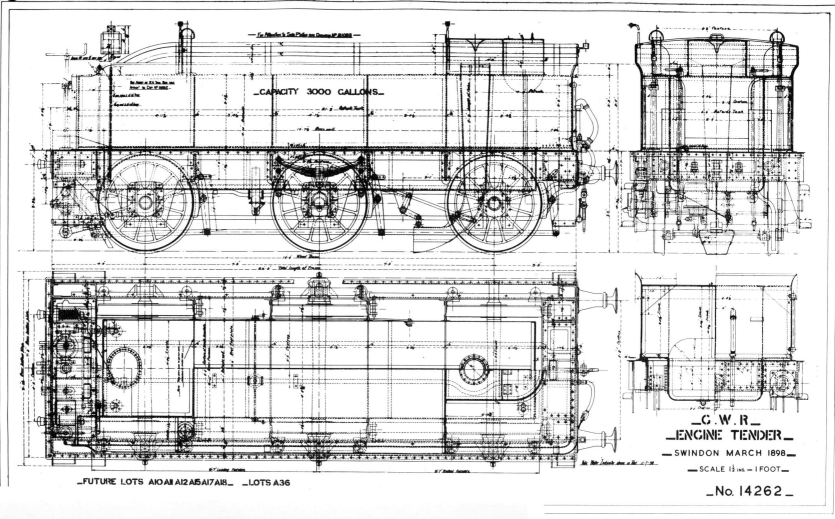

Figure 519

CAPACITY 3000 GALLONS

FUTURE LOTS A10 A11 A12 A15 A17 A18 — LOTS A36

_G.W.R_
_ENGINE TENDER_
— SWINDON MARCH 1898 —
— SCALE 1½ INS. = 1 FOOT —
_No. 14262_

Figure 518

A still larger tender, with a water tank holding 3,000 gallons, *(Figure 518)* shows the big tender built to Lots A10, A11, A12, A15, A17, A18 and A36 in the years from 1890 to 1899.

The picture of *Waterford* in *Figure 519* shows the engine coupled to a tender of this series.

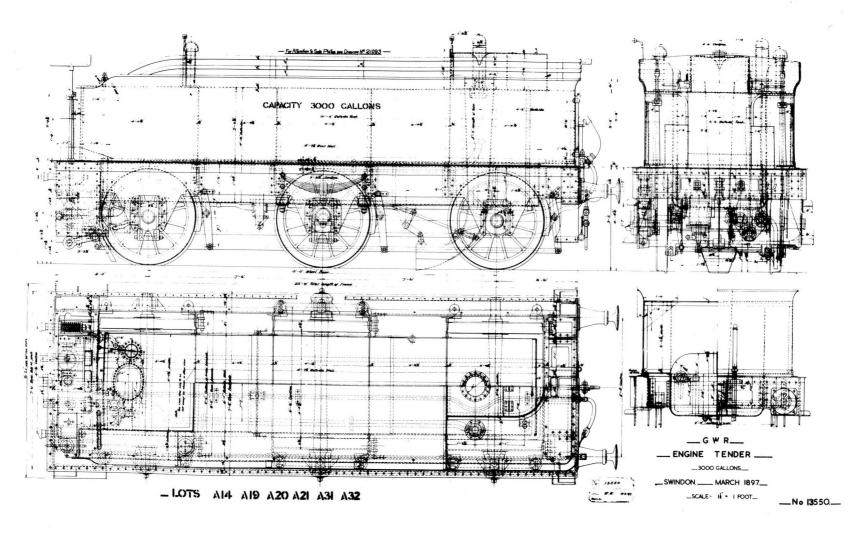

CAPACITY 3000 GALLONS

— LOTS A14 A19 A20 A21 A31 A32

G W R
— ENGINE TENDER —
3000 GALLONS
SWINDON — MARCH 1897
SCALE 1½" = 1 FOOT — No 13550

Figure 520

The tenders built to the Lots A14, A19, A20, A21, A31 and A32, were very similar to the previous class shown on the preceding page with certain exceptions. They were fitted with an overflow pipe and fountain for use with engines which were equipped with crosshead driven water feed pumps. These were built between 1891 and 1899. For illustration see page 51, *Figure 128.*

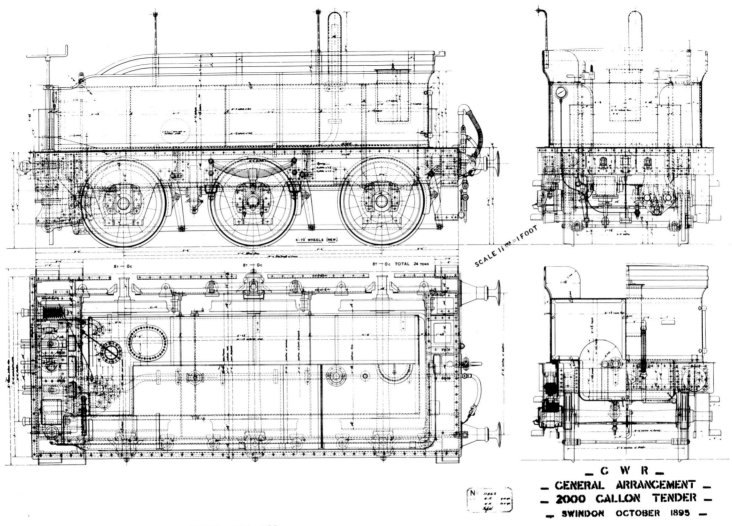

_ G W R _
_ CENERAL ARRANGEMENT _
_ 2000 GALLON TENDER _
_ SWINDON OCTOBER 1895 _

_ LOTS A24 A25

Figure 521

This class of small tender, with a wheelbase of only 11′
was built for use with the '3521' class the 'Stella' series, and
later, the 'Dukes'. When new, the first two Lots had 'Mansell'
solid wheels as can be seen in this drawing of the A24/A25
series, built in 1895 and 1896. Water capacity was only 2,000
gallons. Good pictures of this tender can be seen on page 163.

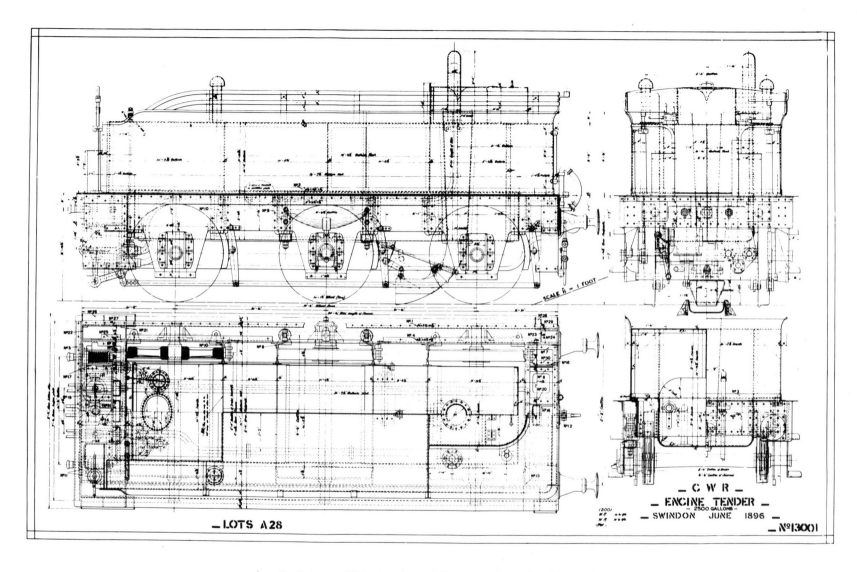

_ LOTS A28 _

_ G W R _
_ ENGINE TENDER _
2500 GALLONS
_ SWINDON   JUNE   1896 _
_ Nº 13001

Figure 522

An intermediate tender, with a capacity of 2,500 gallons and a wheelbase of 13′, is illustrated in *Figure 522*. Only one was built to this order, and used first on the Dean 4-6-0 goods engine No. 36 in 1896. It survived for many years, being coupled to 'Bulldogs' and Dean goods amongst other engines, and was finally scrapped in 1949.

Its running number was 1178. See page 150.

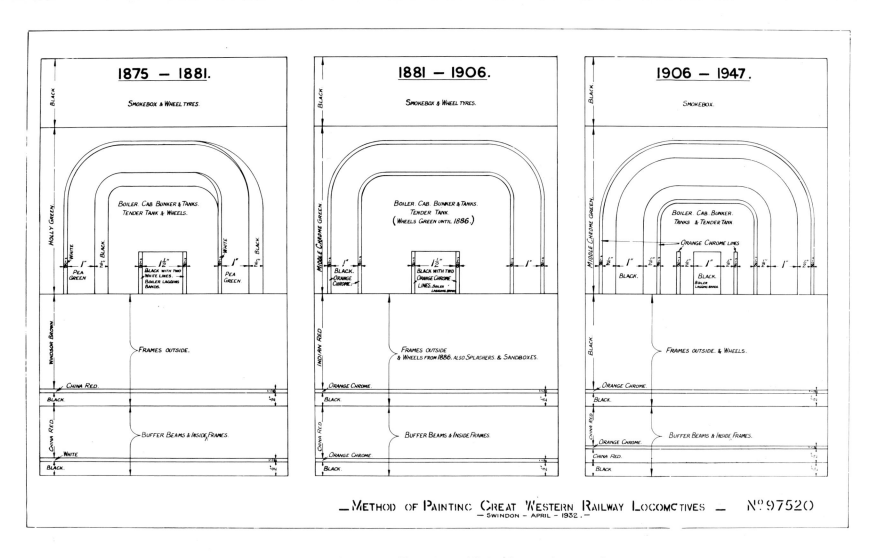

Figure 523

The official drawing of 'painting and lining' locomotives covering the years from 1875 to 1947 is shown on this page. The diagram is self explanatory and was prepared at Swindon in 1932. It is useful to note the correct widths of the various colours!

Before bringing Volume I to a conclusion, there is appended a complete Lot index from the official Diagram book at Swindon, in which can be found all the various classes and types since this system came into being. It should serve as a useful link between the two volumes of this collection.

Note that the Lots with alphabetical letters are the Wolverhampton series, whereas Swindon lots are all numerically ordered.

| Lot | Engine No. | Type | Diagram |
|---|---|---|---|
| A | 372 - 377. 1006 - 1011 | 2-4-0 | I |
| B | 1016 - 1027 | 0-6-0T | I. A.26. B.17. |
| C | 1028 - 1039 | 0-6-0T | I. A.26. B.17. |
| D | 517 - 528 | 0-4-2T | A.B.E.F.H.L. |
| E | 529 - 540 | 0-4-2T | A.B.E.F.H.L. |
| F | 541 - 552 | 0-4-2T | A.B.E.F.H.L. |
| G | 553 - 564 | 0-4-2T | A.B.E.F.H.L. |
| H | 565 - 576 | 0-4-2T | A.B.E.F.H.L. |
| I | 1421 - 1432 | 0-4-2T | A.B.E.F.G.L. |
| J | 1040 - 1051 | 0-6-0T | I. A.28. B.17. |
| K | 1052 - 1063 | 0-6-0T | I. A.28. B.17. |
| L | 1064 - 1075 | 0-6-0T | I. A.28. B.17. |
| M | 633 - 644 | 0-6-0T | A.59. A.62. |
| O | 645 - 654 | 0-6-0T | K. A.35. 40. 41. |
| P | 656. 757 - 763 | 0-6-0T | K. A.35. 40.41. |
| Q | 764 - 766. 768 - 775 | 0-6-0T | K. A.35. 40.41. |
| R | 826 - 837 | 0-4-2T | B.E.F.H.L. |
| S | 838 - 849 | 0-4-2T | F. L. |
| T | 850 - 861 | 0-6-0T | L.A.14. 31. B.51. |
| V | 862 - 873 | 0-6-0T | L.A.14. 31. B.51. |
| W | 1154 - 1165 | 0-4-2T | F.L. |
| X | 987 - 998 | 0-6-0T | L.A.14. 31. B.51. |
| Y | 1216 - 1227 | 0-6-0T | L.A.14. 31. B.51. |
| Z | 202 - 205. 215 - 222 | 0-4-2T | B.F.L. |
| A2 | 1501 - 1512 | 0-6-0T | K.A.35. 40. 41. |
| B2 | 1513 - 1524 | 0-6-0T | K.A.35. 40. 41. |
| C2 | 1433 - 1444 | 0-4-2T | B.E.F.L. |
| D2 | 1525 - 1536 | 0-6-0T | K.A.35. 40. 41. |
| E2 | 1537 - 1548 | 0-6-0T | K.A.35. 40. 41. |
| F2 | 1549 - 1560 | 0-6-0T | K.A.35. 40. 41. |
| G2 | 1801 - 1812 | 0-6-0T | K.A.35. 40. 41. |
| H2 | 45 | 0-4-0T | B |
| J2 | 1901 - 1912 | 0-6-0T | L.A.14. 31. B.51. |
| K2 | 132.135.136.139.141-6 310 - 313. 315 | 0-6-0 | K.Z. |
| L2 | 1913 - 1924 | 0-6-0T | L.A.14.31. B.51. |
| M2 | 1465 - 1476 | 0-4-2T | E.F.G.H.L. |
| O2 | 1925 - 1936 | 0-6-0T | L. A.14. 31. B.51. |
| P2 | 1477 - 1488 | 0-4-2T | A.E.F.G.H. |
| Q2 | 1937 - 1948 | 0-6-0T | L. A.14. 31. B.51. |
| R2 | 1949 - 1960 | 0-6-0T | L. A.14. 31. B.51. |
| S2 | 3226 - 3231 | 2-4-0 | J.V. |
| T2 | 1961 - 1972 | 0-6-0T | L. A.14. 31. B.51. |
| V2 | 1973 - 1984 | 0-6-0T | L. A.14. 31. B.51. |
| W2 | 316 - 318 | 0-6-0 | B. |
| X2 | 1985 - 1996 | 0-6-0T | L. A.14. 31. B.51. |
| Y2 | 1997 - 2008 | 0-6-0T | L. A.14. 31. B.51. |
| Z2 | 2009 - 2020 | 0-6-0T | L. A.14. 31. B.51. |
| A3 | 655. 767. 1741-1750 | 0-6-0T | A.36. 42. B.65. |
| B3 | 1771 - 1790 | 0-6-0T | A.36. 42. B.65. |
| C3 | 3571 - 3580 | 0-4-2T | D.I. |
| D3 | 2021 - 2030 | 0-6-0T | N.O. A.38. B.52. |
| E3 | 2701 - 2720 | 0-6-0T | A.18. 36. 42. B.65. |
| F3 | 2031 - 2040 | 0-6-0T | N. O. A.38. B.52. |
| G3 | 2041 - 2060 | 0-6-0T | N. O. A.38. B.52. |
| H3 | 2061 - 2080 | 0-6-0T | N. O. A.38. B.52. |
| J3 | 2081 - 2100 | 0-6-0T | N. O. A.38. B.52. |
| K3 | 2101 - 2120 | 0-6-0T | N. O. A.38. B.52. |
| L3 | 2121 - 2140 | 0-6-0T | N. O. A.38. B.52. |
| M3 | 2141 - 2160 | 0-6-0T | N. O. A.38. B.52. |
| N3 | 4500 - 4519 | 2-6-2T | K. A.2. |
| 1 | 379 - 382. 384 - 387 | 0-6-0 | A.V. |
| 1st | 57 - 68 | 0-6-0 | B.A.3. |
| 1st renl | 37. 238. 1012 - 1014 | 0-6-0 | C. A.7. |
| 2&3 | 79 - 90. 122 | 0-6-0 | D. A.2. 8. |
| 4 | 119 - 121. 123. 124 | 0-6-0T | A. A.34. |
| 5 | 125 - 130 | 0-6-0T | A. A.34. |
| 6&7 | See K.2. Lot | | |
| 8 | 360 - 369.1001.1015 | 0-6-0 | E. A.6. |
| 9 | 388 - 406 | 0-6-0 | F. A.2. 9. |
| 10 | 26.38.42.407-12.419-25 | " | F. A.2. 9. |
| 11 | 429 - 438 | 0-6-0 | F. A.2. 9. |
| 14 | 439 - 444 | 2-4-0 | A. |
| 15 | 445 - 454 | 0-6-0 | F. A.2. 9. |
| 16 | 370.371.426 - 428 | 0-6-0 | F. A.2. 9. |
| 17 | 41.43.44.46.50 | 0-6-0 | F. A.2. 9. |
| 18 | 3 - 6. 455 - 470 | 2-4-0T | A.K. |
| 19 | 471 - 78.480.577 - 86 | 0-6-0 | A.V. |
| 20 | 12.19.20.54.483.486 | 2-4-0 | B.X. |
| 20 | 489.490. 587 - 592 | 2-4-0 | B.X. |
| 21 | 491 - 516.1082 - 85 | 0-6-0 | F. A.2. 9. |
| 22 | 1076 - 1081 | 0-6-0T | B. A.17. |
| 23 | 593 - 602. 1086 - 1105 | 0-6-0 | F. A.2. 9. |
| 24 | 603 - 612.1106 - 1115 | 0-6-0 | F. A.2. 9. |
| 25 | 613 - 21.623 - 30. 632 | 2-4-0T | B.1. |
| 26 | 24.31.48.51.52.116 | 0-6-0 | F. A.2. 9. |
| 26 | 298. 300. 415. 416 | 0-6-0 | F. A.2. 9. |
| 26 | 657 - 676 | 0-6-0 | F. A.2. 9. |
| 27 | 56 | 2-4-0 | C.T. |
| 28 | 677 - 716 | 0-6-0 | F. A.2. 9. |
| 29 | 717 - 726 | 2-4-0 | C.T. |
| 30 | 727 - 756 | 0-6-0T | B. A.17. |
| 31 | 776 - 805 | 0-6-0 | F. A.2. 9. |
| 32 | 806 - 815. 817 - 825 | 2-4-0 | D. S. |
| 33 | 55 | 2-2-2 | A. |
| 34 | 999.1000. 1116 - 33 | 2-2-2 | A. D. |
| 35 | 874 - 893 | 0-6-0 | F. A.2. 9. |
| 36 | 927 - 946 | 0-6-0 | G. Y. |
| 37 | 947 - 966 | 0-6-0T | B. A.17. 61. |
| 38 | 967 - 986 | 2-4-0T | B.I. |
| 39 | 1134 - 1153 | 0-6-0T | B. A.17. 61. |
| 40 | 1166 - 1185 | 0-6-0T | B. A.17. 61. |
| .41 | 21.22.23.25.27.29. | 0-6-0 | F. A. 2. 9. |
| 41 | 32. 39. 53. 117. | 0-6-0 | F. A. 2. 9. |
| 41 | 1186 - 1195 | 0-6-0 | F. A. 2. 9. |
| 42 | 1196 - 1215 | 0-6-0 | F. A. 2. 9. |
| 43 | 1228 - 1247 | 0-6-0T | B. A.17. 22. |
| 44 | 1248 - 1267 | 0-6-0T | B. A.17. 22. |
| 45 | 1268 - 1297 | 0-6-0T | B. A.17. 22. |
| 46 | 1 | 2-4-0T | D.L. |
| 47 | 1401 - 1420 | 2-4-0T | C.H. |
| 48 | 1561 - 1580 | 0-6-0T | B.A.17.22.61. |
| 49 | 1581 - 1600 | 0-6-0T | B.A.17.22.61. |
| 50 | 1601 - 1620 | 0-6-0T | B.A.17.22.61. |
| 51 | 157 - 166 | 2-2-2 | B. |
| 52 | 1621 - 1640 | 0-6-0T | B. A.17. 22. 61. |
| 54 | 9 | 2-2-2 | B. |
| 55 | 1641 - 1660 | 0-6-0T | B. A.17. 22. 61. |
| 56 | 2201 - 2220 | 2-4-0 | D. S. |
| 57 | 1445 - 1464 | 2-4-0T | B. I. |
| 58 | 1833 | 0-6-0 | H. |
| 59 | 1813 - 1832 | 0-6-0T | C. A.9. 23. 49. B.66. |
| 60 | 1834 - 1853 | 0-6-0T | C. A.9. 23. 49. B.66. |
| 61 | 2301 - 2320 | 0-6-0 | I. T. A.10. |
| 62 | 2321 - 2340 | 0-6-0 | I. T. A.10. |
| 63 | 2341 - 2360 | 0-6-0 | I. T. A.10. |
| 64 | 3501 - 3520 | 2-4-0 | E.O.Y. |
| 65 | 3201 - 3205 | 2-4-0 | E.O.Y. |
| 66 | 10 | 2-2-2 | C. |
| 67 | 2361 - 2380 | 0-6-0 | J. U. A.12. |
| 68 | 7 | 4-4-0 | T. A.4. 12. 26. |
| 69 | 1661 - 1680 | 0-6-0T | D. A.21. 29. 47. |
| 70 | 8 | 4-4-0 | A. A.4. 12. 26. |
| 71 | 1681 - 1700 | 0-6-0T | D. A.21. 29. 47. |
| 72 | 13 | 4-4-0T | A. |
| 73 | 3521 - 3540 | 4-4-0 | BCDUA.3.8.13.20.21.22.27. |
| 74 | 4169. 4170 | 4-4-0 | T. A.4. 12.26. |
| 75 | 3206 - 3225 | 2-4-0 | F.P.A.1. 2. 8. |
| 76 | 3541 - 3560 | 4-4-0 | BCDUA.3.8.13.20.21.22.27. |
| 77 | 28 | 2-4-0 | B |
| 79 | 1854 - 1873 | 0-6-0T | E.A.19.25.45. B.56. |
| 80 | 481. 482. 484. 485 | 2-4-0 | B.X. |
| 81 | 34. 35. | 0-4-4T | A. |
| 82 | 2381 - 2400 | 0-6-0 | I. T. A.10. |
| 83 | 1874 - 1893 | 0-6-0T | E.A.19.25.45. B.56. |
| 84 | 3001 - 3020 | 4-2-2 | A. C. D. F. |
| 85 | 1701 - 1720 | 0-6-0T | E.A.19.25.45. B.56. |
| 86 | 3021 - 3030 | 4-2-2 | A. C. F. |
| 87 | 2401 - 2430 | 0-6-0 | I. T. A.10. |
| 88 | 1721 - 1740 | 0-6-0T | E.A.19.25.45. B.56. |
| 89 | 1751 - 1770 | 0-6-0T | E.A.19.25.45. B.56. |
| 90 | 3232 - 3241 | 2-4-0 | G. Q. A.6. 10. |
| 91 | 1491 - 1500 | 2-4-0T | B.1. |
| 92 | 2431 - 2450 | 0-6-0 | I. T. A.10. |
| 93 | 3242 - 3251 | 2-4-0 | G. Q. A.6. |
| 94 | 3031 - 3040 | 4-2-2 | B. C. F. |

| Lot | Engine No. | Type | Diagram |
|---|---|---|---|
| 95 | 3041 - 3060 | 4-2-2 | B. C. D. F. |
| 96 | 3561 - 3570 | 2-4-0T | B.I. |
| 97 | 3252 | 4-4-0 | E.A.6.9.18.29.30. |
| 97 | 3300 | 4-4-0 | E.H.S.A.2.15.25. |
| 98 | 1791-1800. 1894 -1900 | 0-6-0T | E.A.19.25.45. B.56. |
| 99 | 2451 - 2470 | 0-6-0 | I. T. A.10. |
| 100 | 2471 - 2490 | 0-6-0 | I. T. A.10. |
| 101 | 3253 - 3260 | 4-4-0 | E.A.6.9.18.29.30. |
| 102 | 3261 - 3265 | 4-4-0 | E.A.6.9.18.29.30.A.40. |
| 102 | 3301 - 3305 | 4-4-0 | E.H.S.A.2.15.25. |
| 103 | 69 - 76 | 2-4-0 | H.R. |
| 104 | 2491 - 2510 | 0-6-0 | I. T. A.10. |
| 105 | 3266 - 3280 | 4-4-0 | A.6.9.18.29.30.39. |
| 105 | 3306 - 3310 | 4-4-0 | E.H.S.A.2.15.25. |
| 106 | 36 | 4-6-0 | A. |
| 107 | 2511 - 2530 | 0-6-0 | I. T. A.10. |
| 108 | 2531 - 2550 | 0-6-0 | I. T. A.10. |
| 109 | 4100 - 4119 | 4-4-0 | J.K.Y.A.5.14.24. |
| 110 | 3061 - 3080 | 4-2-2 | B. C. E. F. |
| 111 | 2551 - 2580 | 0-6-0 | I. T. A.10. |
| 112 | 2721 - 2740 | 0-6-0T | F.A.12.20.30.46. B.47.55. |
| 113 | 3281 - 3291 | 4-4-0 | A.6.9.18.29.30. |
| 113 | 3311 - 3319 | 4-4-0 | E.H.S.A.2.15.25. |
| 114 | 1490 | 4-4-0T | B. |
| 115 | 2741 - 2760 | 0-6-0T | F.A.12.20.30.46. B.47.55. |
| 116 | 2601 (see lot 156) | 4-6-0 | B. |
| 116 | 2602 - 2610 (See L.166) | 2-6-0 | A. |
| 117 | 3581 - 3590 | 2-4-0T | C. H. |
| 118 | 3320 - 3339 | 4-4-0 | E.H.S.A.2.15.25. |
| 119 | 3591. 3592. 3594 - | 2-4-0T | C. H. |
| 119 | 3599. 3500 | 2-4-0T | C. H. |
| 119 | 3593 | 2-4-2T | D. I. |
| 120 | 3340 | 4-4-0 | A.2.15.25. |
| 121 | 17. 18 Crane | 0-6-4T | A |
| 122 | 2761 - 2780 | 0-6-0T | F.A.12.20 B47 30.46 B55 |
| 123 | 2611 - 2620 | 2-6-0 | D.F.I.Q. |
| 124 | 3341 - 3360 | 4-4-0 | P.W.A. 11.23 |
| 125 | 4120 - 4138 | 4-4-0 | L.A. 1.24 |
| 126 | 4139 - 4148 | 4-4-0 | L.A. 1.24 |
| 126 | 3700 - 3709 | 4-4-0 | M.Z. A.17. |
| 128 | 2600 | 2-6-0 | F.I.Q. |
| 129 | 2781 - 2799. 2700 | 0-6-0T | G.H.A.11.43 B47 44. B55 |
| 130 | 3600 | 2-4-2T | A.C.H. |
| 131 | 2621 - 2640 | 2-6-0 | C.D.F.I.Q. |
| 132 | 2900 | 4-6-0 | C.P. |
| 133 | 2641 - 2660 | 2-6-0 | C.D.F.I.Q. |
| 134 | 3601 - 3620 | 2-4-2T | B.C.G.H. |
| 135 | 2661 - 2680 | 2-6-0 | D.F.I.Q. |
| 136 | 101 | 0-4-0T | A. |
| 137 | 3361 - 3380 | 4-4-0 | P.W.A. 11.23 |
| 138 | 2998 | 4-6-0 | D.O. |

| Lot | Engine No. | Type | Diagram |
|---|---|---|---|
| 139 | 2800 | 2-8-0 | A.B.C.D. |
| 140 | 3100 | 2-6-2T | A.J.A. 3.7. |
| 141 | 3710 - 3719 | 4-4-0 | M.Z.A.17. |
| 142 | 3381 - 3390 | 4-4-0 | P.W.A. 11.23 |
| 143 | 3621 - 3630 | 2-4-2T | C.G.H. |
| 144 | 4400 | 2-6-2T | C.O.A.4. |
| 145 | 2971 | 4-6-0 | E.O. |
| 146 | 102 | 4-4-2 | A.G.1. |
| 147 | 4401 - 4410 | 2-6-2T | C.O.A.4. |
| 148 | 3391 - 3410 | 4-4-0 | P.W.A. 11.23 |
| 149 | 3800. 3831 - 39 | 4-4-0 | N.X. |
| 150 | 3111 - 3120 | 2-6-2T | B.I.P.R.T.A.7. |
| 151 | 2221 - 2230 | 4-4-2T | A.B.C.E.G. |
| 152 | 3121 - 3130 | 2-6-2T | B.I.P.R.T.A.7. |
| 153 | 2801 - 2810 | 2-8-0 | B.C.D. |
| 154 | 2972 - 2980 | 4-6-0 | E.O. |
| 155 | 2811 - 2820 | 2-8-0 | B. C. D. |
| 156 | 2601 | 2-6-0 | D. F. I. Q. |
| 157 | 103. 104 | 4-4-2 | C. E. H. |
| 158 | 2981 - 2990 | 4-6-0 | O. |
| 159 | 3131 - 3150 | 2-6-2T | B. I. T. A.7. |
| 160 | 2821 - 2830 | 2-8-0 | B. C. D. |
| 161 | 4000 | 4-6-0 | M. T. Y. |
| 162 | 3411 - 3425 | 4-4-0 | P. W. A.11. 23. |
| 163 | 3426 - 3440 | 4-4-0 | P. W. A.11. 23. |
| 164 | 2901 - 2910 | 4-6-0 | F. O. |
| 165 | 3801 - 3820 | 4-4-0 | N. |
| 166 | 2602 - 2610 | 2-6-0 | D. F. I. Q. |
| 167 | 3901 - 3920 | 2-6-2T | F. N. A.8. |
| 168 | 4001 - 4010 | 4-6-0 | H. J. M. T. U. |
| 169 | 3151 - 3170 | 2-6-2T | E. H. L. S. |
| 170 | 2911 - 2930 | 4-6-0 | I. O. |
| 171 | 111 | 4-6-2 | A. B. C. |
| 172 | 3171 - 3190 | 2-6-2T | E. H. L. S. |
| 173 | 4011 - 4020 | 4-6-0 | H. M. T. U. |
| 174 | 4520 - 4529 | 2-6-2T | D. K. A.2. |
| 175 | 2231 - 2240 | 4-4-2T | A. B. C. E. G. |
| 176 | 4149 - 4168 | 4-4-0 | A. 16. 19. |
| 177 | 3441 - 3455 | 4-4-0 | A.7. 11. 23. |
| 178 | 4021 - 4030 | 4-6-0 | M. T. U. |
| 179 | 1361 - 1365 | 0-6-0T | A. 13. |
| 180 | 4031 - 4040 | 4-6-0 | Q. T. U. Y. A.10. |
| 181 | 2831 - 2835 | 2-8-0 | D. |
| 182 | 4201 | 2-8-0T | A. D. |
| 183 | 4301 - 4320 | 2-6-0 | G. L. |
| 184 | 3821 - 3830 | 4-4-0 | A. 10. 28. |
| 185 | 2931 - 2940 | 4-6-0 | R.V. |
| 186 | 2836 - 2845 | 2-8-0 | D. |
| 187 | 4202 - 4221 | 2-8-0T | D.E. |
| 188 | 2241 - 2250 | 4-4-2T | B.C.E.G. |
| 189 | 2941 - 2950 | 4-6-0 | R.V. |
| 190 | 2846 - 2855 | 2-8-0 | D.E. |
| 191 | 4530 - 4539 | 2-6-2T | K.M.A.2. |

| Lot | Engine No. | Type | Diagram |
|---|---|---|---|
| 192 | 2951 - 2955 | 4-6-0 | R.V. |
| 193 | 4321 - 4330 | 2-6-0 | H.K.M. |
| 194 | 4331 - 4340 | 2-6-0 | H.K.M. |
| 195 | 4041 - 4045 | 4-6-0 | Q.S.T.U.A.10 |
| 196 | 4222 - 4231 | 2-8-0T | A.B.D.E. |
| 197 | 4600 | 4-4-2T | D.F. |
| 198 | 4341 - 4360 | 2-6-0 | H.K.M. |
| 199 | 4046 - 4060 | 4-6-0 | S.U.A.10. |
| 200 | 4232 - 4241 | 2-8-0T | B.D.E. |
| 201 | 4540 - 4554 | 2-6-2T | K.A.2. |
| 202 | 4361 - 4380 | 2-6-0 | M. |
| 203 | 4242 - 4261 | 2-8-0T | C.D.E. |
| 204 | 4381 - 4399. 4300 | 2-6-0 | M. |
| 205 | 5300 - 5309 | 2-6-0 | M.P. |
| 206 | 5310 - 5329 | 2-6-0 | M.P. |
| 207 | 5330 - 5349 | 2-6-0 | M.P. |
| 208 | 5350 - 5369 | 2-6-0 | M.P. |
| 209 | 5370 - 5389 | 2-6-0 | M.P. |
| 210 | 2856 - 2883 | 2-8-0 | I. |
| 211 | 5390 - 5399 | 2-6-0 | M.P. |
| 211 | 6300 - 6317 | 2-6-0 | M. |
| 212 | 6318 - 6341 | 2-6-0 | M. |
| 213 | 4262 - 4285 | 2-8-0T | D.E. |
| 214 | 4700 | 2-8-0 | F.H.J.L. |
| 215 | 3000 - 3019 | 2-8-0 | G.K. |
| 216 | 6342 - 6361 | 2-6-0 | M. |
| 217 | 4061 - 4072 | 4-6-0 | U.A.10. |
| 218 | 6370 - 6399 | 2-6-0 | M. |
| 218 | 7300 - 7304 | 2-6-0 | M. |
| 219 | 16 Crane | 0-6-4T | C. |
| 220 | 4200. 4286 - 4299 | 2-8-0T | D. |
| 220 | 5200 - 5204 | 2-8-0T | D. |
| 221 | 4701 - 4708 | 2-8-0 | J. L. |
| 222 | 7305 - 7319 | 2-6-0 | M. |
| 223 | 5205 - 5214 | 2-8-0T | E. |
| 224 | 4073 - 4084 | 4-6-0 | W. Y. |
| 225 | 5215 - 5244 | 2-8-0T | E. |
| 226 | 4555 - 4574 | 2-6-2T | A.2. |
| 227 | 7. 8. | 2-6-2T | A.1. |
| 228 | 5600 - 5649 | 0-6-2T | A.30. |
| 229 | 15 Simplex | 0-4-0 | A. I.C.E. |
| 230 | 6362 - 6369 | 2-6-0 | M. |
| 230 | 7320. 7321 | 2-6-0 | M. |
| 231 | 696. 779. 935. 942 | 0-4-0T | Y.W. |
| 232 | 4083 - 4092 | 4-6-0 | W. Y. A.19.26. |
| 233 | 5245 - 5274 | 2-8-0T | E. |
| 234 | 4093 - 4099 | 4-6-0 | W. Y. A.19. 23. 26. |
| 234 | 5000 - 5012 | 4-6-0 | W. Y. A.19. 23. 26. |
| 235 | 5650 - 5699 | 0-6-2T | A.30. |
| 236 | 280.283.291.296 | 0-6-2T | A.2. 3. 4. 5. |
| 236 | 343. 361. 362. 390 | 0-6-2T | A.2. 3. 4. 5. |
| 236 | 397. 398. 402. 406 | 0-6-2T | A.2. 3. 4. 5. |
| 236 | 435 | 0-6-2T | A.2. 3. 4. 5. |

| Lot | Engine No. | Type | Diagram |
| --- | --- | --- | --- |
| 237 | 143. 238. 246 | 0-6-2T | I. A.1. |
| 238 | 2166. 2196 | 0-6-0T | A. 109. 111. |
| 238 | 21. 33. 48. 54. 83 | 0-6-2T | A.22.B.D.H.M.N.A.32. |
| 238 | 156. 158. 370. 380. | 0-6-2T | A.22.B.D.H.M.N.A.32. |
| 238 | 381. 420 | 0.6.2T | A.22.B.D.H.M.N.A.32. |
| 239 | 701 | 0-4-0T | |
| 240 | 3050 - 3099 | 2-8-0 | G. |
| 241 | 3020 - 3049 | 2-8-0 | G.K. |
| 242 | 4575 - 4599 | 2-6-2T | A.5. |
| 242 | 5500 - 5504 | 2-6-2T | A.5. |
| 243 | 6000 - 6019 | 4-6-0 | Z.A.24 |
| 244 | 6600 - 6629 | 0-6-2T | A.30 |
| 245 | 1331 | 0-6-0T | B.46 |
| 246 | 1101 - 1106 | 0-4-0T | T. |
| 247 | 13 Sentinel | 0-4-0T | |
| 248 | 12 Sentinel | 0-4-0T | |
| 249 | 5505 - 5524 | 2-6-2T | A.5. |
| 250 | 23 Simplex | 0-4-0T | A. (I.C.E.) |
| 251 | 5525 - 5544 | 2-6-2T | A.5. |
| 252 | 6630 - 6649 | 0-6-2T | A.30 |
| 253 | 5545 - 5574 | 2-6-2T | A.5. |
| 254 | 4901 - 4980 | 4-6-0 | A.1.2.3. |
| 255 | 6650 - 6699 | 0-6-2T | A.30. |
| 256 | 5700 - 5749 | 0-6-0T | B 48.74 |
| 257 | 5101 - 5110 | 2-6-2T | A.9. |
| 257 | 5150 - 5159 | 2-6-2T | A.9. |
| 258 | 5750 - 5779 | 0-6-0T | B 48.74 |
| 259 | 5160 - 5189 | 2-6-2T | A.9. |
| 260 | 5780 - 5799 | 0-6-0T | B 48.74 |
| 261 | 2251 - 2270 | 0-6-0 | A.27.29.33. |
| 262 | 6700 - 6724 | 0-6-0T | B.48.74. |
| 263 | 7700 - 7724 | 0-6-0T | B.48.74. |
| 264 | 7725 - 7749 | 0-6-0T | B.48.74. |
| 265 | 6725 - 6749 | 0-6-0T | B.48.74. |
| 266 | 5275 - 5294 | 2-8-0T | F. |
| 267 | 6020 - 6029 | 4-6-0 | Z.A.24. |
| 268 | 4981 - 4999. 5900 | 4-6-0 | A.3. |
| 269 | 6100 - 6129 | 2-6-2T | A.10.11. |
| 270 | | | |
| 271 | 7775 - 7799 | 0-6-0T | B. 48. 74. |
| 272 | 8725 - 8749 | 0-6-0T | B. 48. 74. |
| 273 | 8700 - 8724 | 0-6-0T | B. 48. 74. |
| 274 | 7750 - 7774 | 0-6-0T | B. 48. 74. |
| 275 | 5901 - 5920 | 4-6-0 | A.3. |
| 276 | 9300 - 9319 | 2-6-0 | R. |
| 277 | 5400 - 5419 | 0-6-0T | B. 61. |
| 277 | 6400 - 6409 | 0-6-0T | B. 62. |
| 278 | 6130 - 6159 | 2-6-2T | A. 10. |
| 279 | 1400 - 1429 | 0-4-2T | M. |
| 279 | 5800 - 5819 | 0-4-2T | M. |
| 280 | 5013 - 5022 | 4-6-0 | A. 5. 19. |
| 281 | 5921 - 5940 | 4-6-0 | A. 3. |
| 282 | 9701 - 9710 | 0-6-0T | B. 69. |
| 282 | 8750 - 8798. 8700 | 0-6-0T | B. 73. 75. |
| 283 | 2271 - 2280 | 0-6-0 | A. 27. 29. 33. |
| 284 | 5190 - 5199 | 2-6-2T | A.9. |
| 285 | 8799. 9711 - 9759 | 0-6-0T | B. 73. 75. |
| 286 | 1366 - 1371 | 0-6-0T | B. 68. |
| 287 | 1460 - 1474 | 0-4-2T | M. |
| 288 | 1430 - 1459 | 0-4-2T | M. |
| 289 | No. 1 Diesel | 0-4-0 | B. I.C.E. |
| 290 | 5941 - 5950 | 4-6-0 | A. 3. |
| 291 | 6160 - 6169 | 2-6-2T | A. 10. |
| 292 | 4100 - 4119 | 2-6-2T | A. 9. |
| 293 | 9760 - 9784 | 0-6-0T | B. 73. 75. |
| 294 | 6410 - 6424 | 0-6-0T | B. 62. |
| 295 | 5023 - 5032 | 4-6-0 | A. 5. 19. 23. |
| 296 | 5033 - 5042 | 4-6-0 | A. 5. 19. 23. |
| 297 | 5951 - 5965 | 4-6-0 | A. 3. |
| 298 | 2281 - 2290 | 0-6-0 | A.27.29.33 |
| 299 | 9785 - 9799 | 0-6-0T | B.73.75 |
| 299 | 3700 - 3734 | 0-6-0T | B.73.75 |
| 300 | 6425 - 6429 | 0-6-0T | B.62. |
| 301 | 5420 - 5424 | 0-6-0T | B.61. |
| 302 | No. 2 Diesel | 0-6-0 | C. (I.C.E.) |
| 303 | 5043 - 5067 | 4-6-0 | A.5.23 |
| 304 | 5966 - 5975 | 4-6-0 | A.3. |
| 305 | 6430 - 6439 | 0-6-0T | B.62 |
| 306 | 3735 - 3784 | 0-6-0T | B.73.75. |
| 307 | 7400 - 7429 | 0-6-0T | B.72. |
| 308 | 6800 - 6899 | 4-6-0 | A.8. |
| 309 | 6007 Renewal | 4-6-0 | Z.A.24. |
| 310 | 5068 - 5082 | 4-6-0 | A.5.18.19.26. |
| 311 | 5976 - 5985 | 4-6-0 | A.3. |
| 312 | 2291 - 2299. 2200 | 0-6-0 | A.27.29.33. |
| 313 | 4120 - 4129 | 2-6-2T | A.9 |
| 314 | 3785 - 3799 | 0-6-0T | B.73.75. |
| 314 | 3600 - 3634 | 0-6-0T | B.73.75. |
| 315 | 3200 - 3219 | 4-4-0 | A.43.44.45. |
| 316 | 7800 - 7819 | 4-6-0 | A.9. |
| 317 | 5083 - 5092 | 4-6-0 | A.5.19.26. |
| 318 | 7240 - 7254 | 2-8-2T | C. |
| 319 | 3100 - 3104 | 2-6-2T | A.13. |
| 320 | 8100 - 8109 | 2-6-2T | A.12. |
| 321 | 2884 - 2899 | 2-8-0 | M. |
| 321 | 3800 - 3803 | 2-8-0 | M. |
| 322 | 2201 - 2210 | 0-6-0 | A.27.29.33. |
| 323 | 4130 - 4139 | 2-6-2T | A.9. |
| 324 | 5093 - 5099 | 4-6-0 | A.5.18.23. |
| 324 | | | |
| 325 | 3635 - 3684 | 0-6-0T | B.73.75. |
| 326 | | | |
| 327 | 5986 - 5995 | 4-6-0 | A.3. |
| 328 | 3804 - 3823 | 2-8-0 | M. |
| 329 | 5255 - 5264 | 2-8-0T | F. |
| 330 | 3685 - 3699 | 0-6-0T | B.73.75. |
| 330 | 4600 - 4634 | 0-6-0T | B.73.75. |
| 331 | 3220 - 3239 | 4-4-0 | A.45.44.43. |
| 332 | | | |
| 333 | 5996 - 5999 | 4-6-0 | A.3. |
| 333 | 6900 - 6905 | 4-6-0 | A.3. |
| 334 | 3824 - 3833 | 2-8-0 | M |
| 335 | 4140 - 4149 | 2-6-2T | A.9. |
| 336 | 4635 - 4660 | 0-6-0T | B.73.75. |
| 337 | 2211 - 2230 | 0-6-0 | A.27.33.29 |
| 338 | 6906 - 6915 | 4-6-0 | A.3. |
| 339 | | | |
| 340 | 6916 - 6958 | 4-6-0 | A.3. |
| 341 | 3834 - 3843 | 2-8-0 | M |
| 342 | 5&6 Late WC&P.2&4 | 0-6-0T | B.76. |
| 343 | | | |
| 344 | | | |
| 345 | | | |
| 346 | 3844 - 3866 | 2-8-0 | M |
| 347 | 2231 - 2250 | 0-6-0 | A.33.29.27. |
| 348 | 8400 - 8409 | 2-8-0 | O |
| 349 | 8410 - 8429 | 2-8-0 | O |
| 350 | 6959 - 6970 | 4-6-0 | A.14.15. |
| 351 | 8430 - 8439 | 2-8-0 | O |
| 352 | 4661 - 4699 | 0-6-0T | B.73.75. |
| 352 | 9600 - 9621 | 0-6-0T | B.73.75. |
| 353 | 8440 - 8489 | 2-8-0 | O |
| 354 | 1000 - 1019 | 4-6-0 | A.17.16.21. |
| 355 | 9622 - 9641 | 0-6-0T | B.73.75. |
| 356 | 9642 - 9651 | 0-6-0T | B.73.75. |
| 357 | 5098 - 5099 | 4-6-0 | A.18. |
| 357 | 7000 - 7007 | 4-6-0 | A.18. |
| 358 | 1020 - 1029 | 4-6-0 | A.16. |
| 359 | | | |
| 360 | 3200 - 3219 | 0-6-0 | A.33.29.27. |
| 361 | 4150 - 4159 | 2-6-2T | A.9. |
| 362 | 9652 - 9661 | 0-6-0T | B.73.75 |
| 362 | 6750 - 6759 | 0-6-0T | B.73.75 |
| 363 | Diesel Electric | 0-6-0 | E. I.C.E. |
| 364 | Diesel Electric | 0-6-0 | D. I.C.E. |
| 365 | 9400 - 9409 | 0-6-0T | B. 78.79. |
| 366 | 6971 - 6990 | 4-6-0 | A.14.15. |
| 367 | 7008 - 7027 | 4-6-0 | A.22.23. |
| 368 | 6991 - 6999 | 4-6-0 | A.14.15. |
| 368 | 7900 - 7919 | 4-6-0 | A.25. |
| 369 | 4160 - 4179 | 2-6-2T | A.14.9. |
| 370 | 9662 - 9672 | 0-6-0T | B.73.75 |
| 371 | 7430 - 7439 | 0-6-0T | B.72 |
| 372 | 18000 BB.GT. | 0-6-0-0 | F. I.C.E. |
| 373 | 1500 - 1509 | 0-6-0T | B.80 |
| 374 | 6760 - 6769 | 0-6-0T | B.73.75. |
| 375 | 7028 - 7037 | 4-6-0 | A.22.23. |
| 376 | 7920 - 7929 | 4-6-0 | A.25. |
| 377 | 7820 - 7829 | 4-6-0 | A.9. |
| 378 | 9673 - 9682 | 0-6-0T | B.73.75. |
| 379 | 6770 - 6779 | 0-6-0T | B.73.75. |
| 380 | 7440 - 7449 | 0-6-0T | B.72. |
| 381 | 1600 - 1629 | 0-6-0T | B.81. |
| 382 | 9410 - 9459 | 0-6-0T | B.79. |
| 383 | 9460 - 9489 | 0-6-0T | B.79. |
| 384 | 8400 - 8449 | 0-6-0T | B.79. |
| 385 | 8450 - 8479 | 0-6-0T | B.79. |
| 386 | 8480 - 8499 | 0-6-0T | B.79. |
| 387 | 9490 - 9499 | 0-6-0T | B.79 |
| 387 | 3400 - 3409 | 0-6-0T | B.79 |
| 388 | 18100 M.V.G.T. | Co-Co | G. I.C.E. |
| 389 | 1630 - 1649 | 0-6-0T | B.81. |
| 390 | 75000 - 75009 | 4-6-0 | SL/4B/1 |
| 391 | 75010 - 75019 | 4-6-0 | SL/4B/1 |
| 392 | 82000 - 82009 | 2-6-2T | SL/3VT/1 |
| 393 | 82010 - 82019 | 2-6-2T | SL/3VT/1 |
| 394 | 46503 - 46527 | 2-6-0 | T |
| 395 | 90000 Class | 2-8-0 | Q |
| 396 | 3 engines S & MR | | — |
| 397 | 70015 - 70024 | 4-6-2 | SL/7A/1 |
| 398 | 82020 - 82029 | 2-6-2T | SL/3VT/1 |
| 399 | 82030 - 82034 | 2-6-2T | SL/3VT/1 |
| 400 | 75020 - 75029 | 4-6-0 | SL/4B/1 |
| 401 | 75030 - 75049 | 4-6-0 | SL/4B/1 |
| 402 | 78000 - 78009 | 2-6-0 | SL/2K/1 |
| 403 | 70025 - 70029 | 4-6-2 | SL/7A/1 |
| 404 | 13000 - 13004 D.E. | 0-6-0 | SL/JD/1 |
| 405 | P.W.M.650 D.E. | 0-6-0 | H. I.C.E. |
| 406 | 77000 - 77004 | 2-6-0 | SL/3K/1 |
| 406 | 77010 - 77014 | 2-6-0 | SL/3K/1 |
| 407 | 77005 - 77009 | 2-6-0 | SL/3K/1 |
| 407 | 77015 - 77019 | 2-6-0 | SL/3K/1 |
| 408 | 75050 - 75064 | 4-6-0 | SL/4B/1 |
| 409 | 75065 - 75079 | 4-6-0 | SL/4B/2 |
| 410 | 82035 - 82044 | 2-6-2T | SL/3VT/1 |
| 411 | 92000 - 92007 | 2-10-0 | SL/9R/1 |
| 412 | 13025 - 13039 D.E. | 0-6-0 | SL/JD/1 |
| 413 | 75080 - 75089 | 4-6-0 | SL/4B/ |
| 414 | 77020 - 77024 | 2-6-0 | SL/3K/1 |
| 415 | 82055 - 82062 | 2-6-2T | SL/3VT/1 |
| 416 | 82045 - 82054 | 2-6-2T | SL/3VT/1 |
| 417 | 1650 - 1669 | 0-6-0T | B.81. |
| 418 | 119 locos transferred from L.M.R. | Various | |
| 419 | 13102 - 13116 D.E. | 0-6-0 | SL/JD/1 |
| 420 | 13182 - 13196 D.E. | 0-6-0 | SL/JD/1 |
| 421 | 92087 - 92096 | 2-10-0 | SL/9R/3 |
| 422 | 92178 - 92202 | 2-10-0 | SL/9R/3 |
| 423 | 73125 - 73134 | 4-6-0 | SL/5B/ |
| 424 | 13255 - 13269 D.E. | 0-6-0 | SL/JD/1 |
| 425 | | | |
| 426 | | | |
| 427 | 11187 - 11211 D.M. | 0-6-0 | |
| 428 | | | |
| 429 | 92203 - 92220 | 2-10-0 | |
| 430 | | | |
| 431 | | | |
| 432 | 13352 - 13366 D.E. | 0-6-0 | |
| 432 | 13419 - 13438 D.E. | 0-6-0 | |
| 432 | 13397 - 13407 | 0-6-0 | |